FOOD LOVERS'
GUIDE TO
DENVER &
BOULDER

Help Us Keep This Guide Up to Date

We would love to hear from you concerning your experiences with this guide and how you feel it could be improved and kept up to date. Please send your comments and suggestions to:

editorial@GlobePequot.com

Thanks for your input, and happy travels!

FOOD LOVERS' SERIES

FOOD LOVERS'
GUIDE TO
DENVER &
BOULDER

The Best Restaurants, Markets & Local Culinary Offerings

First Edition

Ruth Tobias

Guilford, Connecticut

Copyright © 2012 Morris Book Publishing, LLC

Editor: Kevin Sirois
Project Editor: Lynn Zelem
Layout Artist: Mary Ballachino
Text Design: Sheryl Kober
Illustrations by Jill Butler with additional art by Carleen Moira Powell and MaryAnn Dubé
Maps: Trailhead Graphics, Inc. © Morris Book Publishing, LLC

ISBN 978-0-7627-7942-0

Printed in the United States of America
10 9 8 7 6 5 4 3 2 1

All the information in this guidebook is subject to change. We recommend that you call ahead
to obtain current information before traveling.

Contents

Introduction, 1

Denver & Boulder: The New Frontier, 1

How to Use This Book, 2

Getting Around, 4

Keeping Up with Food News, 5

Food & Drink Events, 8

Food Trucks & Carts, 13

Denver, 19

North Denver: Berkeley, Sunnyside, Highland, LoHi (aka The Highlands) & Stapleton, 20

Foodie Faves, 21

Landmarks, 48

Specialty Stores, Markets & Producers, 52

Central Denver: Downtown Denver/LoDo, Golden Triangle & Five Points, 60

> Foodie Faves, 61

> Landmarks, 98

> Specialty Stores, Markets & Producers, 105

West Denver: Jefferson Park, Lincoln Park & Federal Boulevard, 112

> Foodie Faves, 113

> Landmarks, 125

> Specialty Stores, Markets & Producers, 127

East Denver: Capitol Hill, Uptown, City Park, Cheesman Park, Congress Park, Park Hill, East Colfax, Cherry Creek & Country Club, 131

> Foodie Faves, 132

> Landmarks, 161

> Specialty Stores, Markets & Producers, 166

South Denver: Baker District, Old South Pearl, Santa Fe Arts District, University, University Hills & Washington Park, 172

    Foodie Faves, 173

    Landmarks, 195

    Specialty Stores, Markets & Producers, 198

Boulder, 205

Boulder, 207

    Foodie Faves, 208

    Landmarks, 243

    Specialty Stores, Markets & Producers, 248

Suburbs, 259

The Best of the 'Burbs, 261

    Foodie Faves, 261

    Landmarks, 282

    Specialty Stores, Markets & Producers, 283

Booze Cruise: Local Breweries, Wineries, Distilleries & Bars, 291

Breweries & Distilleries, 293

Cocktail Lounges, 303

Dive Bars, 308

Pubs, 311

Wine Bars, 315

Recipes, 321

Tapenade (Executive Chef Elise Wiggins of Panzano), 322

Burrata (Frank Bonanno, Executive Chef and Owner of Osteria Marco), 323

Samosas with Roasted Corn Sauce (Chef Matt Selby of Vesta Dipping Grill), 326

Colorado Lamb Sliders (Executive Chef Tyler Wiard of Elway's), 329

Bella! Bella! Benny (Snooze), 330

Grilled Beef Ribeye with Beet Greens and Horseradish Aioli (Eric Skokan, Chef and Owner of Black Cat Bistro), 332

Whole Grilled Trout with Autumn Vegetables in Brown Butter
    (Executive Chef Sheila Lucero of Jax Fish House & Oyster
    Bar), 333

Nut Brown Ale Cake with Caramel Icing (Kim Rosenbarger,
    Co-Owner of Kim & Jake's Cakes), 336

Funnel Cake–Fried Bananas with Peanut-Butter Caramel (Jennifer
    Jasinski, Executive Chef and Partner of Euclid Hall), 338

Sweet-and-Savory Bread Pudding on a Stick (Andrew Novick), 340

Aspen Highland (Bryan Dayton, Owner and Beverage Director of
    OAK at Fourteenth), 342

Pueblo Chili Flip (Justin Cucci, Owner of Root Down), 343

Appendices, 345

Appendix A: Eateries by Cuisine, 346

Appendix B: Specialties & Specialty Food, 355

Index, 362

About the Author

Beginning her career in Boston at the turn of the millennium, Ruth Tobias is a Denver-based food-and-beverage writer, assistant editor at *Sommelier Journal,* and author of the blog Denveater. For more information, please visit www.ruthtobias.com and www.ruthtobias.com/denveater.

Acknowledgments

You'll note that, throughout the chapters that follow, I tend to use the royal "we" instead of the first-person singular. The truth is, this guide owes so much to the guidance and input of others—dear foodie friends and esteemed colleagues like Mark and Amy Antonation, Kristen Browning-Blas, Rebecca Caro, Clay Fong, John Imbergamo, Kazia Jankowski, Kate Lacroix, Mark and Teresa Mañago, Adrian Miller, Robin Moses, Tucker Shaw, and many more. Of course, it wouldn't exist at all if not for Denver/Boulder's extraordinary community of chefs, restaurateurs, and producers—never mind the hearty encouragement of my editor at Globe Pequot Press, Kevin Sirois.

My parents, meanwhile, deserve countless thanks for teaching me at a young age to appreciate everything from oysters and papayas to latkes and tandoori—no small feat in Oklahoma in the 1970s and 1980s.

But my deepest debt of gratitude must be paid to Brit Withey—eater of my leftovers, love of my life.

Introduction

Denver & Boulder: The New Frontier

From the Gold Rush to the green revolution, from yahoos to young guns: in a nutshell, that's the history of the Front Range, as the towns along this southeastern stretch of the Rocky Mountains are collectively called. Settled by prospectors in the late 1850s, Denver started out as a shantytown whose first seat of government was, famously, a saloon—and whose legendary brewing industry, founded by Adolph Coors in 1873, preceded statehood by three years.

Fast forward to today, when some of us can't help but see shades of a double entendre in the nickname Mile High City (though technically it alludes to our altitude). According to Visit Denver, the city's convention and visitors bureau (www.dmcvb.org), the area affectionately known as the Napa Valley of beer ranks number one in the country with respect to production; meanwhile, in just a few short years, microdistilleries have made enormous strides alongside microbreweries (as have wineries, located primarily in western Colorado's fruit basket). So it's no surprise that our bars have quickly risen to the occasion, garnering national attention in the process; some of the winningest bartenders on the craft-cocktail competition circuit reside right here in Denver and Boulder.

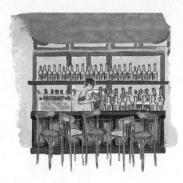

Speaking of the latter—just as Denver has slowly shed its reputation as a cowtown, Boulder has begun to replace its hippy-dippy image with that of an ultra-sophisticated hub for the locavore movement. As the young, well-educated population booms, the restaurant industry in both towns has responded with a remarkable sense of purpose: where, two decades ago, steak houses and tofu huts reigned respectively, dynamism and diversity now define the dining scene to such an extent that blinking means missing something special.

Indeed, to say that, in the months we spent working on this book, eateries were opening at the rate of nearly one a day is no exaggeration. If we could insert a sheaf of blank pages for you, the reader, to jot down all the newcomers that will surely have hit town by the time of publication, we would. As it is, we can only welcome them—and you—with open arms and cutlery at the ready. Dig in.

How to Use This Book

Excepting the chapter on booze and the sidebars, the listings in this book are organized geographically—covering neighborhoods loosely grouped to the north, east, south, and west of central Denver as well as the closest suburbs and, of course, Boulder. (There had to be arbitrary cutoff points somewhere; ours included Boulder to the north and Littleton and Greenwood Village to the south.)

The chapter entries are further arranged according to the following categories:

Foodie Faves

This broadly defined section covers everything from the hottest chef-driven destinations to the homiest holes in the wall.

Landmarks

The Front Range just wouldn't be the Front Range without these old-timers—many of which you'll have to see to believe.

Specialty Stores, Markets & Producers

Here you'll find our favorite indie markets, boutique wine shops, ice cream vendors, and so on, as well as smaller bakeries, coffeehouses, and other specialized sit-down venues. Note that only those with in-store meal service receive price codes; the same goes for the listings in the Booze Cruise chapter.

Price Code

We used the following system to classify restaurants by price, according to the average cost of a single entree—but keep in mind that it's an estimate only; in the era of small plates, from traditional sushi and tapas to their contemporary equivalents, meals (and tabs) are no longer one-size-fits-all.

$ **Less than $10**
$$ **$10 to $20**
$$$ **More than $20**

Getting Around

Eco-minded, two-legged, and/or two-wheeled mobility may be a way of life for Coloradans, but Western sprawl is a fact of life. Denver's pioneering bike-sharing program is admirable but, at the time of this writing, geographically limited—and though trails do crisscross the city, many patches of pavement remain less than hospitable to cyclists; likewise, the RTD Light Rail is only convenient if you're going its south-central way. The bus system is far more extensive—and certainly offers a whirlwind tour of Denver's more colorful side; taking Route 15 down East Colfax can be like going on an urban safari—but visitors who plan to traverse the city to any great degree should, loathe as we are to admit it, seriously consider renting a car. (That said, far be it from us to squelch the spring in your step; if you're so inclined, you'll find plenty of information at www.rtd-denver.com, www.bikedenver.org, and www.denverbike sharing.org.) As for Boulder, being more concentrated, it's naturally more walkable, bikeable, and busable.

Boulder Locavore, www.boulderlocavore.com. Toni Dash's beautifully photographed foray into Boulder's foodscape.

Cafe Society, http://blogs.westword.com/cafesociety. If there's a restaurant-related scoop to be had, indefatigable editor-about-town Lori Midson and her equally tireless, hungry team get it—several times a day. Alt weekly *Westword*'s dining blog is a local chowhound's most indispensable, comprehensive resource.

Colorado Wino, http://colorado.localwinos.com. Founder Jacob Harkins fills a crucial niche with his in-depth coverage of the state's wine industry.

Culinary Colorado, http://culinary-colorado.com. Recognized freelance journalist Claire Walter has maintained this blog since before many of us fully understood what blogs were.

Denveater, www.ruthtobias.com/denveater. This blog by yours truly covers restaurants around town and beyond.

The Denver Dish, http://thedenverdishblog.com. Mike Ross pens this personable ode to the culinary community.

Colorado Grown

Albeit unbeknownst to most nonresidents, Colorado's a cornucopia of produce, with more than 30 million acres devoted to farmland—most notably around the Western Slope (where, not coincidentally, its vineyards are concentrated). In season, you'll find the following—as well as local apricots, apples, pears, and plums—not only in markets but on menus statewide.

Chiles. Their counterparts from Hatch, New Mexico, tend to steal the national spotlight, but chiles from the town of Pueblo, in the southern part of the state, make Coloradans' hearts go pitter-pat. In early fall, you'll smell them roasting in the big drums dotting Federal Boulevard before you even see the stands.

Corn. Practically creamed on the vine: that's how trademarked Olathe Sweet corn tastes to us come late summer.

Melons. The state's melon patch is centered around the southeastern town of Rocky Ford; watermelons and cantaloupes crop up throughout the late summer and early fall.

Hazel Dell mushrooms. Okay, Colorado isn't known for fungi per se. But Hazel Dell founder Jim Hammond's organic mushrooms are ubiquitous in local restaurant kitchens with good reason: they're gorgeous. In addition to shiitakes, oysters, and of course buttons, we love the bulbous, meaty lion's manes.

Peaches. The town of Palisade is practically synonymous with peaches; begin to look for them in late July.

Denver Off the Wagon, www.denveroffthewagon.com. Exuberant booze news from local-industry insiders and enthusiasts alike.

Denver On a Spit, www.denveronaspit.com. There isn't a hole in the wall the anonymous author of this delightful blog won't stick his head into; follow him on his quest for, among other things, the holy grail of tacos al pastor.

The Denver Post, www.denverpost.com/food. The value-added online version of the *Post*'s weekly food section includes recipes and blogposts from acclaimed local chefs and authors as well as restaurant reviews; editor Kristen Browning-Blas oversees it all with aplomb.

Denver Street Food, www.denverstreetfood.com. Though it's not updated as regularly as we insatiable sorts would like, it's nonetheless a major stop on the food-truck trail.

Eat Drink Denver, http://eatdrinkdenver.com. This multi-authored blog founded by the convention and bureau, Visit Denver, features chefs' interviews, recipes, and other newsy tidbits.

Fermentedly Challenged, www.fermentedlychallenged.com. An exhaustive chronicle of craft beer and brewing.

Indie Eats, http://indie-eats.com. A sassy collection of recipes, reviews, and interviews.

Food & Drink Events

Although the mountain towns are home to some of Colorado's most
renowned epicurean extravaganzas—first and foremost the Food &
Wine Classic in Aspen—we've got our share of goings-on
down here along the Front Range. If you're a
passenger on the pop-up dinner bandwagon,
check out **Beware of Dog** (www.bewareofdogs
supperclub.com), **Hush** (http://hushdenver
.com), **Noble Swine Supper Club** (http://
nobleswinesupperclub.com), and **Studio F**
(http://studioflodo.com); if tours are your
bag, head to the **West End Tavern** (p. 240)
to hop on Banjo Billy's seasonal **Boulder Brew Bus** (http://thewest
endtavern.com) or sign up for **Culinary Connectors'** popular restaurant crawls (http://culinaryconnectors.com).

February

Denver Restaurant Week, www.denver.org/denverrestaurant.
The nationwide phenomenon that is Restaurant Week has its under-
standable detractors as well as its devotees; chaos can and does

ensue. But with nearly 300 restaurants in 2011 alone participating for a fortnight straight, serving multicourse menus for two at the wink-wink price of $52.80 (that's the number of feet in a mile, alluding to Denver's altitude), we can't deny that it's an efficient introduction to the local dining scene—particularly if you take it as an opportunity to explore neighborhood gems rather than joining the mobs who treat it as a sort of fire sale on steak house fare.

May

Colorado Beer Week, www.cobeerweek .com. The springtime answer to the GABF (p. 11), which launched in 2011, is an intimate affair, its area-hosted events more locally focused and food-centric: think vertical tastings and hors d'oeuvre pairings.

June

Civic Center EATS Outdoor Cafe, www.civiccenterconservancy .org. From June through September, Civic Center Park turns midday fiesta every Tuesday and Thursday, as some of the city's best trucks line the promenade, live music fills the air, and foodies pack the cafe tables to bask in the sunshine on their lunch breaks. Hopefully they're long lunch breaks, because it can take a good half-hour to survey the array at any given time: brisket chili, chimichurri fries, curried lentils over hominy, organic burgers with Thai-style fixings, lemon-pistachio ice cream–cookie sandwiches, gyros and pizza and noodle bowls . . . If you can name it, you can probably order it here.

Greek Festival, www.thegreekfestival.com. Amid the folk dancers and musicians, goldsmiths and makers of olive-oil soap holding court beneath the gold dome of the Assumption of the Theotokos Greek Orthodox Cathedral, this annual weekend bender offers it all: gyros, pastitso, spanakopita, souvlaki, baklava, and much more, as well as Greek coffee and ouzo to wash it down.

Juneteenth, www.juneteenth-denver.org. Anchored by a parade, this Five Points street fair commemorates the day on which the last official bastion of slavery, Texas, issued its emancipation proclamation. Here, everybody's welcome to pursue one of America's greatest pastimes: chowing down on barbecue.

July

Colorado Dragon Boat Festival, www.cdbf.org. "Taste of Asia" is a bit of a misnomer—the food pavilion at this annual spectacle is no haven of real-deal hawker stalls. But you'll find a few vaguely authentic snacks to tide you over until the last colorful dragon-boat race on Sloan's Lake has ended and you're free to head to Federal Boulevard for dim sum and pho.

August/September

A Taste of Colorado, www.atasteofcolorado.com. There's a nominal Fine Dining Area, but we'd rather slum it at this Labor Day jamboree in Civic Center Park, appeasing our inner brats with the turkey legs, hot dogs, caramel corn, and other junk foods we'll surely regret later—especially if we happen to catch an accidental, stomach-turning glimpse of the ice cream–eating competition.

September/October

Denver Food and Wine, www.colorado restaurant.com. Held at the Metropolitan State College of Denver just off Auraria Parkway at the edge of downtown, this two-day event is a double whammy in that it both hosts its own grand tasting and partners with alt-weekly *Westword* to present the latter's annual chef showcase, Dish.

Denver Beer Fest, www.denver.org/denverbeerfest. Leading up to the GABF (see below), this drink-around packs so many tappings, beer dinners, and workshops into a single week that you yourself could be tapped out before the doors of the convention center even open.

Great American Beer Festival, Colorado Convention Center, 700 14th St., Denver, CO 80202; (303) 447-0816; www.great americanbeerfestival.com. This is it: the mecca to which hundreds of thousands of American craft brewers and connoisseurs alike make pilgrimage each year. In 2011, nearly 2,500 different beers flowed in the jam-packed madhouse that the convention center becomes; swirling around the main event—the Olympian juried competition—are all manner of pavilions hosting tastings, demos, seminars, and so forth. Speaking of competition, general-admission passes routinely sell out within days. Purchase yours early—and don't forget your pretzel necklace.

Harvest Week, http://eatdenver.com. EatDenver, a consortium of local independent restaurateurs, hosts this annual showcase of Colorado products with a series of prix-fixe menus and/or multi-cheffed theme dinners. Commitment to the project is strong, community energy high; some of the most memorable local dishes we've ever encountered were during Harvest Week—Riesling-marinated pork belly with porcini mascarpone and peach gastrique comes to mind, as does bison-liver mousse with corn fritters and gin marmalade—so do keep your eyes on the association's Twitter feed (@EatDenverCO) come early fall for updates.

November

Denver International Wine Fest, www.denverwinefest.com. This still-young festival is growing at a steady pace. In 2011, it moved operations to the Wings Over the Rockies Air & Space Museum (7711 E. Academy Blvd., Denver, CO 80230) to accommodate the lineup of participating wineries, distributors, and chefs, which just keeps getting better—and the caliber of the experts who lead its seminars is especially high for a regional expo.

First Bite Boulder, www.firstbiteboulder.com. Participants in Boulder's alternative to Restaurant Week feature three-course menus for $26 per person; kudos to **Arugula Bar e Ristorante, Pizzeria Basta,** and **Q's Restaurant** (pp. 209, 228, 246), among others, for taking the promotion in stride with stimulating, varied selections.

Food Trucks & Carts

They're here . . . and there, and everywhere. That the food-truck trend hit metro Denver like, well, a semitrailer a few years back was really no surprise; after all, loncheras have long dotted parking lots across town, old-school carts the 16th Street Mall. These days, their spanking-new siblings crisscross the city, lining up at farmer's markets, tap rooms, and, come summer, twice a week at Civic Center among other places. The local fleet is dozens strong; the following roster includes many notables, but truck-chasers would do well to visit **Denver Street Food** and **Westword's Cafe Society,** whose homepages are embedded with Twitter trackers, as well as individual websites for further listings and daily updates (note seasonal schedules—and prepare for pop-up gatherings).

Of course, some of our favorite brick-and-mortars have also launched mobile units, including twin concepts **Fat Sully's New York Pizza** (p. 138; Twitter: @sullyslicetruck) and **Denver Biscuit Co.** (p. 138; Twitter: @DenverBiscuitCo); **Steuben's** (p. 156; Twitter: @SteubensTruck); and **The Über Sausage** (p. 159; Twitter:

@TheUberSausage). As for **Biker Jim's Gourmet Dogs** (p. 62; Twitter: @bikerjimsdogs), the cart that started it all at the corner of 16th and Arapahoe Streets now has a sibling on the Auraria University campus as well as a truck.

Basic Kneads Pizza, http://basickneadspizza.com; Twitter: @ikneadpizza; Pizza; $. Improbable but true: a fervent local following swears that this fraternally run truck, outfitted with a wood-fired oven, makes the best pizza in town. Organic, Colorado-milled flour and a blend of mozzarellas form the base; toppings include everything from beer-laced barbecue sauce and black beans to ratatouille.

Chef Driven, http://thechefdriven.com; Twitter: @TheChefDriven; Contemporary; $. Turning out Korean tacos, Cubanos, Thai-style lettuce wraps, and more, the classically trained chef behind the wheel, Richie Stothard, also offers dandy specials like kabocha squash–wild mushroom soup.

Comida, www.eatcomida.com; Twitter: @eatcomida; Mexican; $. Though the owner of this shocking-pink Mexican mobile has just opened a brick-and-mortar in the 'burbs (721 Confidence Dr., Unit 1, Longmont, CO 80504; 720-204-6455), she's not putting the brakes on her baby, which rolls through Boulder dispensing the fancy-pants likes of gorditas with mushrooms, garlic mashed potatoes, and cotija and beef–sweet potato tacos with pecans and cranberries. Best bet: the prized coconut cake.

Manna From Heaven, www.mannafoodtruck.com; Twitter: @mannafoodtruck; Vietnamese; $. It's best known for its untraditional *bánh mì* (think red-wine teriyaki steak), but we keep our eyes peeled for cold-weather soups like the chicken broth–based "Vietnamese tangy/sour" with rice, pineapple, bamboo shoots, tomato, and cilantro.

Mikes2 Kitchen, www.mikes2kitchen.com; Twitter: @mikes2kitchen; American; $. A little of this, a little of that; Southern here, Mexican there, Italian over there—that's what the two Mikes, Levine and Carlin, dish up from their school bus–yellow vehicle. Scattershot as the repertoire may sound, rest assured the results—obtained entirely from scratch but for baguettes from **The Denver Bread Company** (p. 53) and **Rancho Liborio** (p. 287) tortillas—are anything but. Best bet: po'boys gussied up with roast beef or turkey and unexpected trimmings like marinated tomatoes and prosciutto.

Pinche Tacos, http://pinchetacos.com; Mexican; $. Though it now has a permanent location, complete with full bar, near City Park (1514 York St., Denver, CO 80206; 720-475-1337), our *corazón* still belongs to Pinche's taqueria on wheels; chefly as the toppings are—think tongue with the consistency of prime rib under chile-honey mayo or braised chicken and spinach with chipotle crema—street tacos are street tacos.

Quiero Arepas, http://quieroarepas.com; Twitter: @quieroarepas; Venezuelan; $. Co-founded by a Venezuelan native, this truck specializes in the stuffed corn-dough pockets found in various forms throughout America; here, the fillings range from the traditional (black beans and *queso blanco,* for instance) to the inspired (smoked salmon with avocado and capers).

Shondiz, www.shondiz.com; Middle Eastern; $. In a town that's virtually devoid of Turkish food, this 16th Street Mall cart stands a beacon—the mini-spit turning in the window its powerful beam of light, signaling döner kebabs ahead. The friendly guys who run it use a mixture of lamb and beef to fill their warm pitas, along with veggies, yogurt dressing, and hot sauce; they're a handful. Regulars swear by, of all things, the breakfast burritos, too. Best bet: if you have to ask, you'd better reread.

Stick It to Me, www.stickfood.net; @stickfood; Organic; $. It's "97% organic" and, yes, it's on a stick (or in a bun, or a salad bowl)—what's not to love? Yet this truck's at least as well known for its fried mashed-potato balls and lemon-ricotta doughnut holes as its Italian chicken and Korean beef.

The Tasterie Truck, http://thetasterietruck.com; Twitter: @TasterieTruck; Bakery/Cafe; $. This Boulder-based, four-wheeled sugar shack is the pride and joy of a sweetheart named Shannon Aten, who draws from a sizeable roster of kicky flavors for her daily-changing selection of whoopie pies, "doughnut muffins," danishes, and more—including cupcakes, of course. Best bet: now that we're attuned to the existence of chocolate chip–potato chip cookies, we'd like a childhood do-over.

Thai Food Cart, http://thaifoodcartdowntowndenver.com; Thai; $. Given the iffiness of metro Denver's Thai food offerings in general, it's mind-boggling that the the one-woman wonder behind this 16th Street Mall fixture should deliver the goods with such ferocity. But she manages to do just that—when she's around, that is; now that she's opened a brick-and-mortar (11650 Montview Blvd., Aurora, 80010; 303-587-2293), scoring her killer—and we do mean killer—curries and noodles al fresco is getting harder, so be prepared to implement Plan B. Best bet: the ironically eye-opening drunken noodles.

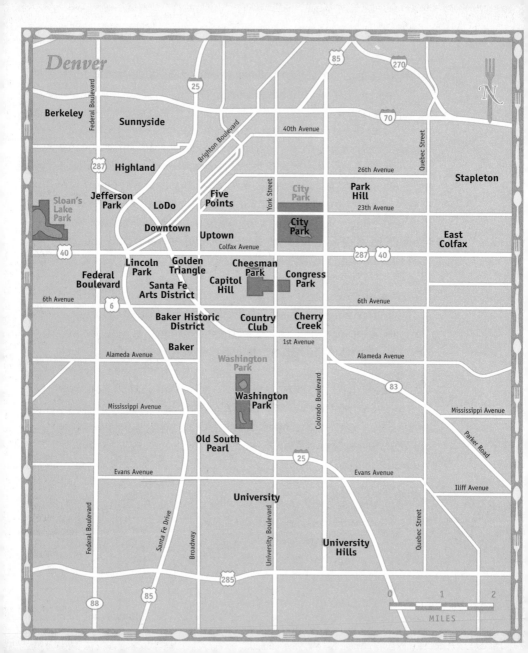

Denver

North Denver

Berkeley, Sunnyside, Highland, LoHi (aka The Highlands) & Stapleton

A salumeria here, a pasticceria there: though its demise began in the postwar era, vestiges of the bygone Italian enclave to which north Denver was once home still remain. These days, however, commercial growth rather than ethnic affiliation delineates the neighborhoods on this side of town. The interlinked Highlands have led the way, dotted with numerous mini-districts where shops and galleries alternate with coffeehouses and restaurants of all stripes, from humble taquerias to buzzing trendsetters; the most established of these is Highlands Square, but the area as a whole is increasingly ripe for discovery.

Foodie Faves

Axios Estiatorio, 3901 Tennyson St., Berkeley, Denver, CO 80212; (720) 328-2225; http://axiosdenver.com; Greek; $$. Neatly filling a conspicuous local void, this upscale Greek eatery—airy and subtly appointed with red-tiled floors and decorative ceramics—trades the stereotypical schlock for refreshing sophistication. We're not saying the servers won't humor you with an "Opa!" or two, especially when bearing a platter of flaming kasseri, but for the most part the mood is as refined as the food. As odd as all-beef meatballs in lamb ragù may sound, don't miss them; called *keftedes,* they're tender and wonderfully seasoned whether sprinkled with sheep's-milk *kefalotiri* and accompanied by warm pita wedges as an appetizer, nestled in a hoagie with provolone, or set atop flatbread or pasta. Dolmades, too, prove distinctive: nearly as big as enchiladas, the tender grape-leaf cylinders are stuffed with rice cooked in red wine, studded with pine nuts, and bathed in a rich but not heavy lemon cream sauce. Of course there are the requisite gyros, spanakopita, and moussaka, but they're complemented by the uncommon likes of braised lamb riblets, zucchini-feta fritters, and tabouli-stuffed roasted peppers, as well as by a knockout, largely high-end Greek wine list (on which retsina—that curious, resinated relic of ancient winemaking—is a sly exception).

bang!, 3472 W. 32nd Ave., Highland, Denver, CO 80211; (303) 455-1117; www.bangdenver.com; American; $$. Off-kilter charm is this Highlands Square long-timer's hallmark. The bright turquoise façade offers a peepshow of the kitchen crew; you have to round the corner to reach the entrance from the cute back patio, where a handful of tables await in two petite dining rooms whose multihued walls— lime, rust, buttercup, and slate—are hung with regularly rotating artworks. No less colorful is the concise, seasonal menu of cafe comforts that speak to diners with a distinct Southern twang: fried chicken and meat loaf, gumbo and cobbler. But it's the fixings that really butter our biscuit—think meatball-size hush puppies with jalapeño tartar sauce or thick slices of toasted sweet-potato bread, paired with easy-drinking wines from an economical list.

The Berkshire, 7352 E. 29th Ave., Stapleton, Denver, CO 80238; (303) 321-4010; www.theberkshirerestaurant.com; American; $$$. Among the quips from such esteemed wits as W.C. Fields and Mark Twain stenciled on the walls of this Stapleton hot spot, owner Andy Ganick's stands out: "Temptation, libation, and a bacon station!" Pork, pork, pork is the kitchen's pride and joy, starting with the signature bacon flight: a strikingly arranged quartet of strips redolent of curry, chipotle, and other spices, supplemented by herbed feta spread. Baby-back ribs, chops, pulled-pork sliders, and more continue the theme—but the menu doesn't end there; in fact, some of its choicest picks are meat-free. Cut from a flash-fried cob basted with lime butter, salty-sweet corn kernels pop; breaded, deep-fried pickle spears retain their crunch; hand-cut french fries come with an entrancing, intense black-garlic aioli. Despite its schtick, then, The Berkshire really does have something for everyone—including oenophiles, who snap up half-priced bottles of wine on Wednesday. (Okay, aesthetes might grumble about the bland ped-mall decor. But once twilight sets in and the lights go way down, even they'll make themselves at home.)

Big Hoss Bar-B-Q, 3961 Tennyson St., Berkeley, Denver, CO 80212; (720) 855-3061; www.bighossbarbq.com; Barbecue; $$. We bet the regulars at this bluesy Berkeley quasi–honky tonk know every word to Garth Brooks's "Friends in Low Places." That's a compliment (we've got the lyrics down cold too); flaunting the slogan "get sauced at Big Hoss," it's the kind of joint where you can kick back, slam down a few brews, and make some chums during the big game without judgment or pressure from the friendly staff. When you do get around to meeting the imperative of alcohol absorption, though, stick with anything dressed in white sauce—the hard-to-find, mayo-based specialty of Alabama will stick right back. The remaining 'cue is hit or miss—sometimes spot-on, sometimes on the dry side (as are the biscuits)—but the signature cheese nips, or batter-fried cheddar nuggets, have never let us down.

Buchi Cafe Cubano, 2651 W. 38th St., Sunnyside, Denver, CO 80211; (303) 458-1328; http://buchicafecubano.com; Sandwiches; $. This oh-so-lucky find on an unsightly stretch of Sunnyside pavement is not only bright as a piñata, it's every bit as full of goodies. The owner, Key West native Emmet Barr, is an unflappably smooth operator who executes a small (but more-than-sufficient) menu with exceptional attention to detail. If you've forgotten, after a string of halfhearted fakes, why Cuban sandwiches moved the needle on the trend-o-meter some years back, Barr's will remind you in an instant; pressed on freshly baked bread, filled with quality ingredients, and smeared with key lime mayo, they satisfy from first bite to last. Which doesn't prevent us from skipping them entirely at times in favor of *pasteles*—tender, ultra-flaky, sugar-sprinkled, house-baked turnovers filled with guava paste and cream cheese—accompanied by a nip of sipping rum. Then again, a traditional shot of Cuban espresso—thick and sweet as liqueur—is dessert enough; true to uncompromising form, Barr ships his proprietary roast from Florida.

Cafe Brazil, 4408 Lowell Blvd., Berkeley, Denver, CO 80211; (303) 480-1877; www.cafebrazildenver.com; Brazilian; $$. Amid lanterns, masks, tiles, and carved wooden screens, glittering tones of ruby, emerald, and sapphire befit this half-hidden jewel. Although the current owners of Cafe Brazil are Colombian, they do their predecessor proud in the form of heady stews and casseroles that are the forte of the cuisine they've adopted—namely multi-meaty *feijoada*, chicken-based *xim xim de galinha*, and our personal favorite, *moqueca* with salt cod and shellfish. It never ceases to amaze us that, using many of the ingredients on which their Southeast Asian counterparts rely—

coconut milk, dried shrimp, black beans, ginger, chiles, garlic, lime, peanuts—Brazilian cooks have developed a repertoire that differs so sharply; in any case, the food here is highly redolent of such stuff. The bar, by contrast, looks beyond Brazil's borders to obtain its fine collection of sipping rums, although it doesn't entirely pooh-pooh homegrown caçhaca in the process.

Chili Verde, 3700 Tejon St., LoHi, Denver, CO 80211; (303) 477-1377; www.chiliverde.net; Mexican; $$. The surrounding residences are eerily quiet; the whitewashed exterior appears a touch sketchy. That this LoHi hideaway is such a sleeper hit, then, attests all the more to the wherewithal of its gracious host, Eder Yañez-Mota, who with his brother and father runs what turns out to be a dapper little spot for a leisurely introduction to the spirited cookery of their native Puebla. The signature *chile en nogada* is a treasure, stuffed with ground beef or cheese and an array of chopped fruits and nuts, then topped with a sweet, walnut-based cream sauce and pomegranate seeds. But its seafood-stuffed cousin is a worthy alternative, as is *puerco en chile morita*—a smoked red variety, not unlike chipotle, that in sauce form gives a jolt to the fried chunks of pork it suffuses. In short, Chili Verde presents a golden opportunity to discover some of Mexico's most intriguing regional specialties (including the acquired taste that is *pulque*). And it all starts with good old chips and a trio of salsas; in particular, the tellingly blood-red *macha* made from dried serranos will unleash your sweat and tears—and you'll love every drop.

Coop de Ville at the Stingray Lounge, 2911 W. 38th Ave., Sunnyside, Denver, CO 80211; (303) 955-0815; American; $$. Style doyenne Leigh Jones and partner Margaret Moore strike again with this dead(pan) ringer for your grandparents' basement, equipped with salvaged sofa sectionals, booths swathed in cheetah print, and two-tone vinyl barstools as well as vintage TV consoles, old bowling trophies, and thrift-store lamps; a pool table awaits at the center of it all, while photos of drag races gone by adorn the walls. Bellying up to the bar, you'll instantly feel yourself one cardigan, some horn-rimmed glasses, and a pair of loafers away from slipping into a time warp; perusing the menu of loaded tater tots, cola-fried chicken, and meat loaf sammies, you'll ask yourself if there aren't worse places to get stuck. Especially since you won't be saddled with the old folks' liquor cabinet—making the lone exception to the retro rule, the bar boasts a fine selection of local microbrews, draft and otherwise.

DJ's Berkeley Cafe, 3838 Tennyson St., Berkeley, Denver, CO 80212; (303) 482-1841; http://djscafe.biz; American; $. For all its vibrant diversity, the Highlands area is relatively devoid of good old, low-key, schtick-free daytime neighborhood joints. Their absence partly explains the popularity of this notable exception to the rule—but only partly; we're willing to wager that DJ's would pack in the patrons no matter its map coordinates. Both the dining room and cute side patio are sunny and comfy, the staff is genuinely kind, and the eats are full of beans. Made with baguettes, the stuffed French toast stands so high and supple it seems spring-loaded; pancakes, by contrast, are unusually thin and lacy. But the Southwestern-style savories are what have us at "hello"—not only the touted New Mexico Benedict with juicy chorizo, charred poblanos, and cheddar polenta but also the salubrious vegetable soup, chunky with tomatoes, potatoes, carrots, and more sausage and topped with poached eggs on crostini. The 3 S's that constitute the lunch menu—soups, salads, sandwiches—make up in quality what they lack in novelty.

Duo, 2413 W. 32nd Ave., LoHi, Denver, CO 80211; (303) 477-4141; http://duodenver.com; Contemporary; $$. A neighborhood trailblazer when it opened several years back, Duo has settled into its role as a Highlands go-to with exceptional grace. As cozy as an old robe and slippers—but much more attractive, with its exposed brick walls, scuffed wood floors, and suspended window frames acting as a peekaboo divider between the bar and a dining room that looks

Spotlight on Mexico

In its vitality and variety, Colorado's Mexican food constitutes a book subject unto itself. Taquerias are as ubiquitous as McDonald's and Starbucks outlets; full-service restaurants specialize in the cookery of Jalisco, Michoacán, Oaxaca, Puebla, Sonora, Veracruz, and Mexico City. We couldn't possibly include them all, but nor could we resist throwing you just a few more *huesos* (bones).

El Olvido, *2200 S. Broadway, Denver, CO 80210; (720) 570-2040;* $$. We're really pulling for this Jaliscan hideaway, occupying as it does a revolving door of a space on traffic-clogged South Broadway. The vibe is sleepy, but the specialty of the house, *carne en su jugo*—a brothy stew of shredded beef, beans, and bacon served with a slew of accompaniments, from lime wedges, chopped onion, and cilantro to fine salsas and tortillas—is sure to put some pep in your step. Best bet: the large order's big enough for two.

El Paraiso, *4690 Harlan St., Denver, CO 80212; (303) 480-0479; http://elparaisomexicanrestaurant.net; Mexican;* $$. Located not far from an old amusement park, this sprawling hacienda fits right into its surroundings with an over-the-top pastiche of painted tiles, murals, Aztec statues, and light-strung palms. The menu, too, screams fiesta, featuring enormous mixed grills (*parilladas*) and boatloads of seafood as well as the usual, foot-long smothered enchiladas and burritos—all done surprisingly well amid the mariachi-and-margarita chaos. Best bet: we have an odd crush on the *machaca con huevos*, a breakfast concoction of dried beef and scrambled eggs—served all day with dreamy spiced beans and rice as well as fresh corn tortillas—that whisks us away to some dusty bygone rancho.

Las Tortas, *5307 Leetsdale Dr., Denver, CO 80246; (720) 379-7269; www.lastortasonline.com; Sandwiches; $.* This trim, bright spot in the dull sprawl of southeast Denver is staffed by a well-meaning crew who may try to steer you, as a newcomer, toward the basics—but will nonetheless cheerfully oblige if you're all set to go for the gusto, Guadalajara-style. Best bet: the *torta ahogada* with succulent, well-marinated carnitas, refried beans, and pickled onions is served on an especially crusty roll that can stand up to the dousing of two salsas: one thin, tart, and tomatoey, the other, called *chile de árbol,* which embodies the cliché that where there's smoke, there's fire.

Patzcuaro's, *2616 W. 32nd Ave., Denver, CO 80211; (303) 455-4389; www.patzcuaros.com; Mexican; $$.* This cozy, long-standing family gathering spot continues to hold its own along an increasingly dynamic stretch of the Highlands. Mexican-style meat-and-threes are its stock in trade; whatever you order—enchiladas, carnitas, chuletas—it'll come with some of the most unctuous frijoles, nearly pink with lard, you've ever tasted . . . and a salsa that won't so much cut through the richness as hack it to bits. Best bet: the giant *cocktel de camaron*—essentially shrimp-and-avocado gazpacho.

Paxia, *4001 Tejon St., Denver, CO 80211; (720) 583-6860; Mexican; $$.* Like the seasoned pros they are, the owners of **Los Carboncitos** (p. 40) deliver on the promise of *alta cocina Mexicana* in a beautifully eclectic, modern setting. Best bets: follow the signature ceviche of oysters and shrimp in hot sauce and cream with *tlacoyos*—oblong, black bean–stuffed, and griddled masa cakes reminiscent of the delightful huaraches served at Paxia's sister kitchens.

onto the kitchen—it's run by seasoned pros who've since branched out with **Olivéa** (p. 146), yet haven't for a moment lost sight of their roots here. As with the interior design, an air of openness characterizes the menu: abundant in produce, John Broening's dishes are seasonal, simple, and honest, revealing a Mediterranean accent that the fairly priced wine list distinctly echoes. And the singularly unfussy desserts of Yasmin Lozada-Hissom ring clear and true. In short, when we want to slip into something more comfortable, we come here.

El Camino, 3628 W. 32nd Ave., Highland, Denver, CO 80211; (720) 889-7946; http://elcaminotavern.t83.net; Mexican; $. From the shocking pink façade to the pendant lamps ringed round with beer cans to the cantina-esque wall designs, this self-styled community tavern plays the vaguely louche (or maybe *lucha libre*) outcast to its mostly yuppie neighbors in Highlands Square with relish—while making its customers feel right at home. Specials are its specialty—popular twice-daily happy hours; brunch that features live flamenco music on Saturday and runs through Sunday to Monday; menus that acknowledge vegetarians and even teetotalers (in the form of housemade ades). Meanwhile, if the tacos, burritos, enchiladas, and so on amount to the usual suspects, they're served with the sort of flair and care that makes happy regulars of us all.

El Original Tacos Jalisco, 4309 W. 38th Ave., Berkeley, Denver, CO 80212; (303) 458-1437; www.original-tacosjalisco.com; Mexican; $$. If there's anything wrong with this old standby, we've yet to discover it; it all feels so right. The dining rooms are cozy and colorful, the air ever-festive—and the food as homey, hearty, and soulful as all get out. Chips and excellent salsa arrive at your table practically before you do, but go easy on them—you've got a heck of a spread ahead. Served in a deep-fried tortilla shell, the warm, gooey blend of melted cheeses and crumbled chorizo that is *queso fundido* is a button-popper in and of itself. Plump, firm-fleshed *camarones adobados*, submerged in a smoky, citrusy, crimson marinade, satisfy in spades, as does a side of what may be the city's best *chicharrónes*—perfectly seasoned, deep-fried, soft-chewy pork rinds to which a little meat still clings. And the margaritas couldn't be trashier—nor should they be otherwise.

Ernie's Bar & Pizza, 2915 W. 44th Ave., Sunnyside, Denver, CO 80211; (303) 955-5580; www.erniesdenver.com; Pizza; $$. Happy days indeed. Tavern-like though this revamped Sunnyside old-timer may be, Ernie's invokes Arnold's at nearly every turn—welcoming the whole neighborhood with fun and games for the kiddos as well as the grown-ups, from skee-ball and chocolate sodas to amaretto sours and bowl games on the big screens. We were rather sorry to see that nifty à la carte assortment of pickled-veggie antipasti go (consider this a call for its reinstatement), but the pies continue to please, their paper-thin crusts defying gravity to support the likes of smoky roasted eggplant and sharp ricotta salata embedded in peppery tomato sauce or chopped clams with garlic and herbs (a Connecticut-style weekend special). The kitchen also uses pizza dough to make airy, fried poppers served with rosettes of prosciutto and schmears of taleggio as an appetizer or sprinkled with cinnamon sugar and accompanied by dipping creams for dessert—but we'll take our extra carbs in the form of stromboli as festive as fruitcake (albeit with chopped meatballs in lieu of maraschinos).

Fuel Cafe, 3455 Ringsby Ct. #105, Denver, CO 80216; (303) 296-4642; www.fuelcafedenver.com; Contemporary; $$. The fuel on which this little engine that could runs is Chef-Owner Bob Blair's own. A man of clear vision and ringing talent, he's turned an inauspicious location in an out-of-the-way studio park into a bona fide destination. Not even odd operating hours (it's open weekdays for lunch and Thurs through Sat only for dinner, with weekend brunch on the way at press time) seem to dissuade the avid droves from descending on the eatery, a model of industrial chic with a patio overlooking the parking lot; nor should you hesitate to seek it out, especially come suppertime. Blair's pastas surpass those of many a trattoria; gnocchi in particular are plump, creamy, perfect little nuggets whether bathed in lamb ragù or herb oil with sherried mushrooms. We've been privy to marvelous quinoa-feta croquettes, wild rice–stuffed calamari shells, and pork loin over spaetzle in bourbon and brown butter as well as to intriguing by-the-glass pours from an ahead-of-the-curve wine list—which, like the mostly organic menu, undergoes regular updates that only up the enchanting ante. Fill 'er up, foodies.

Hash, 2339 W. 44th Ave., Sunnyside, Denver, CO 80211; (303) 477-5406; www.sunnysidehash.com; American; $. Run by a veteran caterer, Heather Hauptman, this darling daytime cafe makes Sunnyside even sunnier. Grogginess is not an option for locals who stumble in only to have their eyelids promptly propped open by, in no particular order, a violet-blue and grass-green color scheme, cheery service, and coffee roasted locally by **Novo** (p. 108). Lack of appetite is also verboten. Obviously, hash, served in individual skillets, is the menu's luscious linchpin—and the gourmet version of the corned-beef classic is downright flawless, with chunks of meat that shred to the touch of a fork under eggs fried to the delicate thinness of crêpes. (Speaking of crêpes, savory or sweet, they're gorgeous too, with a velvety, springy texture.) But it's to Hauptman's credit that hardcore omnivores like us would favor the earthy, filling vegetarian hash made with sweet potatoes, portobellos, and tofu—and that the macadamia-nut sticky buns are worth every extra minute at the gym.

Highland Pacific, 3934 W. 32nd Ave., Highland, Denver, CO 80212; (303) 477-6644; www.highlandpacific.net; Seafood; $$. Something of a neighborhood secret, this two-room seafooder at the edge of Highlands Square has a quirky appeal that's reflected in the diverse happy-hour crowd. Along the bar, trucker-capped hipsters perch next to grandmothers in pearls as a young, energetic crew shucks a slew of oysters for a buck a pop; couples hunker down over bowls of peel-and-eat shrimp or crab legs on special. We're there, too, polishing off yet another order of hot, crunchy, scallion-flecked hush puppies. But on the rare occasions that we manage to resist them, we have fun picking and choosing from a menu that's pleasantly awash in nostalgia: cioppino, shrimp Louis, and linguine Alfredo with crawfish all take us back a ways. And if our reverie lasts, we might just be here long enough to catch a live jam session. It's all very Fisherman's Wharf circa 1985—in a good way.

Highland's Garden Cafe, 3927 W. 32nd Ave., Highland, Denver, CO 80212; (303) 458-5920; www.highlandsgardencafe .com; American; $$$. Unsurpassed quaintness suffuses the twinned Victorian cottages that house Patricia Perry's veritable country inn at the edge of Highlands Square. The architectural and ornamental details that fill each of several small rooms, awash in pastels, simply astonish—fireplaces, antique sideboards, stained-glass inlays, trompe l'oeil murals, and carved crystal; no less breathtaking is the wraparound patio fringed with flowering foliage galore. Not surprisingly, the menu tends to mirror its surroundings—light, delicate, tradition-minded—and when the kitchen's on, that's a very good thing. Creamy soups of celeriac and fennel or watercress gain depth and color from berries and nuts, as do fish dishes—though our favorite is the pan-seared tilapia drenched in lemon butter and topped with smoked bay scallops and capers. The likes of honey-roasted figs with goat-cheese cream or pheasant over wild rice pilaf with cashews possess an almost bygone grace. If your instincts tell you to finish your meal with an apple-based dessert, listen well: the fruit was likely picked from the grounds' own trees. Open seasonally only; call ahead.

Highland Tap & Burger, 2219 W. 32nd St., LoHi, Denver, CO 80211; (720) 287-4493; http://highlandtapdenver.com; Burgers; $. Countless flat-screens and garage door–style windows that open onto a spacious sidewalk patio lure Broncos and Rockies fans by the pack to this LoHi watering hole—which, we're happy to report, otherwise breaks the sports-bar mold whole-heartedly. Devoting 18 of 20 taps to local craft beer—including house exclusives from Fort Collins's acclaimed Odell Brewing Company—the crew behind the stick aims to wet your whistle further with a smallish but shrewd selection of bottled domestics and imports. The kitchen, meanwhile, pledges allegiance to the gastropub flag with a menu that's relatively simple but conscientiously executed. As the name suggests, burgers are its prime-time game—and they're high scorers, piled with every nifty thing from root beer–marinated pulled pork to salt-cured *foie gras*. But they meet their match in starters and sides like terrific potato skins—crunchy without, fluffy within, and ooey-gooey all over with bacon-loaded white cheddar, not to mention buttermilk ranch dip—as well as fat, piping-hot, chewy beer-battered onion rings.

Hops & Pie, 3920 Tennyson St., Berkeley, Denver, CO 80212; (303) 477-7000; www.hopsandpie.com; Pizza; $$. Low-key as it feels, this Berkeley parlor and taproom has made major waves on the Denver dining scene due to the sheer *savoir faire* of Owners Drew and Leah Watson. The ever-evolving beer selection—about 20 on tap and twice that in bottle—reflects their focus on limited-edition and other rare finds: barrel-aged, cask-conditioned, brewed with herbs and fruits and tubers (yams?!), you name it. And anything goes for their pizzas, too. From the seats along the bar, you can watch the kitchen crew toss the dough through a small window to the kitchen; what you can't see coming are the ingredient combos so wacky they just might work (and do): pulled chicken with blackberry barbecue sauce and black-eyed peas, for instance, or steak and mashed potatoes with gruyère (not to mention à la carte smoked ham hocks and tofu). The $3 daily slice borrows toppings from tacos, burritos, and cheeseburgers—while leaving just enough room for a bite of skillet-baked, golden-crumbed, beer-infused mac-and-cheese or a gooey Rice Krispies treat made better with brown butter.

Indulge French Bistro, 4140 W. 38th Ave., Berkeley, Denver, CO 80212; (303) 433-7400; http://indulgefrenchbistro.net; French; $$$. Serendipity: that's how we view the circuitous path that Chef William Wahl, with wife-partner Stéphanie, took from his native Normandy to open this intimate, twinkling bistro in an unlikely location on downmarket 38th Avenue. Centered around a small, marble-topped bar, the dining room presents a distinguished setting—low lights, silken drapes, stained-glass panes, and all—for doing exactly as the name suggests (a flowerbox-lined side patio does likewise). Classic plates and modern updates peacefully coexist on Wahl's seasonal menu; although we tend to favor the former—including perfectly prepared steak au poivre vert and dark, dreamy coq au vin—inspired desserts show an appealingly light touch, as with tea-infused, pistachio-studded orange soup. It's worth noting that "indulge" isn't a euphemism for "splurge" here; the all-French wine list is surprisingly reasonable, containing plenty of finds in the $30 to $40 range, and the Thursday-night mussel special is a steal complete with frites and a glass of wine (we recommend the cream-splashed homage to Wahl's home turf, *moules à la normande*).

Linger, 2030 W. 30th Ave., LoHi, Denver, CO 80211; (303) 993-3120; www.lingerdenver.com; Small Plates/Tapas; $$. Leave it to Justin Cucci to turn a WWII-era mortuary into the liveliest haunt around. The mastermind behind **Root Down** (p. 43) is a finder and a keeper par excellence: reclaimed boxcar parts, church pews, Lite Brite pegboards, cue balls, and more don't merely tie the room together; they animate the entire two-story space (three if you count the almost vertiginous, panorama-blessed rooftop deck). Of course, the ebullient aura the decor creates also imbues Chef Daniel Asher's menu, itself a sort of collection of found objects in that, says Cucci, "it brings the international street foods I love" together in one place—where they tend to undergo a mod metamorphosis. We're addicted to the raw yet somehow toasty "samosas" with cashew yogurt, the deconstructed saag paneer with rhubarb ketchup, the highly irregular but nonetheless delicious take on Moroccan *b'stilla,* and the fava-and-pea-based twist on hummus; seasonal soups and salads are strong points, too. By the same token, we're thrilled with the wine list, fearlessly unconventional and ripe for exploration; meanwhile, the mixology team shakes things up in sassy fashion (and of course they make a mean corpse reviver).

LoHi SteakBar, 3200 Tejon St., LoHi, Denver, CO 80211; www .lohisteakbar.com; (303) 927-6334; Bar & Grill; $$. What's the difference between a steak house and a "steak bar"? Cross the threshold of this neo-tavern and find out. Mellow at times, boisterous at others, it's the hepcat's alternative to the fat cat's cow palace either way, featuring a menu that simultaneously channels the roadside diner and the corner bistro, supplemented by liberal happy-hour and blue-plate specials. Strange as it may sound, our foolproof system for picking the cream of the crop involves ordering anything with either blue cheese or mushrooms. Patted with butter or served over toast, the namesake steaks benefit handsomely from the presence of both, as do jaw-stretching burgers; likewise, for our money, blue-cheese fondue with housemade potato chips and thick-sliced portobellos broiled in garlic butter almost beat out the judiciously oil-slicked, herb-seasoned frites. As for the bar, it's at its best when re-creating the classics from its collection of some 25 gins—which only goes further to show that at LoHi, everything old-school is novel again.

Lola Coastal Mexican, 1575 Boulder St., LoHi, Denver, CO 80211; (720) 570-8686; www.loladenver.com; Mexican; $$$. Boasting killer views of the downtown skyline and a wicked lineup of tequilas and mezcals, this LoHi fixture plays the simultaneous part of rustic cantina and urbane hang for a crowd who can't get enough of its performance. Rightly so; like many of its siblings under the Big Red F banner, Lola exceeds the expectations set by its prime location. Abiding by the philosophy that bolder is better, the kitchen proves it with a seafood-heavy repertoire that's no less consistent for being seasonal. Sprightly tomatillo–green apple salsa sparkles on a sampler that's worth the surcharge, as is guacamole prepared tableside; tropical fruits, tubers and roots, and chiles of all stripes alternately add brightness and depth to soups, ceviches, and hefty mains. And Lola's long been at the top of our list for brunch; be it a plate-size slab of chicken-fried steak in chorizo cream gravy over sweet-potato hash or scrambled egg–topped lobster enchiladas, the selection never lacks for eye-catching inventions. The same goes for a happy-hour menu that eschews a wholesale rehash of dinner-time apps in favor of its own choice tidbits, like fried pickles and asparagus with avocado-buttermilk dip. That's just the way we want it all to stay for our Lola (la-la-la-la Lola . . .).

Los Carboncitos, 3757 Pecos St., LoHi, Denver, CO 80211; (303) 458-0880; www.loscarboncitos.com; Mexican; $$. Unless you're severely color-blind, you can't miss this Mexico City–style mainstay on a heavily trafficked Highlands corner—it's painted flaming orange outside as well as in. But if you are and/or you do, hang a U-turn and try again: Los Carboncitos is well worth the trouble (and we don't say that lightly, given that it lacks a liquor license). The corn-crunchy, tostada-like namesake items smeared with refried beans and cheese alone will convince you we speak the truth, especially if they're topped with char-tipped yet drippingly juicy *carne al pastor*. But so will everything else, from the electrifying red-and-green salsa quartet that accompanies chips to the elliptical griddled masa flatbreads known as *huaraches*—the Cubano is an overloaded hoot—to super *alambres*, effectively south-of-the-border stir-fries scooped into fresh corn tortillas (our favorite is the simple, earthy combo of chopped steak, cactus, and onion). Wash it all down with a frothy *horchata*, soak up the good-natured atmosphere, and you won't even miss your cerveza (much). Additional locations: 720 Sheridan Blvd., Denver, CO 80214; (303) 573-1617; 15210 E. 6th Ave., Aurora, CO 80011; (303) 364-2606.

Lou's Food Bar, 1851 W. 38th Ave., Sunnyside, Denver, CO 80211; (303) 458-0336; http://lousfoodbar.com; American; $$. Retro signage, a simply furnished space, and a relaxed vibe convey an emphasis on comfort that restaurateur-about-town Frank

Bonanno makes explicit: Lou's, he says, serves "the things that I want to eat with my family." Both his Jersey upbringing and his French training influence a menu that pays homage to delis and diners on the one hand, classic bistros on the other—pâtés and rillettes du jour (now pork, now salmon) juxtapose house-cured pastrami and spaghetti with meatballs; roast chicken meets fried; and potpies bump up against pheasant *en croûte*. While Bonanno himself is partial to the classic French dip, we lean toward the blackened fish sandwich on a baguette slathered with celeriac rémoulade. And though we're enchanted by the thought of dipping jalapeño corn bread into a side of chicken *velouté*, we rarely make it past the good old-fashioned garlic bread in practice. Ditto the warm, tangy, bacon-smeared sauerkraut that makes cheddar-flecked venison links our pick from the litter of handsome housemade sausages. The pies are good (Bonanno also owns **Wednesday's Pie**, p. 111), but the brownie bread pudding's even better, and the cocktail program's solid (bonus points for the Mason-jar glassware).

Masterpiece Delicatessen, 1575 Central St., LoHi, Denver, CO 80211; (303) 561-3354; http://masterpiecedeli.com; Sandwiches; $. From the cocksure moniker to two-story-tall walls the startling shade of banana peppers, this LoHi deli heralds the audacity of Chef-Partner Justin Brunson—and the sandwiches justify it. Some are virtual entrees en baguette: much local ink (and drool) has been spilled over the signature slow-braised brisket with melted taleggio, caramelized onions, arugula, and red wine gastrique, while downright elegant specials combine, say, herb-roasted chicken to rival that of any bistro with swirls of creamy-sweet parsnip puree, brought into sharp relief by warm chard and pickled carrots. Even breakfast egg sammies skew sophisto, like sautéed wild mushrooms with swiss (although we're tickled all the pinker by the rare offer of Taylor pork roll, a pop-cult classic from back east). Ditto the materials with which to build your own masterpieces, including chickpeas, sliced pears, tomato tapenade, and locally canned sparkling wine (okay, that comes on the side).

Parisi, 4401 Tennyson St., Berkeley, Denver, CO 80212; (303) 561-0234; www.parisidenver.com; Italian; $. Around every corner of this charmer, whose strung lights and gleaming wood-planked floors emit a warm ochre glow, there's something to see. The deli shelves and cases lining one entire wall contain everything from gelati in flavors like butternut squash to various dolci and fresh loaves of ciabatta to take-out salads to imported Italian cheeses and pantry staples; opposite them stands a cozy wine bar and a stairwell down to the romantic little grotto owners Simone Parisi, a native of Florence, and his wife, Christine, call Firenze a Tavola, open four nights a week for dinner (the menu changes monthly). For Italophiles like us, merely to consider all the offerings is to take a trip *all'onda dei ricordi*: will it be the *gnocchi gorgonzola e noci* (walnuts) to whisk us back to Perugia, or the risotto with sausage and radicchio we recall from Verona? Maybe classic caponata and arancini like we first had in Palermo? We only know we'll keep returning until, eventually, we've relived it all.

Root Down, 1600 W. 33rd Ave., LoHi, Denver, CO 80211; (303) 993-4200; www.rootdowndenver.com; Contemporary; $$. We don't use the word "visionary" lightly, but restaurateur Justin Cucci raised the bar high when he opened this humdinger of a hot spot in 2008. (To learn how he's since cleared it, see **Linger,** p. 37.) In renovating the mid-century service station that Root Down replaced, the intrepid auction hound amassed castoff lamps, sculptures, rotary phones, bathroom scales, cookbooks, and other period pieces to create what is now as much a funky vintage design gallery as it is an ultra-progressive, green-leaning eatery. How the kitchen upholds its ethicurean ideals; accommodates today's vegan, gluten-free, and raw-food diets; and still manages to pull off such a wide-ranging repertoire is beyond us, but we applaud the boldness of such creations as a salad of Asian pear, spaghetti squash, aged gouda, candied walnuts, and pomegranate in star anise vinaigrette or butternut squash-and-ricotta gnocchi with mushrooms, spinach and black currants in both brown butter and sage pesto (whew). When it works, it's fireworks; meanwhile, the bar crew has been slinging the zingers since day one. See Root Down's recipe for **Pueblo Chili Flip** on p. 343.

Spuntino, 2639 W. 32nd Ave., LoHi, Denver, CO 80211; (303) 433-0949; www.spuntinodenver.com; Bakery/Cafe; $. For all the namesake items (spuntino means "snack") on colorful display, it's *sprezzatura*—an Italian synonym for *je ne sais quoi*—that permeates every nook and cranny of this refreshing LoHi find. Crisp, earth-toned digs warmed by copper fixtures and a jazz soundtrack bid you relax awhile, as does the sincere hospitality of co-owner Dorina Miller, whose small crew puts more thought into the most casual nibble than some kitchens do into elaborate multi-coursers. Though sandwiches are Spuntino's house-baked bread and butter (so to speak), our heads are often turned by mouthwatering specials like a passel of short ribs intensely perfumed with fig agrodolce or mini-loaves of *povitica*, a sweet bread swirled with walnut paste. Other times, we go straight to what we ultimately came for: blissful brain freeze. Together, the gelati and the smashing gourmet popsicles form a seasonal rainbow of flavor-bending goodness: if a scoop of subtle Earl Grey and cream or anything-but-subtle cannoli doesn't grab you, peach cobbler or peanut butter-and-jelly on a stick surely will. At press time, Spuntino had just added bistro-style dinner service to its repertoire.

Tocabe: An American Indian Eatery, 3536 W. 44th Ave., Berkeley, Denver, CO 80211; www.tocabe.com; (720) 524-8282; American; $. Think of it as aboriginal soul food. Marked by a triple-handprint logo that symbolizes the three branches of the Osage Nation, this quick-casual counter joint specializes in hot, fresh puffs of fry bread from the owners' family recipe, stuffed or more popularly topped with your choices from a sizable array of items lining the steam table. Of the three meats, three types of beans, and six salsas on offer, shredded buffalo and soupy pintos with chunky hominy-cranberry relish are the way to go, generously layered with shredded cheese, lettuce, tomatoes, red onions, sour cream, and chipotle sauce. But fry bread for dessert ain't half bad either, whether smothered in *wojapi*—essentially fruit compote—or rolled into nuggets dusted with powdered sugar. Except for chili, nachos, and braised bison ribs, that's pretty much it—but believe you us that's more than enough: this stuff will stick to your own ribs all day long.

Trattoria Stella, 3470 W. 32nd Ave., Highland, Denver, CO 80211; (303) 458-1128; http://trattoriastella.squarespace.com; Italian; $$. Graced with both front and back patios, this snug, renovated Victorian cottage is an adorable Highlands Square magnet for the ladies who lunch on greens (paired with Pinot Grigio, of course) and the couples who reenact everyone's favorite scene from *Lady and the Tramp* over dinner. If Stella isn't quite stellar, with a kitchen whose reach sometimes exceeds its grasp, it's certainly likeable. Among the fresh pastas, our favorite is the dense, chewy pipe rigate in peppery vodka sauce with excellent herbed sausage, preceded by a salad—any salad, so long as it comes with that curious lemon-cherry dressing—but daily specials like lasagna layered with green tomatoes are always worth a gander, as are housemade desserts like liqueur-spiked bread pudding. And wines by the bottle are almost unreasonably reasonable, the majority hovering around the $30 mark. (Guess those lunching ladies know a thing or two about a thing or two.) Additional location: 3201 E. Colfax Ave., Denver, CO 80206; (303) 320-8635.

Udi's Bread Cafe, 7357 E. 29th Ave., Stapleton, Denver, CO 80238; (303) 329-8888; http://udisfood.com; Bakery/Cafe; $. If the logo on the signs marking this clean, modern Stapleton cafe strikes you as familiar, it's no wonder: Udi's granola graces market shelves nationwide. The Denver-based company's mini-chain of cafes, however, has yet to expand beyond the Rockies, catering accordingly to Colorado's ultra-health-conscious community. Vegetarian and gluten-free options abound on a menu that starts with sandwiches featuring rustic, fresh-baked breads of all kinds—like the neat twist on the French dip that replaces roast beef with chicken breast and jus. But often, the most intriguing items aren't sandwiches at all; that honor goes instead to dinner specials like kabocha-and-shiitake curry or mushroom-arugula fusilli. Additional locations (hours vary; check the website): 1001 17th St., Denver, CO 80202; (303) 395-7700; 101 E. 70th Ave., Denver, CO 80221; (303) 657-1600; 12700 E. 19th Ave., Bldg. P-15, Aurora, CO 80045; (303) 340-3388; 7600 Grandview Ave., Arvada, CO 80002; (303) 421-8000.

Wooden Spoon Cafe & Bakery, 2418 W. 32nd Ave., LoHi, Denver, CO 80211; (303) 999-0327; http://woodenspoondenver .com; Bakery/Cafe; $. Even if you stumble into this vanilla-colored storefront on a whim, a warm, jammy aroma assures you you've come to the right place. The husband-and-wife proprietors turn out a full array of treats both fun-size and really fun-size: while cakelets and tartlets, enrobed in chocolate or topped with meringue, are just right for one—we're smitten with the pillowy lemon-coconut cubes—the jars and trays are stacked with gingerbread cookies, fruit-chunked scones, and turnovers big enough to share (enor- mous, really). But the savories are astutely conceived too: chive sour cream, it turns out, is a simple BLT's new, mayo-replacing BFF, and we love that we have a choice between ham and cheese and, well, ham and cheese (one country-style with swiss, the other com- bining prosciutto and brie). As for personal-size quiches, with their thick, rustic crusts, they could pass for potpies.

Z Cuisine & À Côté, 2239/2245 W. 30th Ave., LoHi, Denver, CO 80211; (303) 477-1111; www.zcuisineonline.com; French; $$$. We clench our teeth, bite our tongues, and still it escapes: ooh la la! Corny as the interjection is, it encapsulates the swooning that Patrick and Lynnde Dupays's LoHi bistro and adjacent absinthe bar induce night after night. With its blackboard menus and close-set tables, the former evokes a rustic farmhouse kitchen; the latter, by contrast, is a smoldering little boîte where every just-so detail sets the mood indigo: the free-form beaded chandelier, the zinc- topped Art Deco bar paneled with embossed teal enamel, the Busby

Berkeley musicals screening silently on one wall. Equally perfect is, well, anything and everything else. Seemingly effortless charcuterie platters. Delicate whitefish steamed in parchment with spring vegetables. Pork belly that melts on contact with your tongue over lentils that pop like bubbles. Gloriously runny, stinky cheese baked in walnut leaves and paired with supple pumpkin compote. Crusty-creamy apple galettes. A small but unassailable selection of wines by the glass, classic aperitifs, and exquisite cocktails—try the icy, tantalizing La Vie en Rose—as well as poetic absinthe drips. Stop us before we say it again—ooh la . . .

Landmarks

Billy's Inn, 4403 Lowell Blvd., Berkeley, Denver, CO 80211; (303) 455-9733; www.billysinn.com; Bar & Grill; $. Despite extensive renovations in 2008, the spirit of this 1930s-era fixture remains largely intact—its Spanish Colonial Revival style of architecture reinforced by the rough-hewn wood, stucco, and block glass within. (For a glimpse of the good old days, check out the cigarette smoke–shrouded photos of long-gone patrons in the bathroom.) Retro but not old-fashioned, the menu likewise reflects the laid-back atmosphere: peel-and-eat shrimp, chips and dip, deviled eggs, and the like round out fish tacos, textbook burgers (try the one with bacon, swiss, and guacamole), and surprisingly good, bounteous salads. Even more surprising, meanwhile, are the numerous tequilas and

margaritas that steal beer's presumptive limelight. Whatever your poison, though, you'll appreciate the flashbacks that Billy's offers to a time when barkeeps actually asked about your poison without air quotes.

Gaetano's, 3760 Tejon St., LoHi, Denver, CO 80211 (303) 455-9852; http://gaetanositalian.com; Italian; $$. The dishonest-to-goodness racketeers who opened Gaetano's six decades ago are long gone. But this red-sauce joint still plays the part of the shady supper club to the hilt: stained-glass lamps, black vinyl booths, Sinatra tunes, cheerfully sinister motto ("Italian to die for"), and all. We have to confess we don't really come for the food—we come for the cheese. But every once in a while, a heaping platter of sausage and peppers, a glass of Chianti (what else?), and, if we're really in the spirit, a dish of spumoni hit the spot.

The Original Chubby's, 1231 W. 38th Ave., Sunnyside, Denver, CO 80211; (303) 455-9311; http://theoriginalchubbysinc.com; Mexican; $. You could base a telenovela on the family squabbles surrounding this 40-something 6-seater and its more-or-less unauthorized spinoffs. But better you should cut right through all the fuss with one bite of the green chile ladled out of pots the size of oil drums (which you can just make out through the window behind the order counter). Actually, you could cut through steel with this stuff. Thicker—even a little gloppy—and frankly much fattier than most, the unusually tan-colored potage is also among the hottest in town, making your lips thrum and numbing your tongue. Without it, neither the beloved burritos nor the burgers that started it all—the original name was Chubby's Burger Drive-In—would be quite the same. Accept no substitutes, indeed.

Pagliacci's, 1440 W. 33rd Ave., LoHi, Denver, CO 80211; (303) 458-0530; www.ipagliaccio.com; Italian; $$. Old-fashioned swank—twining grapevines, velveteen-cushioned booths, recessed niches painted depicting Italian landscapes—speaks to this candle-lit LoHi ristorante's venerable, nearly 70-year history. But we'd just as soon sit at the more casual bar, where we can study the inventory of imported digestivi little known stateside. After all, we're going to need them—Pagliacci's makes no concessions to 21st-century dietary concerns. Nor should it; its regulars rely on the kitchen's ability to turn back time via such hefty classics as chicken tetrazzini, veal saltimbocca, and manicotti (all heartily accompanied by good old minestrone). For our part, we're enamored with the all-too-rare dish of chicken livers cooked in red wine with mushrooms and onions, which we scoop onto bread—saving some for sopping up the remaining juices, of course; meanwhile, nightly specials like sherry-glazed *maiale* (roast pork) with caponata keep us on our toes. And we're equally appreciative of the all-Italian wine list for bucking the either-or cliché of jug Chianti and big-ticket Piedmontese vintages; interesting pours from smaller vineyards like Alto Adige's Abbazia di Novacella go to show that you can honor tradition without getting stuck there.

Patsy's Inn, 3641 Navajo St., LoHi, Denver, CO 80211; (303) 477-8910; www.patsysinn.com; Italian; $$. Patsy's was old-school before the term existed. Opening in 1921—two decades before its nearby rivals in red sauce, **Gaetano's** (p. 49) and **Pagliacci's** (p. 50)—it has, by the third-generation owners' own account, undergone many changes over the years. That most occurred well before the turn of the millennium is, however, evident at a glance. The long wooden bar in the entranceway, the napkin-covered bread baskets awaiting on red tablecloths beneath the murals of Italian landmarks, the repartee among long-timers—it's all here, and so are the plates overflowing with homemade (a word we think they've earned the right to use over the more accurate "housemade") spaghetti topped with traditional meat sauce or chicken cacciatore. Like the linguine with clams, the vino pretty much comes in red or white—and the list prices are a throwback too, rarely breaking the $25 mark. The only notable exception to Patsy's status quo: the 2009 addition of a tiny pizzeria next door—though the pies themselves are, sure enough, *vecchia scuola.*

Carbone's Italian Sausage Market & Deli, 1221 W. 38th Ave., Sunnyside, Denver, CO 80211; (303) 455-2893. At 40 years and counting, Carbone's doesn't look a day over 50—small and humble, even slightly dingy. In other words, it looks—to anyone who's ever lived in New York or Boston or Chicago or San Francisco (and that, to be sure, includes a lot of newly minted Coloradans)—like every other *salumeria* back home, practically bricked up as it is with traditional cold cuts and cheeses, bags of dried pasta, and canned tomatoes. Tastes the same, too. The combo sandwiches get the most love from locals, but we're partial to the subs with meatballs or sausage marinara, all made daily in house. They come with your choice of cheese—but you'd better choose provolone or mozzarella—and mild or spicy pepperoncini (again, the latter are the only valid option). May the grandkids who now sometimes pop up behind the counter keep this place as real as their nonni have for decades.

Common Grounds, 3484 W. 32nd Ave., Highland, Denver, CO 80211; (303) 458-5248; www.commongroundscoffeehouse.com. Though the beans are house-roasted, it isn't the joe that brings us here. Nor is it the pastries or sandwiches, adequate yet typical. An assortment of bottled beers and wines as well as ice cream from **Liks** (p. 168) are nice touches but not deal-makers. Rather, for 20 years and counting, this Highlands Square coffeehouse has won us over by serving as a sort of community center where neighbors of all ages gather to peruse the free books lining the shelves, get a board game going, or just idly pass the time. Ongoing exhibits by area artists add their local color to the living, breathing, cappuccino-sipping kind.

The Denver Bread Company, 3200 Irving St., Highland, Denver, CO 80211; (303) 455-7194; www.thedenverbreadcompany.com. If you dine out in Denver with any regularity, chances are good you're a loyal customer of this Highlands bakery without even knowing it; its sourdough boules, baguettes, and country Italian loaves are bread-basket staples across town. So you might as well cut out the middleman from time to time, especially since owner Greg Bortz stocks his own shelves with the goods to fill dozens of baskets back home: beer and potato breads, garlic and cinnamon twists, scones, lovely cookies—try the somewhat mochi-like Lemon Lucys—and gorgeous focaccia rounds covered with caramelized onions, chopped walnuts, and gorgonzola. Though Bortz's operation is strictly retail—no coffeehouse-style service awaits—the friendly staff is quick to offer samples.

Happy Cakes Bakeshop, 3434 W. 32nd Ave., Highland, Denver, CO 80211; (303) 477-3556; www.happycakes.com. "I see you looking at my cupcakes," read the sassy message tees stacked in cubbyholes beneath the blackboard menu in the only slightly larger cubbyhole that is this Highlands Square sweets shop. Go ahead and ogle. For all the pretenders that have hopped on the cupcake bandwagon in recent years, Happy Cakes is the real deal—its frosted little babies are as cute and, more important, lip-smacking as they are wildly creative. Most of the flavors change daily and range widely; novelty seekers of all ages will ooh and aah over specials inspired by caramel corn or "dirt cake" with gummy worms, while tipplers hit the jackpot on Friday with boozy concoctions like the Casa Noble—a tequila-soaked peach-and-cherry cake—and the self-explanatory Jack & Coke. Meanwhile, the bubbly staff puts the colored sprinkles on service.

Little Man Ice Cream, 2620 16th St., LoHi, Denver, CO 80211; (303) 455-3811; http://littlemanicecream.com. Shaped like a giant silver milk jug, this two-story-tall ice-cream stand forms a shining beacon for LoHi's sweet of tooth. The handmade scoops—about 20 at any given time, including gelato and sorbet—tend toward the tried-and-true: butter pecan, seasonal candy cane, and so on. But every now and then you'll encounter a brow-raiser like blueberry-cinnamon or salted Oreo. In any case, it's owner Paul Tamburello's dedication to community that really sets the place apart. Out on the surrounding patio, depending on the season, he screens old movies, hosts a roster of local musicians, sells Christmas trees, and—when the temperature dips below zero—offers "pink-cheek pints" for a buck apiece.

Mondo Vino, 3601 W. 32nd Ave., Highland, Denver, CO 80211; (303) 458-3858; www.mondovino.net. The brainchild of a sommelier by the curious name of Duey Kratzer, this Highlands Square boutique barely has enough floor space for browsing, so thoroughly stocked is every nook and cranny. Even so, there's plenty of room to broaden your horizons. Kratzer is a consummate tastemaker; for every big-ticket classic, there's an up-and-comer or two worth exploring. We've scooped up wines from Mexico and Armenia along with bottles from cult producers like Alto Adige's Elena Walch and undersung sparklers like Brachetto d'Acqui—gawking all the while at the uncompromising selection of gift-bottled boutique spirits and craft beers. And when something in particular catches our eye, we don't hesitate to interrogate the highly trained, discreetly attentive staff; there isn't a flagon of rose nectar or unpronounceable Islay scotch they can't answer for.

The Pig & Block Charcuterie, 3326 Tejon St., LoHi, Denver, CO 80211; (720) 628-7192; www.thepigandblock.com. "There are so many old recipes I want to dabble in. I want to get it back into people's heads that [artisanal production] is a way of life," enthuses Jeff Bauman. He and his brother Marc have begun to do just that at their new penny–shiny Highland shop. They cure pancetta and bacon, grind sausages daily—including caul-webbed crépinettes— and make their own duck-leg confit, pâtés, and terrines like the blockbuster forestière with pork liver and wild mushrooms. And what they don't produce in house, they source carefully: locally raised chickens (and their eggs), restaurant-grade chops, hand-tied

A GREEN CHILE PRIMER

Green chile: it's a sauce, it's a stew, it's a way of life. Here in Colorado, as in neighboring New Mexico, styles vary—some are thin, some thick; some contain tomatoes, some don't; ditto pork. (See, for example, two of our diametrically opposed faves at **El Taco de Mexico,** p. 195, and **The Original Chubby's,** p. 49, respectively.) But so long as they contain roasted green chiles, broth, onions, and garlic, they can be worthy of the name. (Red chile, meanwhile, is made with dried pods and little else.)

Still, settling on a definition isn't the same as anointing exemplars thereof; Coloradans dissect the stuff down to the last drop, and debates as to where, exactly, the best green chile is to be found will end when the world does. The following picks are by no means conclusive—but they're ours, and we're sticking to 'em.

Efrain's II, *1630 N. 63rd St., Ste. 10, Boulder, CO 80301; (303) 440-4045; www.efrainsrestaurant.com; Mexican; $.* Oddly, Efrain's second branch is better than the original—and the humble but welcoming cocina at the dreary eastern edge of Boulder certainly creams the college-town competition. We think of its kitchen as a classroom whose cooks teach Green Chile 101: Theirs is a textbook version that's ruddy with tomatoes yet greenly laced with diced chiles, rich in tender nuggets of pork yet bristling with spice that pellets the back of your throat first, then spreads to set your lips atingle. Approaching it with respect is a lesson you'll learn well. Additional locations: 101 E. Cleveland St., Lafayette, CO 80026; (303) 666-7544; 451 S. Platt Pkwy., Longmont, CO 80501; (720) 494-0777.

La Popular, *2033 Lawrence St., Denver, CO 80203; (303) 296-1687; http://lapopular.food.officelive.com/default.aspx.* The owners of this decades-old Five Points tortilleria rightly tout their delish tamales (the beefy red-chile version may be the best buck you ever spent); the shelves flanking the take-out counter are crammed with pineapple and pumpkin empanadas, bolillo rolls, taco shells, and bags of masa for home cooks. Green chile by the pint seems almost an afterthought—but it isn't. Glowing orange with bits of red pepper as well as green, and thick with giant chunks of pork, it departs from the standard recipe, at least in these parts, but it's no less heady for that.

Santiago's, 571 Santa Fe Dr., Denver, CO 80204; (303) 534-5004; www .eatatsantiagos.com; Mexican; $. Though you can order it à la carte, this ubiquitous local chain's green chile is, in the minds of most locals, inseparable from the legendary breakfast burritos. Respectable on its own—orange-tinged, thickish, highly seasoned—it enters a whole new dimension as it melds with the ham, bacon, or chorizo that the kitchen throws in with the tortilla-swaddled eggs, potatoes, and optional cheese on alternating days. Order it spicy and you, too, could be thrust into hyperspace; newbies are advised to start with the half-and-half. Additional locations include 2505 N. Federal Blvd., Denver, CO 80211; (720) 855-8109; 5701 Leetsdale Ave., Denver, CO 80224; (303) 333-5305; and 1325 Broadway #105, Boulder, CO 80302; (303) 245-9365.

Socorro's, 19 E. Bayaud St., Denver, CO 80209; (303) 777-8226; Mexican; $. It may be unsung, but this tiny New Mexican–style taqueria in the Baker District speaks for itself, especially if Carlos is behind the counter. He painstakingly assembles killer tacos al pastor with chunks of fresh pineapple and equally excellent street-style fish tacos slathered with chipotle mayo. And then he ladles up some of the best green chile most Denverites have never had. Just right, indeed: neither too thin nor too thick—with absolutely no tomato, only miniscule shreds of pork, and sporadic pearls of pork fat highlighting its yellow-green, vegetal purity—it's spicy enough to make you sit up straight without blasting you to smithereens.

salamini, and other salumi from acclaimed domestic labels like La Quercia, Olli, and Oldani Bros., as well as imported jamón and prosciutto. A few well-chosen cheeses and condiments complete the neat picture, almost old-fashioned in its neighborly simplicity.

Seafood Landing, 3457 W. 32nd Ave., Highland, Denver, CO 80211; (303) 571-1995. What could this small Highlands Square seafood outlet possibly have that the supermarkets don't? In a word, heart. Proprietor Bruce Johnson, an extremely soft-spoken and kind engineer-turned-fishmonger, embodies the benefits of shopping locally. His inventory sparkles on ice, from glistening grouper fillets and tuna steaks to sea scallops as thick as your wrist to rock lobster tails, softshell crabs, and escargot in the shell. He makes his own cocktail sauce and first-rate Manhattan chowder—light, peppery, and brimming with fresh clams and bacon. Speaking of clams, he offers take-home clambakes; he also stocks an array of seasonings, brings in loaves of sourdough from **Denver Bread Company** down the street, and compiles handy recipe pamphlets. And did we mention he's an absolute peach? Well, it's worth reiterating.

St. Kilian's Cheese Shop, 3211 Lowell Blvd., Highland, Denver, CO 80211; (303) 477-0374; http://stkilianscheeseshop.com. We don't squeeze into this shoebox of a boutique in Highlands Square to be entertained; we go for the gorgeous gourmet goods. Nevertheless, owner Hugh O'Neill always makes us smile—and think. Promoting "the rather radical idea that eating well doesn't have to be a special-occasion thing," he and wife-partner Ionah de Freitas stock exquisite products that "some customers would describe, in a word, as 'smelly.' I prefer 'diverse,' although I admit to a certain pungency in the air." If so, it's no sharper than his wit, ever on display as he nimbly guides a steady stream of customers through the inventory: luscious blues from the world over, little-known Spanish sheep's milk cheeses, logs of locally made chèvre, cheddars from his native Ireland, and more. Accoutrements range from artisanal salumi and crackers to lovely pâtés, preserves, and seasonings; all you'll need to supplement your spread is a bottle of wine from **Mondo Vino** (p. 54) next door—and rest assured O'Neill will have just the pairing suggestion.

Central Denver

Downtown Denver/LoDo, Golden Triangle & Five Points

Had it not been captured for posterity by no lesser bards of the downtrodden than Jack Kerouac and Tom Waits, you'd never know that, not so long ago, downtown Denver was crosshatched with bona fide skid rows. Larimer Street in particular, once "teeming with that undulating beat," as Waits put it in "Drunk on the Moon," now bustles and gleams as it stretches from the promenades of LoDo through the quickly emerging Ballpark neighborhood to the historically colorful and increasingly artsy area known as Five Points. And it sets the paradigm for the central business district in general: converted lofts, eclectic shops, and myriad eateries today run the length and breadth of what was once off-limits after the offices closed. Centered on the pedestrian 16th Street Mall and ringed round by professional sports stadiums, a landmark convention center and performing arts complex, and the museums that mark the Golden Triangle, downtown Denver can only keep moving on up—to a point, anyway. Without those last ramshackle patches, this wouldn't, after all, be the city through which Kerouac, "at lilac evening, walked with every muscle aching"—convinced all the while that anywhere else "was not enough ecstasy for me, not enough life, joy, kicks, darkness, music, not enough night."

Foodie Faves

Ambria, 1201 16th St., LoDo, Denver, CO 80202; (303) 623-8646; www.ambriadenver.com; Mediterranean; $$. A long-overdue exception to the rule of mediocrity on the 16th Street Mall, this Tabor Center sanctuary signals its distinction from the get-go: globe lanterns, sheer drapery, and spice hues convey a respite from the commercial tempest raging beyond its doors (love that corkscrew mobile, too). Though the kitchen is hardly alone in approaching traditional foodways from a contemporary angle, the thoughtful tweaks it gives to Mediterranean classics really do seem new: venison pops in cassoulet, butternut squash in Bolognese, parsnips in hummus, and spinach in falafel. Some of the most striking dishes gesture only vaguely toward their origins, like a refreshing raw-carrot salad that eschews Moroccan ingredients in favor of Marcona almonds, crumbled gorgonzola, curls of frisée, and daubs of celery-leaf pesto; it's light and crunchy with just a hint of funk. Befitting the emphasis on small plates, the bar offers wine by the half-glass to make mixing and matching easy; we wish more restaurants would adopt the logical practice.

Belvedere Restaurant, 323 14th St., Downtown, Denver, CO 80202; (720) 974-4052; Polish; $$. Despite its uncommonly dashing ambiance—behold that wood-paneled, stained glass–trimmed back parlor—**Kinga's Lounge** (1509 Marion St., Denver, CO 80218, 303-830-6922) is a Colfax watering hole first and foremost. So kudos to owner Kinga Klek for putting traditional Polish food in the limelight at her second venture, Belvedere, a haven of Old Country charm on a characterless downtown block. Belvedere's copper tones and rustic accents—a firewood display here, a winding vine there—evoke some cabin hearth around which the rib-sticking repertoire coalesces. Of course there's kielbasa, red or white, and veritable planks of schnitzel; of course there's cabbage—sweet, sour, or stuffed—and spuds in all guises. A butter-slicked pile of tender pierogi contains your choice of fillings; we like the nicely spiced spinach and cheese. Thick, peppery, pork-chunked *zurek polski*—or sour rye soup—is adorably served in a bread bowl on a wooden board, accompanied by two ice-cream scoops of cold herbed mashed potatoes and boiled egg wedges. Finally, a round of vodka shots is inevitable, if only to get a jump on the digestion process—it could take a while. (Make a toast: *Na zdrowie!*)

Biker Jim's Gourmet Dogs, 2148 Larimer St., Five Points, Denver, CO 80205; (720) 746-9355; http://bikerjimsdogs.com; Hot Dogs/Sausages; $. Chowhounds and epicures alike bow down to the charismatic godfather of Denver's flourishing street-food community, Biker Jim Pittenger, whose brick-and-mortar operation only cements the reputation for gleeful innovation he built on his beloved sausage cart. The Five Points joint exudes brash attitude from the schoolyard-brick walls bearing his graffitied skull logo and the bare floors anointed with skidmarks courtesy of his motorcycle buddies to, of course, eats that are to the culinary establishment what slamdancing would be at a cotillion. They start with awesome sausages—not only the notorious jalapeño-cheddar elk, reindeer, and rattlesnake-pheasant but also cilantro-flecked duck, apricot-and-cranberry-studded wild boar, and more. Trimmings and sides catapult them over the top: harissa-roasted cactus, curry jam, and Coca Cola–marinated onions, for instance, plus blistering mac-and-cheese wedges. Above all, the wiener Wellington borders on mad genius—it's a beef brat slathered with mushroom duxelles and Dijon cream, encased in puff pastry, and finished off with bordelaise. That and a beer will convince you, too, that Biker Jim is on the side of angels—hell's and otherwise.

Bistro Vendôme, 1420 Larimer St., LoDo, Denver, CO 80202; (303) 825-3232; www.bistrovendome.com; French; $$$. Though it keeps a lower profile, this *vrai-blu* bistro has shown no less staying power than its celebrated sibling **Rioja** (p. 88). Hidden from street view in a brick-lined Larimer Square courtyard brimming with greenery, it's a startling facsimile of the Parisian template, from the snug bar to the now sun-warmed, now twinkling dining room and terrace. Both the back and the front of the house—overseen by partners Jennifer

Jasinski and Beth Gruitch, respectively—are sufficiently versed in the idiom of the bistro to affirm it spontaneously rather than recite it mechanically. Escargot, pâté, roast chicken, steak frites, croques monsieurs, and kir royales—all are, yes, *comme il faut*, although we tend to make a beeline for the frog's legs and weekly specials like *lapin à la moutarde*. They're complemented, *naturellement*, by wines from Alsace, the Rhône, and the Loire as well as the Big Two—and completed by French press coffee. *Les bisous* all around.

Boney's BBQ, 1555 Champa St. #C, Downtown, Denver, CO 80202; (303) 825-9900; www.boneysbbq.com; Barbecue; $$. This subterranean storefront doesn't look like much—but then, what 'cue hut worth its dry rub does? Damned downhome for being downtown, complete with communal tables covered in red-and-white-checkered cloths, it was first brought to our attention by a leading soul-food expert and certified barbecue judge, the locally based Adrian Miller, who swore by the St. Louis–style spareribs and the pulled pork; sure enough, they're the whole hickory-smoked, ring-marked, sauced-to-order package. But truth be told, we're hooked on the smoked wings, juicy to the bone.

Brava! Pizzeria della Strada, 16th Street Mall at D & F Clock Tower, Downtown, Denver, CO 80202; (303) 619-0802; www.bravapizza.com; Pizza; $. Though it's technically mobile, David

Bravdica parks his beehive-shaped brick oven every weekday nearly year-round at the foot of the historic clock tower on the 16th Street Mall, where he shares a breezy outdoor lounge with Lannie's Clocktower Cabaret—which just so happens to have a liquor license. He has, in short, jerry-rigged quite the nifty setup. But its most alluring feature is his very own presence. What this gifted piz-zaiolo produces in a few square feet of workspace outstrips the output of most brick-and-mortar parlors put together. Crusts are unusually airy, indeed almost flaky, beneath locally sourced toppings of optimal quality (including salumi from **Il Mondo Vecchio;** see p. 203). Our go-to is the Fun Guy with shiitakes, dollops of creamy mozzarella and fresh goat cheese, and drizzles of both garlic and truffle oil; weekly specials laden with sundried tomatoes, roasted green chiles, gorgonzola, dates, and the like tantalize, too. The ultimate garnish, however, is the fact that Bravdica and his crew are super-friendly; they seem as genuinely happy to be here as we are.

Buenos Aires Pizzeria, 1307/1319 22nd St., Five Points, Denver, CO 80205; (303) 296-6710; www.bapizza.com; Argentinian; $$. We still feel pangs about the closure of Buenos Aires Grill a few years back. But as consolation prizes go, its more casual sibling around the corner takes the cake. Or rather pie. This welcoming sit-down parlor is dotted with tango-themed memorabilia from the owners' homeland, but it's their pizzas that convey the feeling you're not in Kansas (okay, Colorado) anymore; toppings like roast

pork and corn, hearts of palm, and golf sauce (a ketchup-mayo blend) capture the carefree spirit of Italo-Argentino cookery. The empanadas, meanwhile, will transport you completely. Baked to order, the circular or crescent-shaped pastries arrive hot and chewy, their thin, blistered crusts nearly splitting with tuna, eggs, and green chiles, say, or blue cheese and onions (to name two of our favorite combos); *canastitas* are their more elaborate, open-faced counterparts. If you get them to go at the take-out counter two doors down, remember to ask for a side of the red chimichurri for dipping—along with a sample of the housemade gelato. Some 30 flavors at any given time may include walnut or *sambayón* (aka *zabaglione*, Italian wine custard).

Cafe Berlin, 1600 Champa St. Unit 230, Downtown, Denver, CO 80202; (303) 377-5896; German; $$. We were darned sorry to see this former haus of Deutschland kitsch decamp for far blander, albeit slightly more upscale, digs on the 16th Street Mall. But where solace must be sought, at least it's quickly found: the staff is as kind as ever, the Paulaner beer sampler as ample as ever, the menu unchanged. This is the stuff that makes you go oof—rootsy, soothing, and huge. We're exceedingly fond of the *wurstteller*—three types of bratwurst forming a heap of browned coins over warm, caramelized sauerkraut—and the seemingly endless jäger-schnitzel smothered in creamy mushroom sauce; rolls, roasts, and

Colorado Raised

Nearly half of Colorado's total acreage is devoted to agriculture, much of it animal husbandry. Buying local meat is, therefore, easy; buying ethically raised meat, however, can present a quandary for even the most educated consumers, as debates about resource management and feeding practices rage. Good thing we've got CliffsNotes—namely the menus of our staunchest advocates for sustainability, including Black Cat Bistro's Eric Skokan, Fruition's Alex Seidel, The Kitchen's Hugo Matheson, Panzano's Elise Wiggins, Potager's Teri Rippeto, and SALT the Bistro's Bradford Heap. If they serve it, we'll try it.

Beef. Though Denver's outgrown the cowtown label in many respects, it remains the case that cattle is the state's number-one agricultural commodity. Look for: Colorado's Best Beef, Lasater Grasslands Beef.

Bison. Given its symbolic pull here on the range—it's the University of Colorado mascot, after all—not to mention its oft-touted healthfulness, you'd think bison would be a more common sight on menus than it is; we take it where we can get it. Look for: Bear Mountain Bison, King Canyon Buffalo.

Lamb. Ranking third in national production, Colorado is renowned worldwide for its lamb, which is both milder and meatier than its Australian and New Zealand counterparts, boasting a larger "eye" (that's the heart of the chop). Look for: Fox Fire Farms, Triple M Bar Ranch.

Trout. Grilled, pan-fried, or smoked, it's the Rocky Mountain region's most famous aquacultural product by far. Look for: E & J Fish Farm and, um, so-called prison trout from the Colorado Correctional Industries fishery. Really.

chops keep the comfort coming. Dumplings are a bit gummy, but a parting shot of fruit schnapps on the house should unstick your lips.

Charcoal Restaurant, 43 W. 9th Ave., Golden Triangle, Denver, CO 80204; (303) 454-0000; www.charcoaldining.com; Contemporary; $$. Though the name alludes to the custom-built grills around which the open kitchen revolves—and though the black-on-brown color scheme casts a smoky glow—this Golden Triangle looker pays no homage to backyard barbecue. While charcoal leaves an indelible mark on the menu, the overriding stamp is that of Chef Jens Patrik Landberg, who presents polished contemporary plates with a European, largely Mediterranean bent. Crackly-skinned, fleshy tournedos of grilled salmon cozy up to vivid pistachio pesto and garlicky greens; grilled vegetables take the form of a napoleon layered with phyllo. Bento-style lunch boxes are as pretty as watercolor palettes and a steal to boot: a ten-spot and change will net you a chunk of protein, veggies, a bowl of rice, another of salad, and a choice of side—including silken but pungent feta mousse. Perhaps most intriguingly, the native Swede in Landberg pops up during weekend brunch to sling the laciest pancakes, lingonberry-tinged meatballs, and gravlax marinated in aquavit. If the wine selection is rather less eclectic, the bar's fennel- and green chile–infused vodkas are all the more electric.

Chlóe Mezze Lounge, 1445 Market St., LoDo, Denver, CO 80202; (303) 825-5111; http://chloe-denver.com; Small Plates/Tapas; $$. Frankly, Chlóe isn't our standard cup of tea—or magnum of Cristal, as the case may be. Named for a mythical catwalk queen, it caters to LoDo's real-life party people in the disco and the firepit-warmed courtyard as well as throughout a lounge that's glam to the core: marble bar, black velvet wallpaper, geometric furnishings. But now and then, we're willing to see and be seen by the willowy ones, so long as the food here remains markedly better than it has to be. Spanning the Mediterranean from Spain to North Africa and the Levant, the selection of small plates is executed with unexpected attention to detail. Lemony, cumin-scented, and paired with a tangy peppadew aioli, the ground beef–filled Moroccan cigars are flaky and crisp; tartare gets a nifty twist from lamb; ditto falafel made with sweet potatoes. Less surprisingly, cocktails skew flirty—but eschew frou-frou.

ChoLon Modern Asian Bistro, 1555 Blake St. Ste. 101, LoDo, Denver, CO 80202; (303) 353-5223; www.cholon.com; Asian Fusion; $$$. It's hard to shake that office building foundation. Though ChoLon is plenty stunning in lavender-gray and black, its hard surfaces and high ceilings, supported by huge concrete pylons, lend it an impersonal feel. All the more kudos, then, go to immensely talented, impressively pedigreed Chef-Owner Lon Symensma, his partners Alicia and Jim Deters, and their well-trained, well-meaning staff for orchestrating one of the most stimulating, satisfying dining experiences not just in LoDo but in the city. Breathtakingly plated dishes range in size and style—some market stall–inspired, others elegant—but not in their ability to make you do an exhilarating double take with every bite. Do we exaggerate? Try the Kaya toast—brioche points glazed with coconut jam and accompanied by soy-touched egg custard for dipping—and decide for yourself. Or the deconstructed green papaya salad à la mode (it's topped, in a flash of brilliance, with tamarind sorbet). Or the black pepper short rib over fresh chow fun. Or even the cheeky cheesesteak wontons. Then cap it all off with a suave-seeming yet roof-raising cocktail—talk about shaking foundations.

Colt & Gray, 1553 Platte St., Downtown, Denver, CO 80202; (303) 477-1447; www.coltandgray.com; Gastropub; $$. Colt & Gray's no Fox & Hound. Nelson Perkins's take on the public house broke ground on day one and has been setting trends ever since. Snug but sharp in ebony and ivory, the Platte Valley rendezvous looks bigger than it is thanks to giant windows and mirrors (note that at the time of this writing, a much-needed expansion was under way); likewise, the plates may be mostly small, but their execution is bold, and the flavors loom large. This kitchen was one of the first in town to champion off-cuts, devoting a whole section of the menu to beef heart, blood sausage, pig trotters, and the like—and earning devotion in turn for its efforts, carefully couched in solid technique. But it also happens to excel at pasta, from luscious pan-fried gnocchi to fresh spaghetti. The bar, for its part, is no sideshow stage; headed by the hugely talented Kevin Burke—a pre-Prohibition scholar and local punch-bowl pioneer—it does wonders with herbs, housemade sodas and syrups, fat washes, and more. And yes, the ice is right.

Coohills, 1400 Wewatta St., LoDo, Denver, CO 80202; (303) 623-5700; http://coohills.com; Contemporary; $$. Having nabbed a space that's surely the envy of their colleagues—with its creekside location overlooking an old truss bridge at the edge of LoDo—Atlanta transplants Tom and Diane Coohill went and did wonders with it to boot. As see-and-be-seen as see-and-be-seen can be, it's swanky to the max but not at all stuffy, with a kitchen-facing chef's table and a pastry counter at the patio-graced entrance, an invitingly spacious bar to one side and a more intimate dining room to the other, all strewn with conversation-piece accents (note the chandelier made from an uprooted grapevine and the built-in firepit outside). The seasonal, Mediterranean-influenced menu, likewise, is surprisingly lighthearted for all its earnest emphasis on local produce and Chef Tom's starry pedigree. Small plates take precedence, be it a *comme-il-faut* duo of pâtés—one wrapped in fatback, country-style, the other a rosy-pink, ultra-creamy spread suggesting chicken-liver semifreddo—or a so-called flatbread that's startlingly like a round sandwich loaf, smeared with a buttery mixture of taleggio and ricotta. Meanwhile, the drink list neatly spans a range of price points, making this the rare high-ender to offer a little something for everyone.

The Corner Office, Curtis Hotel, 1401 Curtis St., Downtown, Denver, CO 80202; (303) 825-6500; www.thecornerofficedenver.com; Contemporary; $$. As with its namesake, everybody loves the view from The Corner Office. Located across from the Denver

Performing Arts Complex on the ground floor of the boutique shrine to pop culture that is the Curtis Hotel, it could serve up swill and slop and still make a mint, luring minglers to what feels like a nonstop soirée in a retro-accented, loungy space with a naughty workplace motif. But CIA-trained Chef Will Cisa is no slouch; his skills ensure that the sheer playfulness of the morning-to-night repertoire doesn't dissolve into self-parody. More or less accurately dubbed "progressive global comfort food," the broad selection of small and large plates yields a number of winners: surprisingly good beer-battered fish tacos with citrus-tinged guacamole, crema, and *curtido*. Fried calamari on overdrive with rock shrimp. Seasoned takes on chicken and waffles, arancini and curried crêpes (the latter just one among many funky specialties Cisa whips up for Sunday's Disco Brunch). Even desserts are thoughtfully crafted—but it's the so-called downward dog, an inspired jumble of pork fu, tsukemono, seaweed, and other Japanese touches, that really sweetens the pot.

Crave Dessert Bar & Lounge, 891 14th St., Ste. 110, Downtown, Denver, CO 80202; (303) 586-4199; http://cravedenver .com; Bakery/Cafe; $. Catering to the workaday crowd before sundown, patrons of the nearby Denver Performing Arts Complex afterward, this dapper downtowner—with its silvery-golden aura and creamy leather upholstery—serves a smattering of savories as well as breakfast pastries and coffee, but its primary focus is on the most important meal of the day: dessert. Beautifully garnished, towering layer cakes, bruléed custards, bubbling crisps, and more come ready for their close-ups, but it's often the accompaniments that reveal the big picture; crème fraîche sorbet adds zing to dainty vanilla doughnuts, while huckleberry preserves nicely contrast a napoleon of pumpkin cheesecake and crisp phyllo. As after-dinner cocktails go, Crave's are, for the most part, admirably light on creamy liqueurs; rye and balsamic vinegar give the raspberry-topped Chocolate Kisses an appreciable edge when it comes to digesting all that sugar.

Cuba Cuba Cafe and Bar, 1173 Delaware St., Golden Triangle, Denver, CO 80204; (303) 605-2822; www.cubacubacafe.com; Cuban; $$. Though it's located in the Golden rather than the Bermuda Triangle, the sense that you're being whisked away on an island escape sets in the moment you lay eyes on Cuba Cuba. Housed in an old double bungalow whose aqua-and-honeysuckle exterior matches the festive interior, with its mambo-themed mural and palm-leaf fans, it enchants immediately and completely; so does prompt, gracious service. The food completes the dreamy picture. Left to our own devices, we'd drink the mojos that accompany the plantain chips—tangy-sweet mango-habañero and almost buttery garlic-lime—straight from the ramekins, but a selection of fine rums suffices where shame fails us. If your entree doesn't come with *fufu*—a sort of plantain pudding studded with pork cracklings—get a side order; it's great. But so are the generous mains themselves: short ribs braised in tomatoes and onions slide off the bone to mingle with pickled carrots; raisins and *maduros* make for a lush picadillo. And a round of *cortaditos* sees you through to the bittersweet end. In a word: sigh.

District Meats, 1625 Wazee St., LoDo, Denver, CO 80202; (303) 623-1630; www.charliepalmer.com; Steak House; $$$. Given the explosive growth of our dining scene, it was only a matter of time before the nation's empire-minded celeb chefs began to zero in on Denver as a conquerable outpost. Enter the prolific Charlie Palmer with this oversize architectural stunner in white and silver, where lamps the size of hot tubs, windowpane dividers, subway tiles, and woodplanks reclaimed from old cable cars and barns combine with an open kitchen and a trio of giant-screen TVs to create a sense of soaring light and movement. Bringing in Chef Jeff Russell from his D.C. steak house, he's centered the menu around chops, including pork, lamb, and so on, as well as beef. But Russell's got plenty of tricks up his sleeve for the grazing rather than gorging set: don't miss the piquillo peppers— roasted to candy-like sweetness and stuffed with brisket or, if you're lucky, pulled pork that surpasses that of most barbecue joints.

EDGE Restaurant & Bar, Four Seasons Hotel Denver, 1111 14th St., Downtown, Denver, CO 80202; (303) 389-3343; www.edge restaurantdenver.com; Steak House; $$$. This being the Four Seasons, you'd expect EDGE to be posh, and it is—gleaming and sculptured and plush through and through. Given the name, how-ever, you can dispense with the assumption that it's stuffy; it isn't. True, the dinner menu sticks closely to the downtown steak house formula, with results as high-notch as any. But for Chef Simon Purvis, it seems, daytime is playtime—and the view from his sandbox is charming. The chicken burger is excellent: juicy, well-seasoned, and chunky with red pepper aioli, feta, and baby spinach under the big top of a fresh sesame bun. So is the glistening ahi tuna steak on focaccia, spunky with pickled red onions, shiitakes, and arugula. And brunch includes a spectacular dessert buffet; EDGE has a secret ace in Pastry Chef Christopher Jordan, whose thoughtful approach yields such sophisticated yet soothing stuff as a layered combo of cheesecake, panna cotta, and blood orange gélee atop a graham-cracker crust.

Elway's, The Ritz-Carlton Denver, 1881 Curtis St., Downtown, Denver, CO 80202; (303) 312-3826; www.elways.com; Steak House; $$$. Sports legend-cum-entrepreneur John Elway scores again with this downtown cow palace—even glitzier and more indulgent than his Cherry Creek flagship (p. 137), from the sparkling sushi bar to the curving wine wall. And since the movers and shakers alight here in even bigger droves, it's a gold mine for us eavesdroppers: we can learn more about the machinations of Capitol Hill over the course of a single happy hour than we could by reading a week's worth of papers—all while sucking down a primo lobster cocktail and a glass of bubbly. Otherwise, we'd just as soon save our spending money for Elway's recurrent multicourse wine or whiskey dinners, when Chef

Robert Bogart really struts his stuff with creations like wine-braised lamb osso buco you could cut with a spoon or sweet potato poutine topped with wild duck confit.

Euclid Hall, 1317 14th St., LoDo, Denver, CO 80202; (303) 595-4255; www.euclidhall.com; Gastropub; $$. Once a den of iniquity, this historic brick two-story at the edge of LoDo is now a dazzling shrine to liquidity—awash in enough craft beer, local and otherwise, to make a suds snob's head spin (including many a large-format one-off). That the food absolutely lives up to the brew comes as no surprise to locals who know that the echoing, clattering loft space is **Rioja**'s sibling (p. 88). Boy wonder Jorel Pierce is a deep-frying, sausage-casing, schnitzel-breading, offal-loving machine; we haven't met the pig ear, cheese curd, beef heart, or foie lobe we didn't adore here. (And the Reubenesque brat burger? Holy moly.) Even the array of house-made pickles and mustards shimmers. And then there are Eric Dale's of-the-moment desserts, the hardcore cocktails, the wines on tap . . . Come to think of it, this place is still a den of iniquity. Teetotalers and health nuts stay out. See Euclid Hall's recipe for **Funnel Cake–Fried Bananas with Peanut Butter Caramel** on p. 338.

1515 Restaurant, 1515 Market St., LoDo, Denver, CO 80202; (303) 571-0011; www.1515restaurant.com; Contemporary; $$$. Novelty being LoDo's hottest commodity, its long-timers are all too easily taken for granted. This one shouldn't be; at its best, it's every bit as good as its trendier counterparts. The urbane, low-lit, two-story space—bar and lounge below, white-cloth dining room above—extends an invitation to ease, one made explicit by eager-to-please waitstaff. Owner Gene Tang's nearly 20-page wine list, meanwhile, elicits intrigue, as does a menu that gestures toward molecular gastronomy without waving off accessibility. Giant scallops, for instance, seared and seasoned just so, gain levity from a cap of Arnold Palmer (that is, tea-and-lemonade) foam, gravity from a smear of almost chocolatey *huitlacoche* sauce. Spoonfuls of hazelnut and mint powder add a whole new kind of spice to an already handsome hunk of sous vide lamb loin and bread pudding–like crab hash. Whether he's rethinking beef carpaccio, anchovies, or even whipped cream, Chef Chuck James is taking some risks worth assuming on your part.

Ghost Plate & Tap, 800 18th St., Ste. 100, Downtown, Denver, CO 80202; (303) 297-1738; www.ghostdenver.com; Gastropub; $$. The good folks behind **Wynkoop Brewing Company** (p. 302) have long made it their mission to rescue historic properties from imminent demise. Joining **The Cherry Cricket, Gaetano's,** and **Wazee Supper Club,** the space in the handsome example of fin-de-siècle architecture that is the Ghost Building—formerly home to the Rocky Mountain Diner—has been resurrected as this wood-ceilinged, warmly lit pub, in whose open kitchen Chef Christopher Cina puts modern twists on tavern fare. Look for the likes of pan-fried sweetbreads with pepper relish, roasted pork belly over cheddar grits with onion jam and jalapeño crème brulée amid the salads and burgers; though they're all made for pairing with beers from Wynkoop and its partner, **Breckenridge Brewery** (p. 294), as well as other local notables, it's worth mentioning that the bar keeps **Infinite Monkey Theorem**'s terrific wines on tap as well (p. 298).

HBurgerCO, 1555 Blake St., #102, LoDo, Denver, CO 80202; (720) 524-4345; http://hburger.com; Burgers; $–$$. This LoDo hot spot rode in on the burger wave a couple of years ago—and it's still hanging ten. Part retro diner, part artsy cafe, it runs on a youthful energy that somehow doesn't translate to culinary immaturity; though the menu is full of fun and games, its execution is in earnest. The signature burger couldn't be better: the combination of smoked cheddar, bacon, roasted chiles, and red pepper–tomato jam as well as the usual lettuce, tomato, and onion may sound like overkill, but it all comes together with a textbook juicy Angus patty on a puffy bun. The fries are groovy too, but we like to shake things up with an order of lightly battered, freshly fried jalapeño coins or crisp, sweet-and-sour apple coleslaw tinged with wasabi and ginger. Speaking of shakes, the liquid-nitrogen milk shakes, with or without booze, are justly ballyhooed—and speaking of booze, the selection's a kick, featuring bourbon cocktails like the Brooklyn Breakfast infused with bacon, maple syrup, and orange juice. Somehow, though, we're always swayed by the so-called champagne on a beer budget—that stemless flute is just too cute. Additional location: 727 Colorado Blvd., Denver, CO 80206; (720) 328-8537.

Hi*Rise, 2162 Larimer St., Five Points, Denver, CO 80205; (303) 296-3656; www.hirisedenver.com; Bakery/Cafe; $. If it were up to us, there'd be a Turkish, Cambodian, or Cape Verdean joint for every other bakery that crowds this town—but Hi*Rise is a keeper. Not, perhaps, for the ambiance, which is a bit too mod-industrial for comfort. Not even, necessarily, for the sweets—although those classic, fat, scored peanut-butter cookies are swell. But for the fresh bagels, none too plentiful in these parts? You bet. (Although your bubbe may roll over in her grave, try the one with green chiles, smeared with bloody-mary cream cheese. She'll roll back when she sees you've cleaned your plate.) And for Waffle Weekends, featuring buttermilk, blueberry, and red-velvet stacks? Bingo.

Hutch & Spoon, 3090 Larimer St., Five Points, Denver, CO 80205; (303) 296-2317; www.hutchandspoon.com; Sandwiches; $. Oh, this place is too darling for words. But wordlessness won't do it justice, either, so here goes. Half-hidden among the studios and warehouses of Five Points, it's a wee, homey thing, sporting all of eight close-set wooden tables; the namesake antique china cabinet and spoon collections, framed and mounted on walls of robin's egg blue, give it the feel of an old kitchen nook. Of course, that's essentially what it is; owner Tracy Zimmer makes almost everything in house, from orange-lavender breakfast bread to rustic soups to stellar, frosty sodas flavored with cucumber and pink grapefruit, pineapple-ginger, and mango-jasmine. But smartly crafted sandwiches are his stock in trade. We heart the homage to French onion soup that is gruyère toasted on rye with caramelized onions, as well as the comfy grilled hunk of meat loaf on sourdough, made even better with good cheddar. As for beverages, when coffee won't cut the morning-after mustard, Zimmer's select assortment of wines and beers surely will.

Jax Fish House & Oyster Bar, 1539 17th St., LoDo, Denver, CO 80202; (303) 292-5767; www.jaxfishhousedenver.com; Seafood; $$$. When Jax replaced the notorious Terminal Bar, it helped mark a turning point in the transformation of LoDo from den of dereliction to hub of enterprise. Going on two decades later, this corner seafooder's still hopping—and we suspect it's those last remaining traces of grit, not their erasure, that count for part of its appeal. With a bar rack shaped like a fish skeleton, snaky black pendant lights, and graffiti-dotted brick walls, the narrow, close-quartered space resembles a cross between an artsy wine bar and an island crab shack. And the kitchen follows suit. Chef Sheila Lucero is one smart cookie, and it shows in a vivacious menu that's jam-packed with things you crave on a gut level. Accompaniments are so intriguing they almost—but don't quite—steal the show: blackened catfish, for instance, makes a glorious comeback with the support of crawfish hush puppies and redeye gravy or buckwheat waffles with root-beer syrup, depending on the season. And oysters shine whether chicken-fried and hot-sauced, broiled in Worcestershire butter, or raw with ever-changing mignonettes. The drink list was designed to complement seafood, so give a glass of proprietary Pinot Noir or a dark 'n' stormy with housemade ginger beer a whirl. (Also see Boulder listing on p. 217).

The Kitchen, 1530 16th St., LoDo, Denver, CO 80202; (303) 623-3127; http://thekitchencommunity.com; Contemporary; $$$. Boasting all of the virtues of the namesake Boulder flagship (see p. 218)—a smart bar program, skillful and eminently shareable farm-to-table plates, and an operational emphasis on sustainability—this instant LoDo hit goes one better, being far more spacious and comfy than its sibling even at its busiest. Don't you dare pass up the burrata spread on thick slabs of grilled bread with dollops of anchoïade.

Le Grand Bistro & Oyster Bar, 1512 Curtis St., Downtown, Denver, CO 80202; (303) 534-1155; www.legranddenver.com; French; $$. Better late than never. Hearkening back to the gay brasseries of fin-de-sìecle Paris, Le Grand is the only convincing take on the genre—rejuvenated at the turn of this millennium by Gotham haunts like Balthazar—that Denver has seen since the closure some years ago of Brasserie Rouge, which "officially registered Francophile" Robert Thompson also owned. He's got the vibe down pat: red awnings, weathered tiles, embossed tin ceilings, leather booths and couches in crimson and black—the whole glittery shebang. And he's enlisted a crew with the chops to keep things hopping. Chef Sergio Romero's cooking is at once soulful and graceful, classically underpinned yet enticingly updated from the shellfish, charcuterie, crêpes, and tarts to the braises, roasts, and stews. Head cheese is heady indeed, made with both beef and pork cheeks. Grilled bread sops up every last drop of the anise-scented broth that lentils topped with coins of garlic sausage leave behind. Grilled salmon uplifts choucroute garni. And crackerjack barmen put their imprint on a skillfully edited list of bières, vins, and genteel cocktails. (At press time, Thompson and Romero were putting the finishing touches on their new Baker District venture, **Punch Bowl Social**; count us in on day one.)

Los Cabos II, 1525 Champa St., Downtown, Denver, CO 80202; (303) 595-3232; www.loscabosii.com; Peruvian; $$. Admittedly, it doesn't look like much; the dining room's dull as dishwater (yes, the cliché fits—even the walls are gray). But come on in—that water's warm. Ceviche is a must: shrimp, octopus, squid, and chunks of whitefish combine with red onion and sweet potato in a sour, sputteringly spicy marinade. *Pollo à la brasa* includes your choice of light or dark meat—juicy either way—plus fries and a chimichurri-like sauce for dipping. And the brunch buffet's a bonanza of *lomo saltado, aji de gallina*, and other Peruvian staples—all for a price as lean as the selection is hearty. Service, for its part, is even sweeter than the coupes of pudding in the dessert case (but you'd better try the *suspiro de limeña* just to be sure).

Marco's Coal-Fired Pizza, 2129 Larimer St., Five Points, Denver, CO 80205; (303) 296-7000; www.marcoscoalfiredpizza.com; Pizza; $$. From out of the blue straight back into the stratosphere: no sooner had Florida transplant Mark Dym opened the doors of this Ballpark-area parlor than the instant groupies—and nationwide accolades—began flooding in. The first Coloradan to have received certification from the Associazione Verace Pizza Napoletana, Dym's been keeping it real ever since. Puffy, perfectly mottled (indeed nearly black-and-white) wood-fired crusts form the striking surface for traditional frescoes of parmesan and mozzarella, prosciutto and salame, and swirls of sauce made with San Marzano tomatoes. (New York–style pies are a tad meatier.) But the eponymous coal-fired oven's reserved for the scene stealers that are plump, limoncello-marinated chicken wings. Stylish decor only highlights the culinary substance, as wrought-iron curlicues punctuate glass-brick mosaics of lime and russet. *Molti saluti, infine,* to the all-Italian wine list. Additional location: 10111 Inverness Main St., Englewood, CO 80112; (303) 790-9000.

Osteria Marco, 1453 Larimer St., LoDo, Denver, CO 80202; (303) 534-5855; www.osteriamarco.com; Italian; $$. Frank Bonanno himself views this LoDo hideaway as the casual mirror image of **Luca d'Italia** (p. 144). But his dark, echoing, brick-walled subterranean funhouse yields more than a mere down-home reflection of *alta cucina*. It's an enoteca; it's a pizzeria; it's a salumeria; it's a dining destination on its own terms. Though there's plenty of seating—wooden tables, wooden booths—we're comfiest at the bar, where we can sip and snack at our leisure. A carafe of wine from the all-Italian wine list; an order of rosy, translucent sliced braesola; and a plush orb of burrata or near-frothy dollop of ricotta with slabs of grilled ciabatta—ah, you could stop there and call it a job well done. Or you could roll up your sleeves and really get to work on a smoky thin-crust pizza or a sandwich laden with meatballs or cold cuts, à la the heroes Bonanno "grew up eating on game day" back in Jersey. You could even knuckle down over Sunday's suckling pig roast. But only after you've polished off a glass of housemade liqueur—be it classic limoncello or its cardamom- or grapefruit-flavored variants—can you truly say your mission is accomplished. See Frank Bonanno's recipe for **Burrata** on p. 323.

Panzano, Hotel Monaco, 909 17th St., Downtown, Denver, CO 80202; (303) 296-3525; www.panzano-denver.com; Italian; $$$. Elise Wiggins is a regular pistol. For her exuberant showmanship as well as her gutsy, soulful cooking, we'd follow her anywhere. Luckily, we don't have to—she's a fixture at the chef's counter of this superb Italian restaurant in the flamboyant Hotel Monaco downtown. Sprawling yet *soigné* from a dining room that twinkles in taupe and ruby to the handsome (and popular) bar—separated by an in-house bakery—it's a mainstay for power breakfasts and lunches. But better you should swing by off the clock to wine and dine at your leisure. Start with the *crespelle ai funghi* (mushroom crêpes) or duck liver mousse with savory *zeppole* (doughnuts)—both luxuriant. Move on to gorgeous fresh pastas; Wiggins's seasonal infusion of tagliatelle or fettuccine with nuts and dried fruits never ceases to impress us. And the pancetta-wrapped, date-stuffed, gorgonzola-sprinkled shrimp over polenta is as swoon-inducing as it sounds. As for dessert, you're on your own—we're only slightly ashamed to admit that our fondness for the sundried-tomato tapenade accompanying the bread basket (see Elise Wiggins's recipe for **Tapenade** on p. 322) takes up all the room we'd otherwise reserve for sweets.

Paris on the Platte, 1553 Platte St., Downtown, Denver, CO 80202; (303) 455-2451; www.parisontheplattecafeandbar.com; Bakery/Cafe; $. The name seems only slightly more apt for the adjacent boîte, where bartenders in natty garb prepare absinthe drips for journal-toting patrons to the strains of live music or open-mic poetry. But if the cafe side lacks Gallic atmosphere, it doesn't want for jazz. Sometimes mellow, sometimes electric, the longtime all-hours haunt—it celebrated its silver anniversary in 2011—bids the coffeehouse crowd work and play, daydream and people-watch not only in the (naturally) funky main room, with its art-splashed red walls and tall black ceilings, but also out on its bookend patios. Get Wi-Fi and wired at the same time with a Crowbar—four shots of espresso mixed with half-and-half; if sugar's your energizer of choice, Italian sodas and milk shakes come in dozens of flavors,

SPOTLIGHT ON PIZZA

For years, Colorado had only one thing to add to the international dialogue regarding pizza—a cheer for honey-dipped whole-wheat crusts that understandably fell on the deaf ears of purists, be they New Yorkers or Neapolitans. But these days, we're cresting a wave of wood-fired masterworks by hardcore pizzaioli—and their hard-nosed city-slicker counterparts. See Appendix A for further listings.

Gennaro's Cafe Italiano, *2598 S. Broadway, Denver, CO 80210; (303) 722-1044; www.gennaroscafeitaliano.com; Italian; $$.* A red-sauce-splattered dive to bring tears to the eyes of homesick East Coast transplants—marked by a Googie-era neon sign complete with tilted martini glass—Gennaro's doesn't tout the fact that its oven produces perfectly bubbly crusts with an abiding chew; it just makes them. It doesn't brag about the excellence or provenance of its toppings; it just adds them, including classic, oregano-scented marinara; cloud-light ricotta; and robust sausage from venerated local producer Polidori. The joint may be a little too crusty—no pun intended—for well-heeled foodies, but it's just right for the rest of us. Best bet: the Tiscanni—and a round of pinball while you wait in the bar.

Lucky Pie Pizza and Tap House, *637 Front St., Louisville, CO 80027; (303) 666-5743; http://luckypiepizza.com; Italian; $$.* The self-applied Neapolitan label doesn't quite stick at this Louisville go-to (though a bumper sticker reading "Baby on Board" would—it's got quite the family following). We're not complaining, mind you—on the contrary, the wildly creative pizza toppings, however untraditional, are precisely what earn Lucky Pie our vote of confidence; we're talking kale, acorn squash, brussels sprouts, pistachios, and more, both here and at the recently opened LoDo offshoot (1610 16th St., Denver, CO 80202; 303-835-1021). Best bet: the Black Forest ham-and-two-cheese pie, subtly accented with caraway and mustard seeds.

The Oven Pizza e Vino, *7167 W. Alaska Dr., Lakewood, CO, 80226; (303) 934-7600; www.theovenpizzaevino.com; Pizza; $$*. That Phoenix-based celebrity Chef Mark Tarbell is a largely absentee owner bodes ill for this rather garish spot in a suburban shopping center. But omens aren't guarantees; as it turns out, Tarbell's crew is up to the task of firing up superior thin-crust pies in the West Coast gourmet tradition with or without him. Best bet: the white-sauce pizza with fresh tomato and spinach, bacon, a fried egg, and a jab of Sriracha.

Proto's Pizzeria Napoletana, *2401 15th St., Denver, CO 80202; (720) 855-9400; www.protospizza.com; Pizza; $$*. Although the competition it's facing these days is downright fierce, Proto's warrants a salute (and a *salute!*, to use the Italian toast) as one of the area's first Neapolitan-style parlors. We get a kick out of the LoDo branch, which, with its exposed pipes, old wood floors, and dough-and-sauce hues, vaguely resembles the inside of a pizza oven. The thinnest of thin crusts are artful when they're not cracker-dry—but on such occasions, a friend taught us to ask for balsamic vinegar on the side, which does wonders for salty combos like the Goombah with prosciutto and capers. Best bet: the Friday night special, clam pizza. Additional locations include 4670 Broadway, Boulder, CO 80304; (720) 565-1050; and 8001 Arista Pl., Broomfield, CO 80021; (303) 466-2112.

The Walnut Room, *3131 Walnut St., Denver, CO 80205; (303) 295-1868; www.thewalnutroom.com; Pizza; $$*. The Five Points flagship (and for that matter its Baker District offshoot) is your standard, likeable neighborhood joint—the beer flows, the patio rollicks, the back room rocks with live music. It would be silly to expect anything other than halfway decent pizzas—but darned if the kitchen doesn't turn out mighty fine ones, with thin yet well-structured crusts and quality toppings. Best bet: the wacky but wonderful Walnut Special with pesto, garlic, red onions, green olives, and, sure enough, walnuts. Additional location: 2 N. Broadway, Denver, CO 80203; (303) 736-6750.

including piña colada and Earl Grey. As the clock spins, snacks and sandwiches supplant breakfast pastries and brunch items, which is too bad only insofar as we could go for the Man in the Moon—toad-in-the-hole made better with cayenne-lemon butter—any old time.

Red Star Deli, 1801 Wynkoop St., Ste. 175, LoDo, Denver, CO 80202; (303) 226-9460; http://redstardeli.com; Sandwiches; $$. White-linen past, brown-bag future—with a golden lining. Long established as a serious chef, James Mazzio has settled in to have some fun at this weekday breakfast-and-lunch joint in the shadow of Coors Field. So should you, whether you fancy a pre-meeting hunk of fresh-baked coffee cake or a lunchtime sammy of classic proportions—house-corned beef on rye, say, or eggplant parm on focaccia. And as long as you're working that jaw, be sure to ask about **Studio F**; in the space just beyond the deli counter, which used to house a cooking school, Mazzio is now hosting pop-up dinners with a local who's who of guest chefs.

Rioja, 1431 Larimer St., LoDo, Denver, CO 80202; (303) 820-2282; www.riojadenver.com; Mediterranean; $$$. Though the LoDo dining scene has grown dramatically since Rioja opened in 2004, its crown jewel remains as polished as ever. The swish flagship of wunderkind Jennifer Jasinski and her front-of-house partner Beth Gruitch is packed nightly with VIPs—but the multifaceted Mediterranean fare, delivered with care by on-the-ball servers, makes everyone feel special, from the best bread basket in town to Eric Dale's comely desserts. A combination of keen vision and technical precision is Jasinski's hallmark. It's evident not only in signatures like the curry-scented square pillow of pork belly bathed in an effervescent green chickpea puree and the tortelloni stuffed with goat cheese and artichoke mousse but also seasonal treats: silky chestnut soup served in a gourd with a crostino of *foie gras*–smeared brioche here, seared tuna ably supporting a rainbow of fennel, figs, citrus, and mustard greens there. As the name suggests, Spanish wines take precedence, but the drink list is well-rounded—we've even been wowed by the occasional cocktail.

Row 14 Bistro & Wine Bar, 891 14th St., Downtown, Denver, CO 80202; (303) 825-0100; www.row14denver.com. Effortlessness born of savvy: that's Row 14 in a nutshell. The right place at the right time conveys casual glamour from every angle of the dining room, tied together with reclaimed pinewood, exposed carpet tiles, and gleaming metallic accents. By the same token, the smart crew in the kitchen and behind the lively bar delivers contemporary plates and potations (get a load of those globular ice cubes!) with panache. Up-and-coming toque Jensen Cummings confidently maintains a global outlook, eyeing in particular the Mediterranean and the Pacific Rim, without losing sight of his local sources—or compromising his playful nature. Though entrees are hardly to be sniffed at—fish dishes in particular beckon—he has a special way with snacks, be it a ring of puffy fried avocado wedges over sweet chili crema, a taco special fit for connsoisseurs, or even, if you're lucky, Hawaiian-style Spam musubi. Meanwhile, a list of wines by the glass that's nearly as long as the bottle list displays Owner-Sommelier David Schneider's commitment to wine education through exploration. Make him proud; study hard.

Russell's Smokehouse, 1422 Larimer St., LoDo, Denver, CO 80202; (720) 524-8050; www.russellssmokehouse.com; Barbecue; $$. There's nary a pie that go-getter Frank Bonanno doesn't have his finger in (including pie itself—see **Wednesday's Pie**, p. 111). And why shouldn't he poke and prod? His touch is firm, as this underground but upscale, dim-lit but lively barbecue venue in Larimer Square shows no less than do its seven siblings. Here as there, the pleasure's in the inimitable details. Lamb ribs or neck pieces and delicate rabbit sliders serve as alternatives to ultra-moist pulled pork and chicken, sliced brisket, and baby-back racks. Smoky baked beans yield fat bacon bits; spinach is creamed with goat cheese. Baked mushroom dynamite proves every iota as tangy and luscious as its seafood-and-mayo-based Japanese namesake. And the drink list thoughtfully and ably covers every angle: virgin sippers like pineapple lassi, house pours in four sizes, and tapped beer in three round out a selection of cocktails that continues what adjacent "speakeasy" **Green Russell** (p. 305) started. It goes without saying that there's pie for dessert—but praise for the tender-crusted, sky-high caramel-apple bears repeating.

Snooze, 2262 Larimer St., Five Points, Denver, CO 80205; (303) 297-0700; www.snoozeeatery.com; American; $. You Snooze, you anything but lose: This daytime diner is an eye-opener on myriad levels. With its Technicolor riffs on Space Age architecture—all starbursts and tailfin swoops—the Ballpark-area flagship of what brothers Jon and Adam Schlegel call their "anti-chain" awakens fierce nostalgia for an optimistic era in the throngs who thrive on the equally kicky food (not to mention the proprietary Guatemalan coffee and souped-up bloodies). The seasonal menu's jam-packed with neat-to-eat treats—first and foremost wacky, wonderful flap-jacks: pineapple upside-down, blue corn with piñon butter and chili syrup, cherry cobbler (our favorite), et cetera. But there are also eggs Benedict inspired by Caprese salads and chilaquiles (the best variants involve killer smoked-cheddar hollandaise). Biscuits and gravy in potpie form. And French toast sticks stuffed with peanut-butter cream cheese, Nutella, and bacon (whew). Rev your engines, folks; this is the culinary equiva-lent of a joyride in a T-Bird. Additional locations: 700 N. Colorado Blvd., Denver, CO 80206; (303) 736-6200; 1617 Pearl St., Boulder, CO 80302; (303) 225-7344. See Snooze's recipe for **Bella! Bella! Benny** on p. 330.

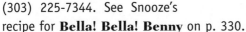

Sushi Sasa, 2401 15th St., Downtown, Denver, CO 80202; (303) 433-7272; www.sushisasadenver.com; Japanese/Sushi; $$$. If Sasa isn't the best Japanese eatery in Denver—the debate that pits it against Chef-Owner Wayne Conwell's former place of employ,

Sushi Den (p. 197), never ends—it's certainly the most chic. Sparklingly white-on-white but for sleek bamboo appointments, the conjoined dining rooms are jewels of minimalism that reflect seductively on their well-heeled occupants—and, of course, on the gorgeous small plates from the kitchen as well as the sushi bar. We're not in the habit of throwing around the word "sublime," but as adjectives go it's apropos for almost everything from the simplest nigiri to the most intricate specialty. For that reason, we tend to postpone our outings to Sasa until we're feeling sufficiently flush to splurge on *omakase* (or chef's tasting), when the anticipation preceding each course is nearly as delicious as the food itself. Flying-fish carpaccio with strawberries, capers and mozzarella in a pool of truffled soy sauce? Black cod soup served French onion–style with gruyère and a seaweed-flecked rice "crouton"? Kabocha tempura, raw monkfish liver on brioche . . . wasabi cheesecake? *Hai, kudasai.*

TAG, 1441 Larimer St., LoDo, Denver, CO 80202; (303) 996-9985; http://tag-restaurant.com; Asian Fusion; $$$. Truth be told, TAG's tagline—"Continental Social Food"—is doubly misleading. First, Chef-Owner Troy Guard's clearest influence is no European chef but former mentor Roy Yamaguchi—a pioneer of intercontinental, Pacific Rim cuisine. Second, if Guard truly means to encourage sharing, then he needs to work (or rather stop working) on his execution, because it's too good for its own good. We hoard every last nibble of the bursting French onion–soup dumplings and seafood potstickers slicked with *gochujang*-spiked butter sauce, every last drop of the icy-hot kumquat-jalapeño mojito. And all the while, the East-West juxtapositions on the seasonal menu continue to startle: *li hing mui* and guacamole, stout and miso, poblanos and shiitakes. But to be fair, maybe the glamour gangs who gather here trade forkfuls more freely than we gluttons. After all, the supper-clubby Larimer Square digs—a mix of communal seating and peekaboo nooks—do seem to sizzle with convivial heat.

TAG | Raw Bar, 1423 Larimer St., LoDo, Denver, CO 80202; (303) 996-2685; http://tagrawbar.com; Small Plates/Tapas; $$. Poppycock! That's the greeting you'll get—in both verbal and edible forms—when you step from the subterranean breezeway into what looks like a glorified snack bar, all gleaming white tiles and juicy orange accents. In fact, **TAG**'s (see preceding entry) little sibling is a full-tilt chef's counter—whose shrewd crew, in full view, whips up tidbits that, though largely raw, are anything but crude. On the contrary, most are highly polished. The kangaroo tartare's sensational if surprisingly delicate, garnished with a quail egg and *foie gras*-infused foam. Far-flung influences and ingredients achieve synthesis in the seafood dishes: think nervy sushi tacos sprinkled with corn nuts or the contrast of wasabi peas, beets, and hearts of palm with salmon (not to mention the sweet muffins flavored with lobster stock that sometimes grace the small display case of baked goods). The talent that saturates this recently expanded space suffuses the cocktails, too; that said, the best drink on offer may be limeade spiked with cinnamon syrup and aloe juice. (They should call it cocky pop.)

Tamayo, 1400 Larimer St., LoDo, Denver, CO 80202; (720) 946-1433; Mexican; $$$. Along with the Latin-Asian fusion he showcases at **Zengo** (see p. 97), Richard Sandoval is known internationally for the style of cookery he calls "modern Mexican." Denverites, for their part, associate this Larimer Square anchor above all with its festive rooftop terrace, a LoDo rarity (the view at the long bar flanking the ground-level dining room is swell as well, bedecked with a colorful Picassoeqsue mosaic). That's not to imply that the food isn't beguiling; it often is. The best dishes prove as complex as they are lively: intensely musky *huitlacoche* crêpes, *carne asada* complemented by a *chicharrón*-stuffed gordita and a mélange of green beans and cactus, chicken mole enriched by a dollop of truffle-habañero butter. Still, well-made margaritas infused with hibiscus or prickly pear and guacamole served in a lava-rock *molcajete* more than suffice to get this party started.

Trillium, 2134 Larimer St., Five Points, Denver, CO 80205; (303) 379-9759; www.trilliumdenver.com; Contemporary; $$$. The look is spare and cool—clean lines, white walls, light woods, and blue accents; one naturally assumes that it's a reflection of the Scandinavian influence on the menu. Not so. Certainly, Chef-Owner Ryan Leinonen's cooking is marked by Northern clarity and precision—but also by sparkling warmth, even buoyancy. The balance he strikes between sweet and savory, tart-fruit and earthy notes is itself striking, as in the bold juxtaposition of *foie gras* mousse, cloudberry jam, and pickled chanterelles served with a dark flatbread called *rieska* (the recipe was Leinonen's grandmother's) or a velvety, robust bread pudding with fresh cheese curds, apples, and rosemary. Not a dish lacks for his distinctive combination of sharp wit and deep soul, from buttermilk-and-cornmeal-fried smelts with lemon-vodka tartar sauce to a grilled pork chop with havarti polenta and cardamom applesauce. But we could live on raw oysters whose flavor is only heightened by a dash of ginger-aquavit mignonette—and his carrot cake is the moistest, most intense we've tasted in recent memory. Color us wildly impressed.

twelve restaurant, 2233 Larimer St., Five Points, Denver, CO 80205; (303) 293-0287; Contemporary; $$$. Twelve is a oner not only in the still-gentrifying Ballpark/Five Points area but on Denver's young, brash dining scene as a whole: mature, tranquil, subtly progressive. Simply decorated in beiges, browns, and blacks, LA-born Chef-Owner Jeff Osaka's low-lit little hideaway invites contemplation—until his monthly changing menu commands your full attention. To a plate, it's composed of the sorts of highly intelligent dishes you find yourself analyzing as you go: what inspired this? How did he do that? Which isn't to say they aren't sensual. Osaka's pork belly unfolds like a ribbon of crisp silk; his sweetbreads aren't showpieces but rather integral parts of a whole, which may include a meltingly soft cake of grits and warm black-eyed peas or a poached egg. Roasted cherry tomatoes so sweet they taste like tiny peaches, along with sauteed mushrooms, walnuts, and figs, adorn a deconstructed phyllo "tart." Even the house-baked bread is uncommon (honey-wheat flavored with cardamom and espresso, for instance). Though a meal here isn't exactly cheap, especially paired with wine, it's a gift considering its level of execution.

Vesta Dipping Grill, 1822 Blake St., LoDo, Denver, CO 80202; (303) 296-1970; www.vestagrill.com; Contemporary; $$$. Vesta burst onto the fledgling LoDo dining scene in 1997—and the energy it generated hasn't dipped since. On the contrary, dipping is the very source of its magnetism. Swooping lines, blown glass, and a copper glow lend the outsize, brick-walled old warehouse space a rollicking yet somehow romantic vibe that reflects the menu, which is built on a stirring array of sauces, salsas, marmalades, vinaigrettes, and so on. Mixing, matching, and sharing are its objective: samplers with tortilla chips or pita wedges are a starting point and a highlight (don't pass up the smoky bacon aioli or roasted-corn cream). Venison frites—the loin marinated in curry, grilled, enriched with dried-cherry butter, and topped with oyster mushrooms sauteed in ginger ale—is a must, as are the oh-so-evocative stacked lamb riblets crusted in a mixture of pistachios and mint and accompanied by rose-scented yogurt. Add in the enormous list of libations, and it's guaranteed you'll never have anything close to the same experience twice here. Young guns yet old hands, partners Josh Wolkon and Matt Selby—who also own **Steuben's**

(p. 156)—simply keep their fingers on the pulse of this city more firmly than anyone. See Matt Selby's recipe for **Samosas with Roasted Corn Sauce** on p. 326.

Wazee Wood Fire Pizza, 1631 Wazee St., LoDo, Denver, CO 80202; (303) 623-2105; www.charliepalmer .com; Pizza; $$. As snug and cozy as its adjoining sibling, **District Meats** (p. 74), is big and shiny, this LoDo parlor constitutes celeb Chef Charlie Palmer's stake in the Neapolitan pizza tournament that so many culinary high-rollers seem to be playing these days. Along with bags of imported pasta and jars of squash and beans, cans of San Marzano tomatoes and bags of Caputo flour line the wall-mounted shelves, serving as decoration as well as true-to-trend key ingredients in the pies. That said, pizzaiolo Jeff Russell doesn't limit himself to traditional Italian toppings; specialty combos like the Defendorf—ground veal and brussels sprouts with gruyère—are downright chefly. At the same time, he nods to New York style with offerings by the slice as well as the round.

Zengo, 1610 Little Raven St., Downtown, Denver, CO 80202; (720) 904-0965; www.richardsandoval.com; Asian Fusion; $$$. Though born in Mexico, Richard Sandoval is now a global citizen, with more than 25 restaurants worldwide that reflect his broad culinary outlook (see also **Tamayo,** p. 94). Among his earlier ventures, this outpost of Asian-Latin fusion overlooking Riverfront Park remains a red-hot spot with an aesthetic to match: flaming hues highlight a profusion of zany design elements whose overall effect is at once mod and sexy. It's almost enough to upstage the food—but not quite. More often than not, sparks fly as the two vigorous cuisines meld flamboyantly—tempuras meeting tacos, Peking duck Hatch chiles. An assortment of intricate ceviches and tiraditos mesh pickled plum and ponzu with hearts of palm and guanabana. The signature black cod's dreamy—the fleshy, creamy fillet broiled in chipotle miso and zigzagged with seven-spice aioli. So, usually, is *foie gras* in any form—seared with poached mango or tucked into hot-and-sour soup dumplings. As for booze, a word to the wise: leave the fusion to the professionals. Tequila and sake are a volatile mix.

Landmarks

The Broker Restaurant, 821 17th St., Downtown, Denver, CO 80202; (303) 292-5065; www.thebrokerrestaurant.com; Steak House; $$$. Located below street level in a 100-year-old bank vault complete with enormous, circular steel door, this decades-old chophouse is so magnificent as to be unreal—like a backdrop from the golden age of the silver screen. Cherrywood and leather, gold leaf and stained glass, towering vases and candlesticks, and a warren of private rooms set the stage for old-school surf and turf in every possible combination. But for all the lobster tails, crab legs, fillets, and medallions drenched in béarnaise and bordelaise, regulars still set the utmost store by giant bowls of peel-and-eat shrimp at the bar (which just so happens to offer boffo happy-hour deals).

Ellyngton's, The Brown Palace Hotel, 321 17th St., Downtown, Denver, CO 80202; (303) 297-3111; www.brownpalace.com; American; $$. The original Palm Court–inspired interior is long gone, but The Brown's signature daytime haunt doesn't lack for ostentation. Posh and awash in heraldic patterns of ochre, burgundy, and teal, Ellyngton's remains a business-class tradition, where deals get inked over Bloody Marys and crêpes Florentine or Champagne and Kobe burgers (why not?). Speaking of Champagne, the Dom Perignón Sunday brunch is an affair extraordinaire: cold and hot stations galore include a sushi bar and abundant desserts against a backdrop of live jazz.

Le Central, 112 E. 8th Ave., Golden Triangle, Denver, CO 80203; (303) 863-8094; www.lecentral.com; French; $$. For 30 years and counting, Robert Tournier's Golden Triangle institution has been charming *les chausettes* off Denverites in this way and that. Occupying an old row house, the several-room bistro is brightly painted with murals on the outside, cozy amid plants and vintage posters within. Along with an all-French wine list, the menu fits the homey vibe to a T: there's escargot in puff pastry and bouillabaisse, pan-seared veal liver in cream sauce and seasonal cassoulet made with goose, brunchtime croques monsieurs and crêpes, profiteroles and even *îles flottantes* for dessert. And of course there are steamed mussels—11 different kinds, in fact, alongside all-you-can-eat frites. The icing on the *gâteau*? Reasonable prices—just as you'd find at a true Parisian working man's daily haunt.

The Market, 1445 Larimer St., LoDo, Denver, CO 80202; (303) 534-5140; http://themarketatlarimer.com; Bakery/Cafe; $. Well before Larimer Square became a dining destination and laptops replaced notebooks, this cute and comfy cafe doubled as a workspace and meeting place for anyone and everyone with business to attend to downtown. Though it's since been hemmed in by some of the city's best eateries, its rank as a grub—and gab—hub hasn't declined one iota (even in winter, the patio beneath the striped blue awnings rarely sits empty). If anything, its popularity has only grown with the addition of a bakery that produces both the plate-size pastries lining the coffee bar in front and the towering desserts on display at the long deli counter in back, where case after case stands crammed with salads of all kinds, quiches, blintzes, savory turnovers, pastas, fried chicken, and pot roast—supplemented by no fewer than five soups du jour and sandwiches by the dozens. Plunking down at a two-top flanked by plant-dotted grocery shelves, you may suddenly flash back to some old Main Street general store—the vibe's that genuinely communal.

My Brother's Bar, 2376 15th St., Downtown, Denver, CO 80202; (303) 455-9991; Bar & Grill; $. Though it hasn't always been My Brother's Bar, this joint at the corner of 15th and Platte—unmarked but for a couple of small copper plaques bearing its piano logo—has been slinging drinks since 1873, which arguably makes it the oldest continuously operating saloon in the city. Like **Charlie Brown's** (p. 163), it counts Jack Kerouac and Neal Cassady among its one-time patrons; unlike Charlie Brown's (and despite the logo), it does not contain a piano, though it does pipe classical music and only classical music throughout the two-room space—whose embossed-tin ceiling tiles, wood paneling, black-and-white photos, stained-glass windows, and lace curtains speak all the more charmingly to its old age. In short, this place has character with a capital C. That the bartenders pour a fine pint and the fry cooks flip a fine burger—the J.C.B. with jalapeños and cream cheese is legendary in and of itself—only gilds the lily. Same goes for the trellised back patio.

Palace Arms, The Brown Palace Hotel, 321 17th St., Downtown, Denver, CO 80202; (303) 297-3111; www.brownpalace.com; Contemporary; $$$. Just off the opulent lobby of Denver's most iconic landmark, Palace Arms looks every inch a bastion of pomp and circumstance—woody and gilded amid museum-ready displays of antiques and flags from the Napoleonic era (indeed, a few choice artifacts belonged to the emperor himself, according to the hotel's historian). And in some ways, that's what it is: the service is as kid-glove as ever, the Caesar salad's still prepared tableside, and the extraordinary wine list abounds as it must in grand and premier crus, rare liqueurs, and other mortgage-denting trophies. But with young, Thailand-born Chef Thanawat Bates at its head, the kitchen, at least, is entering the 21st century with gusto. Dispensing with Continentalism, Bates is bringing global influences to bear on the menu: think *chicharrón*-crusted scallops with holy-basil pesto or crabcakes laced with coconut and lemongrass. "This place can have fun with you," he insists. We say bring on the octopus, lime paste, and piloncillo.

Restaurant Kevin Taylor, Hotel Teatro, 1106 14th St., Downtown, Denver, CO 80202; (303) 820-2600; www.ktrg.net; Contemporary; $$$. As dramatic as befits its proximity to the Denver Performing Arts Complex, this soaring, mezzanine-lined downtowner exudes elegance in ivory and jet, accentuated by abalone chandeliers and gilt-edged mirrors. For its sheer luster, Kevin Taylor received national recognition as a pioneer of fine dining in Denver at the turn of the millennium; today his namesake venue stands a pillar of haute cuisine. Presentations are impeccable, preparations irreproachable. Butternut gnocchi goes from hearty to arty with roasted apple and microcelery, blue-cheese cream and fresh truffle; milk-fed veal two ways—loin and cheek—finds contrast in smoked leeks, chorizo, and brandy; and nary a dish lacks for some delicacy or other—wild game, caviar, edible flowers, exotic produce. In that light, it goes without saying that the wine cellar is one giant trophy case. If it's all a tad too rich for your blood, Taylor's slightly less-spendy Italian alternative, Prima, awaits just across the lobby.

Sam's No. 3, 1500 Curtis St., Downtown, Denver, CO 80202; (303) 534-1927; American; $. Though this downtown diner sits a few doors down from its original site, you can't tell by looking that it wasn't built in 1927. Cheerfully cluttered and ever hustling, it comes about as close as Denver gets to the rickety Greek-American hash houses that anchor every New York City block, departing from the model only in its extra emphasis on Mexican grub—and in the casual Western hospitality of the waitstaff. The "kickin' green chile" with pork and tomatoes is aptly named, well worth a try alone or on a burrito that flops over the rim of the plate. Otherwise, the eggs, dogs, and blue plates are a mixed bag—sometimes gratifying, sometimes merely adequate. But given a menu this huge, and portions this huge, and Bloody Marys this huge, and cups of coffee this bottomless, you've got to love Sam's for serving up surefire hangover cures with an extra dose of goodwill.

Ship Tavern, The Brown Palace Hotel, 321 17th St., Downtown, Denver, CO 80202; (303) 297-3111; www.brownpalace.com; Bar & Grill; $$$. Centered around a carved wooden pillar resembling a mainmast, The Brown's most casual eatery sports a nautical motif from stem to stern. The model ships, navigational maps, and mermaid imagery don't, however, signal the theme of the menu; pub fare, not seafood per se, is the focus. So be it; we're here primarily for the ultra-cozy vibe and a pint of the house ale, brewed exclusively by Great Divide, anyway. Should hunger strike, however, a half-dozen oysters Rockefeller and prime rib on rye strike back. To be sure, they come at a premium, but the historic setting's priceless.

Tom's Home Cookin', 800 E. 26th Ave., Five Points, Denver, CO 80205; (303) 388-8035; Southern; $$. As far as Denverites are concerned, the timeworn shacks that dot the byways of the Deep South have nothing on this Five Points joint. Though it opened in 1999, its veneer of roadside memorabilia appears to be as vintage as its crusty schtick is thick (note the surcharges for high-maintenance attitude and cellphone use listed on the chalkboard above the steam table). Meanwhile, the grub it dishes up every weekday from 11 a.m. "until it's gone"—or 2:30 p.m. at the latest—is all it's cracked up to be. Chicken-fried, barbecued, smothered, mashed, and candied: the rotating menu items cover the five basic food groups in all their meaty, gooey, saucy, sassy glory. The mac-and-cheese is duly vaunted, but as far as yellow goo goes, we've got to give top prize to Tom's banana pudding. We've also got to warn you: bring cash, grab napkins, and make time for a nap—you're gonna need them all.

Wazee Supper Club, 1600 15th St., LoDo, Denver, CO 80202; (303) 623-9518; www.wazeesupperclub.com; Bar & Grill; $$. When the Wazee opened nearly 40 years ago, it was an oasis in a vice zone; now it's a shelter from the yuppie storm. Your waitress may remember when the 15th Street Viaduct still eclipsed this checkerboard-floored time capsule, luring customers who, in the words of one, "weren't used to natural light." That was back when the vintage bric-a-brac was just bric-a-brac; these days, the taps dispense local craft brews; the pizza toppings skew "gourmet"; and, as of press time, interior renovations are underway. But ultimately, a pint and a pie—thin-crusted and cornmeal-dusted—come pretty much the same as they ever did, complete with a bonus slice of life.

Specialty Stores, Markets & Producers

Cook's Fresh Market, 1600 Glenarm Pl., Ste. 120, Downtown, Denver, CO 80202 (303) 893-2277; http://cooksfreshmarket.com. Downtown Denver doesn't have a supermarket, but it does have a super market. This bright, airy high-end grocery on the 16th Street Mall boasts a full-service meat and seafood counter, deli, bakery, salad bar, and coffee bar (which even pours wine and beer); nifty finds are everywhere. At any given time, you can stock up or dine in on the likes of house-smoked salmon, portobello-brie soup, chicken salad with blue cheese and pecans, and white chocolate–pistachio truffles while priming your palate for the exotic: butcher Bill Roehl will specially order everything from antelope to wood pigeon. Before you sail out with all the makings of a gourmet meal, check the cheese case; wrapped ends occasion a quick nosh no one but you and the counter clerk need to know about. If you feel guilty nonetheless, throw in a bouquet—that's what the small flower display is there for.

Crema Coffee House, 2862 Larimer St., Five Points, Denver, CO 80205; (720) 284-9648; www.cremacoffeehouse.net. A proponent of the movement known as the Third Wave of Coffee, Crema co-owner Noah Price takes his java seriously—the provenance of the beans, the quality of the roasting, the art of the brew, and the ambiance it demands. Where the chains dole out those candy-striped milk shake equivalents alongside limp, prepurchased pastries, Price pours for purists, offering the likes of oak-aged, cold-brewed toddies in stoppered brown bottles (okay, the oatmeal latte is a tummy-warming exception to the rule) while a real live chef prepares grapefuit bruléed in rose sugar or "PB&Js" with almond butter and date-balsamic jam. And where the chains can only imitate the community-studio ethos of the urban coffeehouse, Crema wholly embodies it. All over its walls, the coolest artworks. On its stereo, the coolest music. At its tables, the coolest people reading the coolest books—or even engaged in art projects of their own. Oh, and the crema itself? Picture perfect. (With partner Jonathan Power, Price will be upping the neighborhood's hipness quotient even further with the opening of the gastropubby **Populist** in summer 2012.)

EVOO Marketplace, 1338 15th St., LoDo, Denver, CO 80202; (303) 974-5784; www.evoomarketplace.com. Tall, arched windows, high ceilings, and wood-planked floors frame a display of steel cannisters that evokes an art exhibit in its streamlined chic. Hands-on owner Mick Major plays the part of curator of this gallery of sorts, guiding customers through a detailed tasting of his exquisite wares: first-press olive oils and nut oils from around the world, aged balsamic vinegars, and all their fused and infused variants. His pairing suggestions are astute—our favorite being Persian lime oil and red-apple balsamic—but once you get the hang of it you'll thrill to discover your own. How about wild mushroom–sage and honey-ginger? Or almond and lavender? Or chipotle and dark chocolate? Since Major and his wife, Carolyn, also sell imported pastas and sauces, French mustards, and other sundries from Colorado's own **34°** (p. 251) and **MM Local** (p. 251) among others, you can practically stock your whole pantry in one fell swoop.

Huckleberry Roasters, 2830 Larimer St., Five Points, Denver, CO 80205; (720) 381-2504; www.huckleberryroasters.com. The north end of Larimer is becoming quite the roasters' row; joining **Crema Coffee House** (p. 106) and **Novo Coffee** (see next listing),

Huckleberry works on a micro-scale, sourcing small quantities of mostly single-origin beans (though they do offer one signature blend, Blue Orchid Espresso) and roasting them in batches no bigger than 5 pounds. The retail counter and tasting room is open only a few days a week for a few hours at a time, so check the website for details and catch the friendly owners while you can.

Novo Coffee, 3008 Larimer St., Five Points, Denver, CO 80205; (303) 295-7678; www.novocoffee.com. Once you've spotted the Novo logo on coffeehouse urns, bakery shelves, and restaurant menus all around town, you may start to notice it in the national media—and conclude that this roasting company is the local equivalent of Intelligentsia or Stumptown. You'd be right, but for the fact that it's got no stake in the chain game. Admirably, the owners are wholly focused on the goal of sourcing single-origin beans through direct trade and roasting them to their fullest expression, period—opening their Five Points warehouse to the public only for cuppings every Friday, when they lead guests through a comparative tasting of four to five pours. The $15 fee includes a take-home bag of coffee; reservations are required (see website for details).

Pacific Mercantile, 1925 Lawrence St., Downtown, Denver, CO 80202; (303) 295-0293; www.pacificeastwest.com. Pac Merc, as we like to call it, isn't the biggest Asian market in metro Denver—far from it. It doesn't have a full-service deli or bakery. But what the Sakura Square grocery at the edge of downtown does have is charm aplenty. You'll have a field day at the seafood counter, sparkling with squid, sea urchin, shark, smelt roe, and more. You'll marvel at the myriad pickled products in the refrigerated cases: eggplant, mushroom, lotus root, burdock root, cabbage. You'll

scour the rice bins; ponder the panoply of potables, from milk tea to marble sodas; and peruse Japanese crisps, crackers, cookies, and candies galore. You'll survey the emporium of colorful tablewares in back. And finally, you'll walk out with an assortment of items so random it'll make you giggle. We've boggled our own minds upon finding bags of *li hing* powder, frozen *takoyaki* (fried octopus balls), and dried cuttlefish in our possession. Such are the joys of intrepid chowhounding.

Savory Spice Shop, 1537 Platte St., Downtown, Denver, CO 80202; (303) 477-3322; www.savoryspiceshop.com. Asafetida and *mahlab*. Ajowan seeds and crushed Urfa pepper. Dried rosebuds from Pakistan and aged black garlic from Korea. Blade mace and kaffir lime leaves. On shelf upon shelf, dozens and dozens of salts, masalas, rubs, hard-to-find extracts, proprietary seasoning blends, and cheese powders that have curried favor (no pun intended) among local chefs. That the flagship of this Denver-based spice retailer has spawned a multistate franchise comes as no surprise to its longtime devotees (nor to Food Network fans who caught owners Mike and Janet Johnston's mini-series, *Spice & Easy*). Not only is the inventory simply dazzling, but it's housed in a charmingly rustic space—old wood-planked flooring, antique cabinets—staffed by well-trained clerks who know their frankincense tears from their grains of paradise. Additional locations: 200 Quebec St., Unit 101, Denver, CO 80230; (303) 364-2188; 2041 Broadway, Boulder, CO 80302; (303) 444-0668; 2650 W. Main St., Littleton, CO 80120; (720) 283-2232.

Tony's Market, 950 Broadway, Golden Triangle, Denver, CO 80203; (720) 880-4501; www.tonysmarket.com. It started with a tiny butcher shop; it culminates with this Golden Triangle grocery, deli, bakery, and sunny in-store "bistro." Tony Rosacci and family cater to just about everybody here, stocking all the raw materials ambitious cooks require, including fresh produce, as well as all the heat-and-serve and take-out items their time-strapped counterparts swear by. Not that we advocate rushing in and rushing out—it's just too much fun to browse, to ponder the possibilities. Crab-stuffed mushrooms, perhaps, or shredded barbecue beef? Brick-size bierocks or fried ravioli? And maybe caramel-pecan bars or cherry-lime-chipotle pie for dessert? Here's a thought: if you do your shopping on your lunch hour, then you just might have a moment to sit down for a meatball sub. You won't miss a shred of breakroom gossip more satisfyingly juicy than that. Additional location: 7421 W. Bowles Ave., Littleton, CO 80123; (720) 377-3680.

Wednesday's Pie, 1422 Larimer St., LoDo, Denver, CO 80202; (720) 524-8050; http://wednesdayspie.com. When Frank Bonanno launched this sweet, petite underground shop as a front during the hush-hush construction phase of **Green Russell**, his speakeasy-style cocktail bar in Larimer Square, the name fit: it hawked its fresh-baked pies on hump day only. Now that the space doubles as the host stand for **Russell's Smokehouse** (p. 90), however, it's open daily to serve up meaty wedges in weekly changing flavors: apple, peach, cherry, key lime, banana cream, peanut butter–chocolate, and more. Vanilla bean–infused whipped cream and caramel or chocolate sauce are yours for the asking; coffee's a buck a bottomless cup. On blue Monday—or any day—you couldn't ask for more.

West Denver

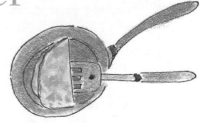

This is it, chow pilgrims—the promised land. The part of town whose streets are paved with tortillas and rice paper. Where every other storefront for block after block is a taqueria, pho shop, or dim-sum joint—and myriad oddities squeeze their way in between. The Columbine Steak House and Lounge, for instance—a true-blue dive that, from the looks of it, hasn't changed one iota since it opened in the middle of the last century. Or its mirror image, Cowbobas—likewise a Texas toast–toting steak house, but also a boba smoothie bar (go figure). Or, for that matter, half the city's entire fleet of loncheras and seasonal chile–roasting stands. Welcome to Federal Boulevard and beyond.

DaLat Vietnamese Cuisine, 940 S. Federal Blvd., Denver, CO 80219; (303) 935-4141; www.dalatdenver.com; Vietnamese; $$. With rather less ado than its neighbors, this family-run spot—unassuming but spruce, even serene, at least when the karaoke videos aren't blasting—serves up a slew of mighty fine surprises. Take the Vietnamese omelet: at once fluffy and crunchy, folded like a crêpe over bean sprouts and onions and served with a light, sweet dipping sauce. Or tiny, rosebud-delicate snails in a mild, lemongrass-scented curry. Or the deceptively named "salty shrimp"—appealingly crunchy, shell-on delights in a darkly savory-sweet, barbecue-like marinade, sauteed with bell peppers and onions. Or superbly saucy chopped pork spareribs. Goat and venison make cameo appearances to pique the gamey of palate, while even the most jaded gastronomes are bound to be bowled over by the signature combination salad—a riot of more snails, jellyfish, chicken feet, pig ears, squid, sea cactus, lotus root, papaya, and then some. DaLat is, in sum, a real sleeper.

JJ Chinese Seafood Restaurant, 2500 W. Alameda Ave., Denver, CO 80219; (303) 934-8888; www.jjrestaurant.com; Chinese/Taiwanese; $$. Watch that menu—it's a doozy, spanning dozens of pages, each more awe-inspiring than the last. Merely to scan it all is to have a field day fantasizing about duck's tongue, pig's feet, goose intestine, fish maw, fresh turtle, and so on; indeed, the repertoire of Chef-Owner Kevin Ho—who grew up and trained in

Guangzhou, aka Canton—is so dazzling that actually ordering from among the hot pots, stir-fries, noodle dishes, rice bowls, and porridges (congee) can feel like an infringement of potential. But you'll get over the frustration once you start tackling the likes of pungent fried smelt laced with sliced chilies, followed by heady casseroles of steamed pork minced with salted fish or chopped spareribs and eggplant. Of course, as the name, the koi-patterned wallpaper in the foyer, and the crustacean-filled tanks that line one wall all suggest, seafood is Ho's particular pride—and it will be your joy to dig into Cantonese classics like oysters in black bean sauce or lobster poached with ginger and green onions. And if, in the end, all the dishes that got away are still nagging at your conscience, come back for dim sum and have what the chefs are having—chances are you'll be surrounded by industry peeps.

King's Land Chinese Seafood Restaurant, 2200 W. Alameda Blvd., #44, Federal Blvd., Denver, CO 80223; (303) 975-2399; Chinese/Taiwanese; $$. For years, this sprawling Cantonese banquet hall has been locked in a cross-parking-lot showdown with **Super Star** (p. 122); at stake is no less than dim-sum supremacy. Let them wage their turf war—the winner in any case is you. After all, each outshines the other in its own way, whether you stick strictly to the treasure troves that are the circulating carts or mine the full menu for further nuggets. King's Land, in our view, takes top honors for its turnip cake, dry-fried salt-and-pepper shrimp, fried shrimp balls on sugar-cane sticks, roast duck, and *siu mai*, especially those filled with pork and black mushrooms; sticky, chewy sliced pineapple bun hits the last remaining spot. Due to its size, King's Land is also better equipped to handle crowds—no hour-long wait times here—so it's the place to be for Chinese New Year celebrations, preferably in the company of a pal who speaks the language.

Lao Wang Noodle House, 945 S. Federal Blvd., Denver, CO 80219; (303) 975-2497; Chinese/Taiwanese; $. You can't come up with a Top Ten list that we won't try to sneak this itty-bitty storefront jewel into somewhere, somehow. The sweet Taiwanese mom and pop who run it simply don't serve anything they haven't perfected: silken, hauntingly scented, broth-spurting *xiao long bao*. Potstickers worthy of the name, their flat bottoms pan-fried to a golden-brown crisp while their midsections burst with juicy pork filling. Paper-thin wontons that unfold like origami in a peanutty broth, accompanied by a dish of red chili sauce to stir in at your will (and peril). Dan-dan noodles to blow your stack and keep you coming back for more. Pungent, five-spiced sliced beef shank. To top it all off, the owners' son, Danny Wang—a cofounder, as it happens, of CAUTION: Brewing Co.—fills the taps with Lao Wang Lager, whose proprietary blend of spices his parents concocted. Talk about sterling family values.

Las Tortugas, 1549 W. Alameda Ave., Federal Blvd., Denver, CO 80223; (303) 744-0767; Sandwiches; $. *Tortuga,* in Spanish, means "turtle" or "slowpoke," but rest assured this torta vendor means business in any language: the no-nonsense line cooks behind the counter assemble what may be the meanest sandwiches this side of the border. Available in some 30 combinations of meats and cheeses, stacked with sliced avocado, tomato, and onion on a fluffy grilled roll that's in turn smeared with refried beans, mayo, and chipotle sauce, they're easily the size of bricks—until, that is, you start squeezing them into the thrillingly drippy messes that fill your mouth (and, probably, spill down your chin and shirt). The sensational Norteña in particular—chock-a-block with well-seasoned, breaded beef cutlet, pan-fried ground chorizo, and *quesillo* that stretches for inches—leaves us giddy. So do *aguas frescas* and *licuados* in flavors like cucumber and papaya. Sipping one to a mariachi beat, you'll feel as though you've stepped right into one of the black-and-white street-market scenes that bedeck the flashy orange walls of the stool-lined seating area. In a way, you have. Additional locations: 7600 Hwy. 2, Commerce City, CO 80022; (720) 389-8439; 712 Peoria St., Aurora, CO 80011; (303) 367-1123.

New Saigon, 630 S. Federal Blvd., Denver, CO 80219; (303) 936-4954; www.newsaigon.com; Vietnamese; $$. Fenced in for miles by the strip-mall pho joints that line Federal Boulevard, this seemingly nondescript long-timer stands alone—literally and otherwise. Soup's just a drop in the bucket of a menu that spilleth over to reveal the many regional dimensions of Vietnamese cuisine. As you peruse page after page, look for the phrase *cà ri*—which, of course, means curry; here, it signifies a rustic stew, chunky yet creamy with potatoes, squash, carrots, and coconut milk. Frog's legs may jump out at you too, with good reason: they're plump and juicy and tinged with lemongrass, onion, and garlic. And the list goes on: for every stir-fry or noodle bowl you know and love, there are two or three things you don't but will: duck sauteed with pineapple, say, or a fondue pot bubbling with a butter-and-vinegar-based broth for dipping slices of raw beef into, shabu shabu–style. (A newly opened bakery annex yields even more delights.) Too bad there's also a slew of items listed in Vietnamese you may never discover: the servers tend to discourage English speakers from going there, at least on the first try.

Pho Duy, 945 S. Federal Blvd., Denver, CO 80219; (303) 937-1609; Vietnamese; $. Almost directly across the street from **Pho 95** (see next review) sits its archrival for the noodle-bowl throne. Occupying a slightly lighter, brighter storefront dotted with watercolor murals, Pho Duy also differentiates itself with a menu that's devoted almost entirely to the namesake soup, along with a selection of more than 20 boba shakes. The broth here is richer and meatier, an advantage entirely depending on your tastes; the prices are a smidge lower, an advantage by any measure. As for the crowds taking said advantage, they're no less constant than they are at Pho 95—but somehow the place always seems more sub-dued; whether the relative quietude is a pro or a con rests on your mood. Ultimately, we

SPOTLIGHT ON VIETNAM

The majority of Denver's sizable Vietnamese population coalesces primarily around Federal Boulevard—and so, therefore, do its restaurants and bakeries. But keep your eyes peeled in every other direction as well—it's a pho frontier out there.

Ba Le Sandwich, *1044 S. Federal Blvd., Denver, CO 80219; (303) 922-9129; Sandwiches; $.* Slapping some 15 variations on the classic *bánh mì* together in virtually seconds flat, the sweet young things behind the counter of this strip-mall sandwich and frozen-yogurt outlet offer everything from sardines to shredded pork skin between the bread. The quality is second to that of **Vinh Xuong** (p. 129), we think, but the variety is tops. Best bet: the pâté, washed down with barley-and-fruit-filled *sam bo luong* or a can of refreshing grass-jelly drink from the cooler.

Chez Thuy, *2655 28th St., Boulder, CO 80301; (303) 442-1700; www .chezthuy.com; Vietnamese; $$.* Boulder's woefully ill-equipped with Vietnamese restaurants; this rather pretty spot, dotted with ornate, Chinese-influenced artworks, is the most established thanks to a well-developed repertoire that keeps noodle bowls, though available, on the back burner in favor of a profusion of grilled and stir-fried dishes.

judge this competition a toss-up—and dare you to compare back-to-back bowls for the sake of your own verdict. Additional locations: 3371 Peoria St., Denver, CO 80010; (303) 367-9884; 6600 W. 120th Ave., Unit B, Broomfield, CO 80021; (303) 438-7197.

Best bet: pork meatballs (*nem nuong*) followed by seafood-stuffed tofu (*tau hu don*).

Pho-natic, *229 E. Colfax Ave., Denver, CO 80203; (303) 832-3154; www.phodenver.com; Vietnamese; $.* Attractively mod, pastel-toned decor sets this Capitol Hill outlier even further apart from the Federal Boulevard pack. The menu, however, is wholly traditional: spring rolls, broken-rice plates, rice noodle bowls, and of course pho are about all there is, folks—and all a midday restorative need entail. Best bet: sprightly, crunchy *bun cha gio.*

T-Wa Inn, *555 S. Federal Blvd., Denver, CO 80219; (303) 922-2378; www.twainn.com; Vietnamese; $$.* A sentimental fave for many a local, this light, bright, comfy long-timer just keeps on keeping on. Best bet: catfish in black-bean sauce (*ca kho tuong*).

Viet's, *333 S. Federal Blvd., Denver, CO 80219; (303) 922-5774; www.vietsrestaurant.com; Vietnamese; $$.* Smaller and quieter than its neighbor **Saigon Bowl**, Viet's deserves as much consideration, especially from the venturesome—spying as they will *bánh khot* (not unlike mini-quiches) and stir-fried eel among some 200 dishes. Best bet: anything from the section labeled "Viet's Special," including marinated, roasted quail (*chim cut roti*).

Pho 95 Noodle House, 1002 S. Federal Blvd., Denver, CO 80219; (303) 936-3322; Vietnamese; $. At the end of a strip mall that contains a few Vietnamese soup shops, on a boulevard that boasts dozens of them, Pho 95 does the briskest business by far. We're not sure what they put in that light-bodied broth to earn such loyalty, but the aroma evokes tea; the flavor is slightly sweet, à la five-spice. It makes for an addictive bowl of pho—comme-il-pho, you might say, with slivered green and white onions, bean sprouts, jalapeño slices, water spinach, basil, and, of course, gobs of rice noodles and your choice of beef (we recommend it rare and marinated in chili sauce). What really floors us, however, are the works of art that the spring rolls resemble—wrapped so tightly the rice paper's nearly invisible, revealing the slices of roast pork and shrimp within, and accompanied by fruity, carrot-flecked peanut sauce. Though service is efficient, you'll have just enough time to sip a glass of salty lemonade and take in the scenery: the ever-packed house is really rather charming, painted lilac, lined with maroon booths, and scattered with scrolls and seascapes.

The Red Claw, 472 S. Federal Blvd., Denver, CO 80219; (720) 328-3620; http://theredclawdenver.com; Asian Fusion; $$. Since this delightful harbinger of the emerging genre that is the Vietnamese-Cajun boiling point, as Louisiana's crawfish shacks are called, opened in 2010, it's been joined by The Crawling Crab (781 S. Federal Blvd., Denver, CO 80219; 303-936-0123) and The Asian Cajun (2400 W. Alameda Ave., Denver, CO 80223; 303-922-0699). But The Red Claw remains by far the best of the bunch. The dining room's a bit bare—a few trawl nets and fishing poles about do it for themed decor—but then, the shellfish boils, seasoned to order and brought to plastic-lined table in overflowing tin pails, supply visuals aplenty. Meanwhile, the rest of the menu brims with curiosities you won't find anywhere else in town. Especially exhilarating is the section devoted to *mon nhau* ("drinking food"), featuring intense curries based on hefty chunks of goat meat, frog's legs, or eel as well as steamed mollusks of all kinds (including periwinkles). And the glossy, crackling, juicy wings marinated in fish sauce outshine their sports-bar counterparts by magnitudes.

Saigon Bowl (aka Dong Khanh), 333 S. Federal Blvd., Denver, CO 80219; (303) 935-2427; Vietnamese; $. With a menu that lists nearly 300 items, this comfy Far East Center staple still can't quite top **New Saigon** (p. 116) in the variety department. But it comes close, with results that are every bit as reliable and generally cheaper. Salads here are invigorating, especially the *goi tom thit*—a tangle of sprouts, cabbage, slivered jalapeños and red onions, basil and mint leaves, peanuts, and more, topped with cold sliced roast pork and shrimp in a spunky, citrusy fish sauce–based dressing. The signature sampler's party central, heaped with grilled pork and chicken strips, fried shrimp paste wedges, crunchy egg rolls, and the crown jewel of softshell crab, plus cucumber and carrot slices, a bundle of fresh herbs, chopped peanuts, and rice paper rounds—all accompanied, of course, by a bowl of warm water for dipping and rolling. *Hu tieu* (glass-noodle soup) amounts to a liquid menagerie of shellfish, poultry, and pork alike. And refreshingly sweet-tart jackfruit smoothies double as dessert.

Star Kitchen, 2917 W. Mississippi Ave., Federal Blvd., Denver, CO 80219; (303) 936-0089; www.starkitchendenver.com; Chinese/Taiwanese; $$. It may not look like a contender, but the moment it opens for dim-sum service—even on weekdays—this borderline drab but nonetheless hot Cantonese spot lines 'em up and knocks 'em for a loop. Dumplings galore pack its biggest punch: spheres or pouches, steamed, pan-fried, or deep-fried and filled with shellfish, chicken, or greens, they're simply among the best we've encountered—whereas the savory-sweet sticky-rice fritters stuffed with pork and mushrooms are unlike anything we've had the pleasure of munching elsewhere. *Baozi* (buns), too, seem just a bit fresher and more finely crafted here. Meanwhile, the regular menu's no afterthought; on the contrary, it's laden with otherwise hard-to-find regional specialties like oyster pancakes, caramel pork, and the ever-elusive Chinese fried chicken as well as fine sizzling platters (we're partial to the chopped beef rib with eggplant in black-pepper sauce).

Super Star Asian Cuisine, 2200 W. Alameda Ave., Ste. 5A, Federal Blvd., Denver, CO 80238; (303) 727-9889; Chinese/Taiwanese; $$. Following a much-needed expansion, Super Star is no longer dwarfed in size by its dim-sum rival across the way, **King's Land** (see p. 114). Nor was it ever eclipsed in terms of quality; indeed, scores of Denverites give it the slight edge overall. Though our own jury's still out, here as there we can declare a few winners: giant pan-fried leek dumplings and shrimp-stuffed eggplant, for instance;

soothing seafood congee and fried rice flecked with shredded egg and peanuts; textbook pork-blood cubes and, by worthwhile special order, plump snails in the shell, richly sauteed with peppers and onions. We're also fond of the ambiance—which is that there is no ambiance, save for the buzz of the crowds packing the dining room to tuck into two-for-one lobsters at all hours. Just like a genuine Chinatown hole in the wall.

Tacos y Salsas #3, 910 S. Federal Blvd., Denver, CO 80219; (303) 922-9400; www.tacosandsalsasrestaurants.com; Mexican; $. Setting foot inside this taqueria-plus is like clambering onto a carousel: the colors whirl, the mariachi tunes play, and everyone's smiling—at least everyone behind the counter. The customers parked in the wildly painted chairs and booths are mostly heads down, too engrossed in their bowls of seafood soup or giant burritos stuffed with boiled *chicharrónes* to bother with friendly gestures. We know just how they feel, especially in the all-consuming face of *tostadas de lengua*—piled with tender chunks of the best tongue in town, smeared with luscious refried beans and sprinkled with the confetti of shredded *queso,* lettuce, and tomatoes. Ditto the model *tacos de carnitas* assembled on hand-pressed tortillas; if they look a little bare, look harder. A dedicated condiment bar is inches away, lined with six house salsas—three green, three red, all powerful—as well as chopped limes, onions, radishes, and cilantro.

Speaking of bars, there's a full one in the back room—which is even splashier than the front, lined with ceramic lanterns and tiles. Best of all, this merry-go-round almost never stops, closing only in the wee hours. Additional locations include 1531 Stout St., Denver, CO 80202; (720) 287-7060; 2184 S. Chambers Rd., Aurora, CO 80014; (303) 283-1616; and 6895 E. 72nd Avd., Commerce City, CO 80022; (720) 542-9519; see website for more.

Tarasco's New Latin Cuisine, 470 S. Federal Blvd., Denver, CO 80219; (303) 922-2387; Mexican; $. This easy-to-miss but hard-to-dismiss seven-table charmer is clearly a labor of love for gregarious Chef-Owner Noe Bermudez, whose painstaking efforts to re-create the specialties of his native Michoacán pay off in the form of delicious deviations from the taco-centric norm. Here you'll encounter simple yet compelling *morisqueta,* a mound of steamed rice topped with dollops of refried beans, salsas *verde y rojo, queso fresco,* and crema. And meltingly soft, soothingly sweet *uchepos,* or corn tamales. And rich, creamy, poblano-based *mole verde* over chicken, as well as *mole siete chiles—* which requires some 30 ingredients and 48 hours of prep time, as its complex flavor attests. Even the virgin pick-me-ups are uncommon: Bermudez whips up nearly 50 *jugos* and *licuados* that contain everything from spinach, garlic, and ginseng to granola and bee pollen. "If you get sick," he says of his elixirs, "you need to come see me." That goes double in flu season, when mugs of *champurrado*—a warm, thick sipper based on corn and chocolate—will chase any chills that bowls of *caldo de mollejas* fail to dispel.

Landmarks

The Buckhorn Exchange, 1000 Osage St., Lincoln Park, Denver, CO 80204; (303) 534-9505; www.buckhorn.com; Steak House; $$$. Although you can bone up on the notorious lore of this National Historic Landmark by perusing its website, better you should belly up to the oak-paneled lounge on the second floor, where your barkeep will wax nostalgic about its founder, a compadre of Buffalo Bill; the 542 hunting trophies covering every square inch of wall space, along with mounted displays of antique firearms and Native American artifacts; and every other vestige of the Buckhorn's Wild West beginnings circa 1893. Thus enlightened, you can repair to a parlor chair or a table on the covered roof deck while the resident autoharpist croons cowboy tunes—or head back downstairs to sup under the watchful eyes of the very creatures whose descendants adorn the menu: elk and quail, alligator and buffalo, even the occasional yak or ostrich fillet. (As for cattle, the up-to-4-pound steaks may be signature, but the batter-fried Rocky Mountain oysters are downright unforgettable, for better or worse.) What you can't do is go home feeling anything less than awestruck—that's simply impossible.

Domo, 1365 Osage St., Lincoln Park, Denver, CO 80204; (303) 595-3666; www.domorestaurant.com; Japanese/Sushi; $$. The overused phrase "hidden gem" doesn't begin to do justice to the dreamscape that Domo Chef-Owner Gaku Homma has lovingly conjured along a dusty stretch of Lincoln Park. The very picture of a woodcutter's rural cottage in shogun-era Japan, his restaurant doubles as a breathtaking gallery of artifacts and other wonders (behold the jar of pit viper wine on one ledge), which leads to a rock garden centered around an arch-bridged lily pond as well as to an actual museum of folk relics. It's a magical setting in whose foreground Homma artfully places what he calls "country food" without compromise (above all, extra condiments are not yours for the asking). *Nabemono* (hot pots), *donburi* (rice bowls), teriyaki,  and our favorite—soupy, omelet-like *tojimono*—as well as the trademark Wankosushi, served chirashi-style, comprise the menu in various combinations, preceded by an array of small plates reminiscent of Korean *panchan* (if you're lucky, you'll get gravied meatballs; soba noodles are swell, too). Sake selected by the house comes in the traditional *masu* (wooden box) or *tokkuri* (ceramic jug), rounding out an experience that's as edifying as it is enchanting.

Jack-n-Grill, 2524 N. Federal Blvd., Jefferson Park, Denver, CO 80211; (303) 964-9544; www.jackngrill.com; Mexican; $$. What makes Jack-n-Grill's flagship the stuff of local legend is not age (it opened in 2000). Nor is it the old two-story building that is, however, notable in its cluttered way—the walls plastered with memorabilia and Polaroids of the daredevils who've polished off the 7-pound burrito. Even said burrito, for all the coverage it's received on national TV, only gets partial credit. No, this family-run *casa de comida* really owes its place in the canon to a workhorse kitchen that rustles up Mexican, and more specifically New Mexican, grub as consistently satisfying as the portions are behemoth. Whatever you choose—be it a honking stuffed sopaipilla, tortilla-wrapped burger, or traditionally stacked enchilada platter—be sure to do as Albuquerqueans do and ask for both green and red chile (aka Christmas) on top: the former wins all the awards, but the latter deserves to, nearly black and intensely smoky. Additional locations: 2630 W. Belleview Ave., Littleton, CO 80123; (303) 474-4242; 9310 Sheridan Blvd., Westminster, CO 80031; (303) 428-4788.

Specialty Stores, Markets & Producers

Celestial Bakery, Deli & BBQ, 333 S. Federal Blvd., Unit 207, Denver, CO 80219; (303) 936-2339. We always knew heaven was a hole in the wall. There's barely room for you inside this tiny take-out joint, but the grandiose name nonetheless fits: it's crammed with more goodies than the night sky is with stars. Over there, hung by their necks behind glass, whole roast poultry glistens. Over here, pastries both savory and sweet abound. Fluffy, slightly sweet steamed and baked buns (*baozi*) and dumplings (*jiaozi*) spill with terrific fillings—chunks of roast chicken mixed with mushrooms and herbs around a whole hard-cooked egg, perhaps, or diced pork in a rich, savory gravy. Lotus leaf packets hold a mixture of more juicy pork and sticky rice so soft and dense it's basically a thick, spoon-able paste. And beautifully decorated moon cakes burst with sweet-ened red-bean paste. Denver may lack a Chinatown, but it's got a world of Chinese culinary tradition right here, in a few square feet.

Little Saigon Supermarket, 375 S. Federal Blvd., #104, Denver, CO 80219; (303) 937-8860. There are no two ways about the fact that **Pacific Ocean Marketplace** (see next entry) down the street is much bigger, brighter, and better organized. But the utter disarray in which this Far East Center grocery usually stands—boxes everywhere, dusty shelves stocked to the ceiling—is precisely what makes it such a ball to navigate. We never know what we'll find

here: jars of lavender syrup or pickled mudfish cream, cans of banana blossoms in brine or puffball mushrooms, wrapped styrofoam packages of pork uterus or (ahem) calf fries, whole rabbit fish or giant featherbacks on ice. Half the time, we don't even know what we've purchased once we get it home. Nor do we much care; we'll figure it out eventually, and in the meantime, we've got what appears to be mackerel stir-fry from the tiny, signless hot buffet to sustain us. So long as it doesn't contain pork bung, we'll be happy campers (not to sniff at another man's delicacy; if you're in the market for digestive tract, Little Saigon delivers).

Pacific Ocean Marketplace, 2200 W. Alameda Ave., Federal Blvd., Denver, CO 80223; (303) 936-4845. For shopping on the cheap and browsing for free, it's hard to top Denver proper's biggest Asian market by far. You need skate wing? They've got skate wing. Fresh dragonfruit, green-bean popsicles, or gingko nuts? They've got those, too. Shiitakes for half the price you pay elsewhere, pickled plums for a song? Yep—not to mention hundreds upon hundreds of items from the grocery, deli and meat and seafood counters you didn't even know you needed, like jarred *halo halo,* preserved *krachai* or dried sea cucumbers, snail heads, and abalone (but heads up—that latter costs more than just about everything else in the store combined, running you $300 a pound). Additional location: 6600 W. 120th Ave., Denver, CO 80020; (303) 410-8168.

Vinh Xuong Bakery, 375 S. Federal Blvd., #112, Denver, CO 80219; (303) 922-4968. Now here's what we call a diamond in the rough. At the end of the Far East Center, this mom-and-pop shop sits a bit forlorn, a tad shabby, its display cases perhaps more haphazardly stocked than some with pastel-colored cake rolls, glistening crullers, and the like. Never you mind: it's the content that counts. We'd pit Vinh Xuong's ridiculously cheap *bánh mì* against **Ba Le**'s (p. 118) any day; the mayo-slathered baguette's just as fresh and crusty, and it's more generously layered with perfectly textured roast pork, pâté, and head cheese plus all the trimmings (pickled, julienned daikon and carrot; thick slices of cucumber and jalapeño; cilantro stems). By comparison, the elegantly embossed mooncakes may seem pricey at $7 a pop, but once you've sunk your teeth into the equally elaborate, chewy mosaic of candied winter melon and other fruits, almonds, cashews, sesame seeds, and even, sometimes, hard-cooked egg yolk, you'll deem them a steal. Of the numerous, rainbow-bright variations on *chè* (pudding), meanwhile, our favorite's the thick, creamy, coconutty vehicle for both red and black beans. Now if, after all that, spiffiness still matters, you're in luck: the owners' son runs a spanking-new spinoff just blocks away (2370 W. Alameda Ave., #15, Denver, CO 80223; 303-922-0999).

East Denver

Capitol Hill, Uptown, City Park, Cheesman Park, Congress Park, Park Hill, East Colfax, Cherry Creek & Country Club

Deep contrasts mark the neighborhoods to the east of downtown Denver. Huge estates and high gates indicate the long-established affluence of Cherry Creek and Country Club. Uptown and Capitol Hill are where the party's at, projecting a come-as-you-are vitality. And as for the areas around East Colfax—well, no less an authority than *Playboy* once dubbed the 26-mile avenue "the longest, wickedest street in America." Although some attempts at gentrification have been successful, it remains nothing if not colorful, for better or worse. Certainly for foodies, it's just as well. After all, this is where they'll find the vast majority of Ethiopian restaurants, side by side with legendary dive bars. But they'll also stumble upon lovely little surprises like the antiques-filled Denver Tea Room (www.thedenver tearoom.com)—tucked away in a historic bed-and-breakfast off City Park—and Prohibition (www.prohibitiondenver.com), a gastropubby oasis in the gritty midst of it all. Such surprising diversity is what Denver's all about.

Foodie Faves

Abyssinia, 4116 E. Colfax Ave., Park Hill, Denver, CO 80220; (303) 316-8830; Ethiopian; $$. Pay-by-the-scoop buffets get a bad rap for good reason—they're mostly slop. Not so at Abyssinia, where $1.75 will get you a lot more than a scoop of the very same, very good stuff that comprises the regular menu. And you'll still get to enjoy it while seated at a trinket-filled *mesob* (traditional basket table)—along with a glass of honey wine if you're feeling frisky. Kindly Chef-Manager Gideon Fanta makes a dandy *doro wot*, with egg-plump drumsticks stewed in a thick red gravy distinguished by *berbere* (Ethiopia's answer to *garam masala*). Its vegetarian counterpart, featuring red lentils, is just as fine. Bear in mind, however, that full-service dining guarantees a greater selection; Fanta even offers a couple of fish dishes, a rarity among the many Ethiopian joints that dot East Colfax.

Aria, 250 Josephine St., Cherry Creek, Denver, CO 80206; (303) 377-4012; www.dinearia.com; Contemporary; $$. We're rooting for this Cherry Creek underdog. Occupying as it does a proverbially cursed space, it shares with **Opus** (p. 274)—its better known Littleton sibling—a classy, warm-toned vibe, but here Chef-Partner

Michael Long is putting his considerable creativity to the test of a mid-priced menu. And so far, he's succeeding. His signature bison short ribs, braised in Dr Pepper, are saucy and tender to the bone. The fish and chips have got a brand-new bag: tempura-light salmon belly strips come with stacked, fried sweet-potato wedges and a zingy aioli combining wasabi and chopped cornichons. Depending on the season, Long may roll out goat-cheese gnocchi enriched by drippings from the bacon-fat candle David Burke made famous. Or Italian tamales—filled with sausage and polenta, topped with lemon and pine nuts. Or deep-fried chocolate-chip cookie–dough spring rolls accompanied by candied ginger dip, of all things. Here's to tempting fate with chutzpah.

Barolo Grill, 3030 E. 6th Ave., Country Club, Denver, CO 80206; (303) 393-1040; www.barologrilldenver.com; Italian; $$$. In a young town where peace and quiet are vastly underrated, this one's for the grown-ups. Low lights, white linens, and soft amber tones set the stage for wining and fine dining in tranquility; both the luxurious seasonal menu and owner Blair Taylor's extraordinary wine list are steeped in the traditions of *alta cucina*. The latter stands testament to one of the city's deepest cellars, with some 10,000 bottles in all—among them an astounding 300 Barolos. (If your pockets are equally deep, ask wine director Ryan Fletter about vineyard verticals.) The former, meanwhile, reveals Chef Darrel Truett's intimate familiarity with the whole earthy, hearty spectrum of northern Italian cookery. Fowl is a specialty—look not just for the signature duck braised with wine and olives but also pheasant and quail. Also noteworthy are soufflés and fresh pastas tossed with chestnuts, wild mushrooms, mascarpone, and other delights. If ever there were an occasion to splurge on a tasting menu, however, a trip to Barolo Grill might be it; for one thing, it's surprisingly well-priced, and for another, it's even richer in game and delicacies than its à la carte counterpart.

Bones, 701 Grant St., Capitol Hill, Denver, CO 80203; (303) 860-2929; www.bonesdenver.com; Asian Fusion; $$. Frank Bonanno scored a three-peat when he opened this snappy noodle bar on the corner of 7th and Grant, smack between its swankier siblings **Mizuna** (p. 145) and **Luca d'Italia** (p. 144). An open kitchen takes up half the room, which is as stripped down as the name suggests—all clean lines, picture windows, and shades of oyster gray. Meanwhile, the succinct menu makes no bones about its unorthodox slant. For every two traditionally Asian ingredients or techniques represented in the signature bowls, there's a classical

French or modern American counterpart: thus the ramen comes chock-full of poached lobster as well as edamame, while egg noodles may derive their rich savor from duck confit or homegrown corn and miso-cilantro butter. Luscious small plates follow the same model—buttery escargot potstickers are an unforgettable highlight, as is roast bone marrow (which no one in this town dared to serve before Bonanno took the plunge). The sake's craft, the cocktails are bespoke (three cheers for a slug of local gin with housemade lemongrass tonic)—and the ice cream is, of all things, soft-serve.

City, O' City, 206 E. 13th Ave., Capitol Hill, Denver, CO 80203; (303) 861-6443; www.cityocitydenver.com; Vegetarian; $$. **Together** with the poetic name, the slogan—"An ode, a lament"—serves as a clue to the emphatically offbeat attitudes that inform this all-day and late-night mainstay on Capitol Hill. But it's the decor that speaks volumes: swoops and swirls of ochre and teal paint, chandeliers of beaded silver fringe, communal tables overlooking an open kitchen, a coffee bar clad in rusted metal salvaged from an antique trailer. And the menu finally spells it all out for you—staunchly vegetarian, largely organic, and community oriented, just like that of its nearby sibling, **WaterCourse Foods** (which supplies its giant baked goods, including the wonderfully thick, crunchy, chocolate-dipped sweet-potato cookie with coconut; see p. 160). Indeed, a few old WaterCourse favorites have migrated here, most notably the oddly addictive arugula salad topped with onion rings in maple-dijon dressing. But the rest is all City's own, from the mix-and-match array of fried veggies with dipping sauces to the lively thin-crust pizzas (think brie with apricots and green olives). As for beverages, the java's locally roasted, the bar is full, and the kombucha's on tap—we kid you not.

CoraFaye's Cafe, 2861 Colorado Blvd., Park Hill, Denver, CO 80207; (303) 333-5551; http://corafayes.com; Southern; $$. Bearing the name of the family matriarch, this two-room country kitchen in Park Hill is so picture-perfect that cynics could be forgiven for thinking it's all an act. But once they've surveyed the clutter of antiques, the flea-market finds, the historic photos, and the multigenerational crowds, and once they've settled upon a table draped in mismatched linens and lace to the strains of some throaty blues chanteuse, they'll be welcomed by Priscilla Smith and family with a graciousness to make their hard hearts melt. The repertoire includes everything a homesick—or would-be—Southerner could hope for. Frog's legs. Rib tips. Fried chicken. Pig's ears, feet, and tails on Wednesday. Oxtails over rice and smothered rabbit on Sunday. Black-eyed peas, fried okra, banana pudding, fruit cobbler, sweet tea, and Kool-Aid—the list goes on. And if actual tears of gratitude spring to your eyes once you get a bite of those incredible, pink-centered, fork-tender pork necks; textbook collards with shreds of ham hock and a splash of cider vinegar; richly spiced, not cloying candied yams; and corn bread with the moist crumb of cake—well, we sympathize. We were skeptics once, too.

D Bar Desserts, 1475 E. 17th Ave., Uptown, Denver, CO 80210; (303) 861-4710; www.dbardesserts.com; Bakery/Cafe; $. When much-decorated celebrity Pastry Chef Keegan Gerhard and his equally gifted partner Lisa Bailey opened this Uptown dessert lounge in 2008, expectations were sky-high citywide. The dynamic duo has been fulfilling, if not surpassing, them ever since. In a space as sleek and chic as an art gallery, awash in robin's egg blue, they oversee the execution of a constantly changing menu that's no less graceful for being cheeky. Its biggest claim to fame is the nostalgia-tinted cake and shake—the name says it all—but gorgeously plated novelties proliferate. The lowliest cheesecake-swirled brownie or frosted cupcake is a work of art, never mind the flamboyant, even avant-garde approaches to bananas foster or French toast, Mexican churros or Belgian waffles. But it all starts with savories: the vinaigrette-and-pesto-slicked pizza salad sandwich is as chewy and gooey as any dessert, oozing with two cheeses, while garlic sauce brings a trio of doughnut holes, thumbprinted with steak tartare, into high relief. It's all handsomely paired with a brief but shrewd list of wines by the half- or full glass as well as stickies and ports by the ounce.

Elway's, 2500 E. 1st Ave., Cherry Creek, Denver, CO 80206; (303) 399-5353; www.elways.com; Steak House; $$$. With a name like Elway's, it doesn't have to be good: football fans would flock to the Broncos quarterback-turned-restaurateur's woody, white-cloth flagship chophouse just to say they'd been regardless. (And well-heeled singles would still throng the bar, a mini-mecca for people-watching and spirited mingling.) But with a name like Tyler Wiard in the kitchen, area foodies know that this Cherry Creek fixture is, in fact, very good. Colorado is as Colorado does, so while hand-cut steaks with all the trimmings are the meat of the matter (along with a massive wine list), the rest of the menu is what puts this place on the map at brunch and lunch as well as dinner; Wiard's a wizard with locally sourced ingredients—not just lamb and buffalo but corn, green chiles, and more. There's no shame, then, in stopping by for a bite rather than a blow-out, be it killer chili, a damn fine burger, a burrito stuffed with chicken-fried steak (oof), or even fried rice with king crab (you read that right). Trust us—we do it all the time. See Executive Chef Tyler Wiard's recipe for **Colorado Lamb Sliders** on p. 329.

Fat Sully's New York Pizza/Denver Biscuit Co., 3237 E. Colfax Ave., City Park, Denver, CO 80206; (303) 377-7900/(303) 333-4440; www.fatsullyspizza.com/www.denbisco.com; Pizza/Southern; $–$$. This place is a riot. Tucked under the giant umbrella that is the Atomic Cowboy—an artsy, rollicking, brick-walled warehouse of a bar whose name is reflected in the wacky paintings of rocket-riding dudettes—are a wink-wink Southern kitchen on the one hand and a street-smart pizzeria on the other. By way of explanation, says General Manager Jake Riederer, "We're Atomic Cowboy all the time, but in the morning we're also the Denver Biscuit Company, and in the evening we're also Fat Sully's." So long as Jonathan Larsen, the chef who oversees both ventures for owners Drew and Ashleigh Shader, can keep it straight, we're happy. And he can. In this town, Sully's alone has New York–style pie by the slice down pat; fancy it isn't, but just right it is, chewy and gooey yet sturdy enough to fold. And there's no skimping on the fixins' for the biscuits: condiments are housemade down to the pickles. So whether they're smothered in chicken potpie filling or shiitake mushroom gravy, topped with shrimp and grits or cornmeal-fried catfish and tartar sauce, they hit the spot.

Fruition, 1313 E. 6th Ave., Country Club, Denver, CO 80218; (303) 831-1962; www.fruitionrestaurant.com; Contemporary; $$$. "I want people to understand what's in front of them," insists Alex Seidel, a young chef with an old soul—and a nationally celebrated restaurant to show for it. Though he thrives on "trying things I've never done before" (hence the recent launch of Fruition Farm), the results are notable above all for their balance and restraint, based on traditions "that have provided memories for people." Exquisite cavatelli carbonara with house-cured pork belly and a perfectly poached egg in parmesan broth is a special case in point—but then, so is virtually everything on the menu. Consider Seidel's mesmerizing take on French onion soup, centered around a crouton-topped short rib drizzled with gruyère cream;

move on to his plump duck breast, its skin the color of polished walnut, over risotto in a pool of intense red-onion marmalade; top them off with lemon meringue pie or carrot cake with cream-cheese ice cream. It's all served with care in a low-ceilinged Country Club row house renovated to resemble a country inn, complete with old wine racks and framed watercolors. "People celebrate 50th anniversaries here," observes Seidel, "but they also walk in wearing shorts and flip-flops—and that's what I wanted."

Il Posto, 2011 E. 17th Ave., City Park, Denver, CO 80206; (303) 394-0100; www.ilpostodenver.com; Italian; $$$. Unlike its coastal counterparts, this city's not exactly rife with neighborhood trattorias. So we tend to treasure the few we've got—including this crisply modern City Park spot run by seasoned Milanese Chef Andrea Frizzi. What isn't housemade is carefully sourced, resulting in a concise but daily updated repertoire characterized by the open kitchen's light touch. Seasonal produce appears where you least expect it: pluots, roasted corn, or orange cauliflower may pop up in risotto served traditionally in a wide, shallow bowl, while carrot tops or green beans strew silken stuffed calamari. Pastas are an invitation to explore; if you've never tasted garganelli or reginette, here's your opportunity. And though it's tweaked from time to time, there's a reason the juicy, pan-roasted chicken, burrata-stuffed and laced with pancetta and oyster mushrooms, is rarely erased from the blackboard menu. Service can be slow, but there are worse ways to kill time than by brushing up on your Italian varietals—here's to Corvina, Friulano, and the triumphant return of Lambrusco.

Jelly, 600 E. 13th St., Capitol Hill, Denver, CO 80203; (303) 831-6301; http://eatmorejelly.com; American; $. We'd say that the name says it all, but it doesn't. Sure, the look of this daytime corner joint on Capitol Hill is marmalade bright and sunny-side-up cheerful—but it's got its sly side, what with modest chandeliers and a Plexiglass display of vintage cereal boxes. And sure, the kitchen jars its own preserves in classic array: mixed berry, peach, strawberry-rhubarb. But novelty is the key to much of the menu. There are five types of eggs Benedict, six of hash (including chorizo–sweet potato), and seven burgers—a fave being the one with jalapeño jelly and cream cheese. There are pancakes that riff on cereal bowls, flecked with Frosted Flakes and bananas, plus hair-of-the-dog beer cocktails from the full bar. Best of all, there are breakfast sliders—darling indulgences like fluffy, lace-edged goat cheese-and-bacon mini-frittatas atop soft buns smeared with spinach-walnut pesto. (At press time, a second location was under construction at 1700 Evans Ave., near DU.)

Jonesy's EatBar, 400 E. 20th Ave., Uptown, Denver, CO 80205; (303) 863-7473; http://jeatbar.com; Gastropub; $$. Irrepressible designer/entrepreneur Leigh Jones has put her eclectic stamp on many a local lounge, but this self-styled gastropub and billiards bar in the shadow of downtown has struck a major chord. Within its violet and burgundy walls, folks from all walks congregate at the handsome bar of inlaid wood from the Art Deco era, in the vinyl booths lit by paper lanterns, and around the pool table, dartboards, and mounted jukebox; every room's a gallery of wild paintings and old family photos. Granted, no one's here merely for the ambiance—they've come for a menu that captured the zeitgeist from day one. First up are the mac-and-cheese fries: a whole chunky, funky pile, topped with diced bacon. Then come the sliders: lamby joes win the popularity contest, but we're always intrigued by the vegetarian one-off, be it falafel with pineapple-chili sauce or black-bean patties with ghost-pepper cream. Of course, burgers and fries aren't the half of it: you've got to love comeback-kid rumaki (new and improved with pineapple chutney), cola-glazed meat loaf, brunchtime chicken-fried pork, PB & J bread pudding, and cocktails slung by bartenders whose generosity is commensurate with their skill.

Lala's Wine Bar + Pizzeria, 410 E. 7th Ave., Capitol Hill, Denver, CO 80203; (303) 861-9463; www.lalaswinebar.com; Italian; $. Terra-cotta hues and pendant lamps set this gathering spot at the edge of Capitol Hill aglow come sunset, luring locals by the swarm to its veritable hive of booths and bar tables, open-ending onto the popular patio. Easygoing amid the buzz of first dates and families alike, it turns out an array of pizzas, panini and antipasti that's much more thoughtfully executed than you'd expect given the high demand placed on the kitchen. Blade-thin, black-bubbled

crusts come topped with such nifty stuff as lamb pancetta, candy-sweet peppadew peppers, and grilled apples; if we had to pick a favorite, ours might be the Diavolo with fontina, dry-cured chorizo, and chopped, roasted poblano. Other musts include the Insalata Susina with dried plums, pumpkin seeds, and excellent sheep's milk cheese; robust hunks of stromboli stuffed with lamb-risotto balls and spinach; and warm flatbread accompanied by a luxuriant duo of arugula pesto and mascarpone. Dispensed by pros who also make a mean cocktail or two, the multifaceted and user-friendly wine list is arranged by type; pours are generous enough to last you awhile—maybe right through seasonal desserts like sweet potato–cherry cobbler.

La Merise, 2700 E. 3rd Ave., Cherry Creek, Denver, CO 80206; (720) 596-4360; http://lamerisefrenchcuisine.com; French; $$$. Run by two women from Latvia and Lithuania, respectively, this *charmante* bistro is a postcard realized via wood trim and white linens, shelves neatly lined with signed wine bottles and tiny paintings of Parisian street scenes. The menu, meanwhile, is a *lettre d'amour* to the classics—escargots and pâté, *oui*; trout grenobloise and boeuf bourguignon, *mais oui*; crème brulée and chocolate mousse, *bien sûr*—that happens to be penned with uncommon grace (and delivered in similar fashion by lovely servers). Depth of flavor meets lightness of touch in well-integrated dishes like the elegantly simple baked chicken croquettes, which skim a pool of frothy dilled cream alongside tenderly caramelized root vegetables—dotted, strikingly, with grapes—and expertly scalloped potatoes; the same goes for the eggy, béchamel-spread crêpe filled with turkey, cranberries, fried eggs, and swiss. (Another crêpe, topped with more swiss, sliced ham, and poached eggs under a blanket of hollandaise, is heavier handed but tasty nonetheless.) Add a largely French wine list that's very well-priced, especially for Cherry Creek, and you can bet that come summer you'll find us out on the brick patio, soaking up the atmosphere over oysters and a bottle of Muscadet.

Luca d'Italia, 711 Grant St., Capitol Hill, Denver, CO 80203; (303) 832-6600; www.lucadenver.com; Italian; $$$. One of Denver's most prominent chef-restaurateurs, Frank Bonanno is also one of its most visionary. Ever at the forefront of trends, he turned tradition on its head when he opened this posh ristorante around the corner from his flagship, **Mizuna** (p. 145), at the edge of Capitol Hill in 2003, introducing locals to the seemingly radical notion of in-house production. The kitchen cured its own salumi, made its own cheeses and pastas from scratch, and dared to serve the then-unheard-of likes of offal, burrata, and lardo. Of course, it still does: to this day the menu is exquisitely artisanal, pushing boundaries without losing sight of its roots. Bonanno invariably does wonders with octopus and rabbit, boldly showcases lesser known pastas—think *caramelle* with roast goat in onion fonduta and poppy-seed *brodo*—and still makes a mean meatball. Desserts are no less multifaceted paired with house-infused grappa—and we love the uncompromising, pan-regional Italian wine list.

Mataam Fez, 4609 E. Colfax Ave., Park Hill, Denver, CO 80220; (303) 399-9282; www.mataamfez-denver.com; Moroccan; $$$. Fraternal owners Mouhcine and Abedelilah Mouhieddine were born in Rabat, but their ancestors hail from Fez—and so do the extravagant, jewel-toned rugs, cushions, lanterns, and tiles that cover every square inch of this longtime escape from Park Hill. Amid the swirl of belly dancers, five-course set pieces include lentil soup, salad, *b'stella,* and mint tea poured in titillatingly grand Moroccan fashion. But they're centered on entrees rich in all the floral and bitter, savory-sweet contrasts for which North African cuisine is known. Cornish hen bathed in juices enhanced by pre-served lemons and green olives is a standby, but Mouhcine is so proud of his rabbit—cut into large pieces and coated in a sauce that glows red with cinnamon and paprika—that, he swears, "We'll give you another plate if you don't like it." No worries there. Still, should you need liquid courage, a glass (or two) of the signature layered wine—white, rosé, and red—just might do the trick.

Mizuna, 225 E. 7th Ave., Capitol Hill, Denver, CO 80203; (303) 832-4778; http://mizunadenver.com; Contemporary; $$$. Now in its second decade, the flagship in powerhouse Chef-Restaurateur Frank Bonanno's local fleet just keeps sailing right along. For funky Capitol Hill, the look of this special-occasion destination is unusually stately; dark woods, crisp linens, and corn-yellow walls belie the French-inflected yet utterly contemporary experience that lies ahead. Mizuna's gift to the Denver dining scene was and is its ultrasophistication. The precise seasonal menu abounds in terminology that reads like erotica to gastronauts—but for those who may not know their annatto from their agnolotti, impeccably trained servers are there to help (that goes double for the wide-ranging wine list). Of course, the dishes themselves serve as the best and brightest explanations. In summer, white-bean croquettes and garden produce add their homey two cents to seared diver scallops in Champagne buerre blanc, for instance, while in winter, venison loin gains textural contrast from sweet potato cannelloni and roasted chestnuts. Desserts, for their part, rarely require clarification, from pound cake to peanut butter cups.

Olivéa, 719 E. 17th Ave., Uptown, Denver, CO 80203; (303) 861-5050; www.olivearestaurant.com; Mediterranean; $$. Stylish but subdued in gray tones, the dining room of this Uptown gem suggests a clean canvas on which the talented quartet behind **Duo** (p. 27) can paint their Mediterranean land- and seascapes in bold strokes and sheer swirls. Color conveys the depth of flavor Chef John Broening achieves: green (olives, pistachios, and capers), red (saffron, beets, and blood oranges), and golden-brown (fregola, polenta, and flatbread) enliven the chiaroscuro created by citrus-marinated scallops, lightly smoked trout, fat boudin blanc, and toasty lamb sausage, among other things. On the sweet side, rising pastry star Yasmin Lozada-Hissom has earned just accolades for her salted caramel–chocolate tart, but her custards deserve stars too (one word: semifreddo). Meanwhile, Stephanie Bonin's wine list is admirably focused but wisely balanced between bottles from coastal Spain, France, and Italy and those from celebrated land-locked regions. Though not expensive, Olivéa's too good for a first date. Reward a second.

Ondo's Spanish Tapas Bar, 250 Steele St., Cherry Creek, Denver, CO 80206; (303) 975-6514; www.ondostapas.com; Small Plates/Tapas; $. Cherry Creek may be upscale, but it frankly lacks character. Set below street level amid the commerical whitewash, this rather plain-looking eatery unfortunately would seem to blend right in—until, that is, you get a taste of its tapas. Trained in Spain, Chef-Owners Curt and Deicy Steinbecker turn out sterling small plates, charmingly rustic and highly polished by turns, whose authenticity emanates from every last bite. The classics are rarely less than exemplary: you'll relish the *solomillo*, juicy beef tenderloin in velvety blue-cheese sauce, and the melting, heaven-scented spinach-and-pine nut croquetas. But seasonal surprises absolutely warm the cockles. *Cazuelitas*, or clay-pot casseroles, come chock-full of saucy, slow-cooked morsels (look for the one with oyster mushrooms). Pungent *pinxtos* (essentially Spanish bruschetta) and *conservas*

Farmers' Markets

As eco-pioneering as it is agriculturally blessed, Colorado should be a double whammy when it comes to farmers' markets. To be sure, there's nary a community without one—but locals frequently, and fairly, protest the low ratio of produce vendors to, well, just about every other type of huckster out there. Still, there's nothing like being out in the Rocky Mountain sunshine with some kimchi from the Hmong vendor in one hand, a steaming tamale in the other. Most markets run May or June through October; see websites for details.

Boulder Farmers' Market, *www.boulderfarmers.org; Twitter: @ BCFMarkets.* Naturally, greener-than-thou Boulder adheres to the strictest standards of vendor membership; this twice-weekly market on 13th Street is a producer-only, Colorado-only, zero-waste affair (as is its Longmont sibling, which pops up Saturday at the Boulder County Fairgrounds).

Cherry Creek Fresh Market, *www.coloradofreshmarkets.com.* Set in the parking lot of the Cherry Creek Mall, this is definitely Denver's biggest and busiest bazaar—more like a twice-a-week carnival than a farmers' market per se, with countless prepared food stands and trucks, wine tastings, live music, and so on. Come Wednesday rather than Saturday to avoid the sheer, discombobulating chaos.

City Park Esplanade Fresh Market, *www.coloradofreshmarkets .com.* We actually prefer Cherry Creek Fresh Market's little sibling, open Sunday mornings on the Colfax-facing side of City Park—mainly because there's more breathing room and much better people-watching.

Denver Urban Homesteading Indoor Farmers Market, *www .denverurbanhomesteading.com.* Essentially a community center for urban agriculturalists, this wonderful organization (200 Santa Fe Dr., Denver, CO 80223) holds a market Thursday and Friday evenings as well as Saturday, where organic spices, raw cow's and goat's milk shares, and biodynamic wines, among more obvious things, are yours for the asking; DUH also hosts regular chicken swaps.

South Pearl Street Farmer's Market, *www.oldsouthpearlstreet .com; Twitter: @SouthPearlSt.* This small Sunday-only market may be Denver's most picturesque, flanked as it is by the boutiques and eateries that line Old South Pearl for blocks. If the downside is that produce picks don't peak until late in the season, the upside is that you can grouse about it over bottomless mimosas within spitting distance of the vendors.

 pique bold palates with superb imported seafood. And if the poached egg with chorizo and mascarpone is available, don't order one—get two; it's small yet sumptuous. The all-Spanish list of wines and sherries warrants further kudos, while happy hour at the bar, lined with canapés galore, is a frankly underappreciated steal.

Parallel 17, 1600 E. 17th Ave., City Park, Denver, CO 80218; (303) 399-0988; www.parallelseventeen.com; Vietnamese; $$. Everything about this modern Vietnamese eatery on the border between Uptown and City Park is fetching, starting with Chef-Owner Mary Nguyen. A woman of supreme taste, she turned what could have been a stereotypically urbane corner space—high ceilings, exposed brick walls, wood floors—into a light-filled stunner, hung with umbrella skeletons and pendant sculptures of hand-blown clay. And she does the same for a menu that nimbly sidesteps the clichés of both the gritty soup kitchen and the glittering shrine to fusion cuisine that too often define Vietnamese cuisine stateside. A rare combination of grace and moxie characterizes her plates: a coffee-rubbed short rib slides off the bone onto coconut rice here, pesto and aioli give naturally vibrant *bánh mì* a sun kiss there. From a charcuterie plate (head cheese, please!) to an Asian food–friendly drink list to cheesecake-filled doughnuts scented with Saigon cinnamon, Nguyen honors and breaks tradition with equal glee. "What is this?" she asks rhetorically, and answers in kind: "Does it matter? Is it good?" That it is.

Phat Thai, 2900 E. 2nd Ave., Cherry Creek, Denver, CO 80206; (303) 388-7428; www.phatthai.com; Thai; $$. Mark Fischer, the celebrated chef-owner of **six89** and **Phat Thai** in Carbondale, made a shrewd move to Cherry Creek with a second branch of the latter: it's just what the neighborhood needed. The enormous, mezzanine-lined space, industrial in scope yet splashed with mango and chili hues, has an upscale, upbeat vibe to keep affluent locals well within their comfort zone; the contemporary repertoire follows suit without blurring the contours of Thai cooking tradition. Tables are set with condiment trays for seasoning to taste—red-pepper flakes, sugar, housemade nam pla—but the dishes themselves carefully overlap spicy, salty, tart, sweet and herbaceous, be they light bites like the zingy salad of grilled calamari and pomelo segments tossed with mint and cilantro or as deep, dark, and hearty as *kaeng Massaman pae*, with chunks of goat and sweet potato in a coconut curry topped with crushed peanuts. A full bar whips up fitting cocktails redolent of ginger and lemongrass, but in lieu of booze, don't shy away from the drinking vinegars infused with tamarind, blackberry, and more; served with a splash of soda, they're brilliantly refreshing.

Phoenician Kabob, 5709 E. Colfax Ave., Park Hill, Denver, CO 80220; (303) 355-7213; www.pkabob.com; Middle Eastern; $$. Saffron and paprika hues, tablecloths, classical music on the stereo, a full bar, and a twinkly-eyed staff: one of the city's very best Middle Eastern restaurants is also one of its most inviting. So sit back and relax as Lebanese-born owner Ibrahim Dahleh and crew re-create family recipes with love from carefully garnished start to finish. Served with house-baked, charcoal-dusted pita that steams and crackles on arrival, the whipped garlic dip is a head-clearing thrill; the warm, chewy pastries known as *fatayer* soothe with a filling of lamb or spinach, onions, and pine nuts. Succulent kabobs come with ultra-creamy *lebni* and perfectly cooked, sumac-sprinkled rice. And daily specials like *kusa* (beef-and-rice-stuffed squash) or *dajaj* (chicken stew with potatoes and peppers) cover culinary territory that's little explored stateside, while tender baklava baked from scratch leads your tastebuds back to familiar ground.

Potager, 1109 Ogden St., Capitol Hill, Denver, CO 80218; (303) 832-5788; www.potagerrestaurant.com; Contemporary; $$$. Long before "field-to-fork" became a household adjective, father-and-daughter restaurateurs Tom and Teri Rippeto were applying it without fanfare to this understated refuge on Capitol Hill. Chef Teri's monthly changing menu reads like a pastoral ode to her purveyors—and while it may strike meat-and-potatoes types as a bit long-winded, even they will see the light with a bite of her rainbow-bright creations: each plate is a veritable cornucopia of burstingly fresh produce, grass-fed meats, and sustainable seafood. Sprightly handmade pastas are always a highlight—gnocchi in particular pops. Lobster's spectacular, butter-roasted chunks studding a summery tumble of corn, peaches, and melon. And cassoulet is an annual event starring duck confit, cubed lamb, pork sausage, and ham hocks. In keeping with the artisanal spirit—which extends to the wine program—the space evokes a crumbling old farmhouse: stone floors and high ceilings, light woods and a cement-topped bar, mismatched parlor furniture and, above all, a lush back patio onto the garden that lends the restaurant its name.

Queen of Sheba, 7225 E. Colfax Ave., Park Hill, Denver, CO 80220, (303) 399-9442; Ethiopian; $. Situated in a strip mall along a grubby stretch of East Colfax, this trim little storefront, its celadon walls dotted with colorful folk art, is a breath of fresh air. We suggest you take that breath before Addis-born Chef-Owner Zewditu Aboye steals it away. You'll have a little time to do so; her kitchen is a one-woman operation, so you may as well sit back with a glass of wine or Ethiopian beer and enjoy the show through the open doorway. When your food finally arrives, though, you'll be transported. The menu doesn't depart much from the norm—*tibs*, *gored gored*, *doro wot*, *yebeg wot*, split peas, lentils—but Aboye's execution is superlative. Here you'll find the laciest *injera*, the most invigorating *fit-fit*, the tenderest cabbage with carrots—and by far the best *kitfo* in town. It may look, startlingly enough, like a mound of plain raw beef, but it's perfumed with the heavily spiced, clarified butter that makes every bite an increasingly excruciating delight.

Rise & Shine Biscuit Kitchen & Cafe, 330 Holly St., Denver, CO 80220; (303) 322-5832; http://riseandshinedenver.com; Bakery/Cafe; $$. Lanky and laid-back, Seth Rubin is one of those immediately likeable guy's guys whose modus operandi is to "make it up as we go along." It's working: the bite-size space he shares with a local pizza joint near Cherry Creek saw success enough in its first year of business to spawn an offshoot (3930 W. 32nd Ave., Denver, CO 80212; 303-477-5400). Inspired by a college-town favorite back in his home state of North Carolina, Rubin makes one thing and one thing only—large, flaky, buttery biscuits. (Even the raisin-studded, cinnamon-swirled rolls, served with thimblesful of icing on the side, are made with biscuit dough.) But there's more to this story, since he also has a knack for coming up with wicked daily flavors like pinto-bean, cheddar-corn, ranch, and even basil-pear; on Friday, he infuses his dough with local craft beers. The ultimate kick in the pants, though, is the Chapel Hill—pepper-fried chicken on a warm, fresh biscuit, no more and no less.

Satchel's on 6th, 1710 E. 6th Ave., Country Club, Denver, CO 80128; (303) 399-2560; http://satchelson6th.com; Contemporary; $$. Dimly lit, cozy, and funky in hues of slate and crimson, this adorable Country Club storefront is the ultimate neighborhood place. Owner Andrew Casalini and his front-of-house crew tend to the handful of tables surrounding the three-sided bar as though they're hosting a dinner party, exuding genuine warmth and professionalism, while the kitchen turns out contemporary plates that burst with personality, at once studied and robust. The menu's always evolving, but respect for ingredients is steadfast. Something as simple as a properly cooked pork chop serves as a revelation; toasted gnocchi actually smack of the lemon and fresh ricotta from which they're made; lusty risottos absorb a dash of chili sauce here, the sweetness of maple and butternut squash there. Skillet hash in any form, at dinner or brunch, is artfully executed, crunchy on the outside and creamy within—as are duck fat fries topped with porcini and parmesan. In short, this is food that tastes exactly the way it's supposed to taste. Casalini's boutique wine list, emphasizing Mediterranean and West Coast producers, enhances it all.

Second Home Kitchen + Bar, JW Marriott, 150 Clayton Ln., Cherry Creek, Denver, CO 80206; (303) 253-3000; www.second homedenver.com; Contemporary; $$. Ensconced in a Cherry Creek hotel, Second Home stands a bit of an open secret among the neighborhood's leisure set. Glossy as a design catalog from the swanky dining room to the lounge plush with low-slung, pillow-lined banquettes, ottomans, and wingbacks to the hidden patio complete with firepit, it makes for one sexy getaway come cocktail hour (the savvy libations are, we think, underrated). But the tireless kitchen, overseen by CIA-trained Chef Jeff Bolton and outfitted with a rotisserie and a brick oven, subverts its own bar-snack schtick to execute comfort food on a grand scale. Keep your eyes peeled for excellent housemade sausages, for instance, or variations on potted fish—salmon rillettes, smoked trout dip. Meanwhile, every last homestyle standard is tricked out in some way, shape, or form, from chicken-fried steak and tuna-noodle casserole to the serious chopped salad with roast chicken and celery-seed dressing. The overall effect is downright glam—in keeping with a wine list as extensive as the menu.

Solera, 5410 E. Colfax Ave., Park Hill, Denver, CO 80220; (303) 388-8429; www.solerarestaurant.com; Mediterranean; $$$. The blare and glare of East Colfax recedes the moment you set foot in Goose Sorensen's handsome sanctuary, which extends from a low-ceilinged, grotto-like lounge packed with devotees who can tell you what's what to a refined yet inviting dining room in saturated hues to a magical, candlelit patio. Solera's popularity after a decade in business has everything to do with its dependability: drawing mainly (though not strictly) from Spain, the menu has been polished to a mellow sheen. It's a fine place, then, to revisit the classics—and neoclassics. In a cloud of scented steam, juicy mussels by themselves or in paella are forever. Spot-on white-truffle mac-and-cheese speckled with peas and almonds justifies its staying power, as do tight ringlets of fried calamari tossed with peanuts, scallions, mint, and sweet chili sauce. And the wine list, relatively light on unknowns, is tailored less for intrepid exploration than sheer enjoyment—although Wednesday wine tastings aim to offer the best of both worlds.

Steuben's, 523 E. 17th Ave., Uptown, Denver, CO 80203; (303) 830-1001; www.steubens.com; American; $$. **It's funny. Even**

though this Uptown hang takes after a mid-century supper club way back in Beantown, it feels one-of-a-kind—at once retro and progressive, a pioneer on the local cocktail scene, and a keeper of the cross-country culinary faith. The menu reads like a trucker's to-do list: Maine lobster rolls and New York–style egg creams, check; Philly cheesesteaks and Chicago dogs, check; chicken-fried steak, huevos rancheros, and classic California Cobb salads, check, check, check. It's all thanks to the crew's sheer energy, which permeates the memorabilia-dotted space—check out the vintage tiki punchbowls lining the shelves above the bar, likewise graced with jars of housemade maraschino cherries—and spreads to the diverse crowd. Chef Brandon Biederman's knowing take on fried chicken and waffles packs a punch (ask for the red-eye syrup), while his sugar-dusted hush puppies will whisk you back to a childhood you only wish you had.

Steve's Snappin' Dogs, 3525 E. Colfax Ave., City Park, Denver, CO 80206; (303) 333-7627; www.stevessnappindogs.com; Hot Dogs/Sausages; $. Crayon colors and corrugated tin, picnic tables and peppy service: this City Park hot dog stand brings the mid-century drive-ins of the Eastern Seaboard—touchingly depicted in the old black-and-white photos that cover its walls—back to life. In many ways, it's tried and true: gregarious Connecticut transplant

Steve Ballas serves up first and foremost the pork-and-beef franks he grew up with, including his personal favorite, the Jersey Dog with bacon and caraway-touched sauerkraut. But the counter also caters to the tastes of 21st-century Denver. The burrito dog comes swaddled in a tortilla beneath thick, extra-meaty chili, cheddar jack, and jalapeños; there are vegetarian, kosher, gluten-free, and low-carb options. In addition to loaded fries and rings, Ballas also tosses green beans and carrot sticks into the deep fryer for a light blister—and he'll even give your dog a hot-oil bath. No wonder Ballas counts chefs as well as civilians among his fans: Matt Selby of **Vesta Dipping Grill** (p. 96) says he had his first true Chicago dog, complete with neon relish, sport peppers, and celery salt, years ago and has been "hooked ever since."

Syrup, 300 Josephine St., #20, Cherry Creek, Denver, CO 80206; (720) 945-1111; http://syrupdenver.com; American; $. Coffee schmoffee. The real eye-opener at this jaunty, pistachio-green Cherry Creek pancake house is the sheer array of hand-crafted syrups—which co-owner Tim Doherty proudly approaches "just like a wine list." Signature flavors range from butterscotch and blackberry to caramel and apple-cinnamon; seasonal specials include mango and apricot. Paired with compound butters like bourbon-pecan or peanut butter-and-jelly, they transform a simple stack of flapjacks into one sweet wake-up call. Syrup also serves savories—salads and sandwiches as well as omelets—but we'd just as soon stick to the sticky stuff.

Table 6, 609 Corona St., Denver, CO 80218; (303) 831-8800; www
.table6denver.com; Contemporary; $$. A little bit country, a little
bit rock-and-roll? Try a whole lot of both. (In fact, make it folk
and punk.) Occupying a blink-and-you'll-miss-it storefront just
steps from the heavy traffic along 6th Avenue, Table 6 is hard to
pinpoint in every sense of the word. Scuffed wood floors, copper
accents, and rooster figurines evoke some Lyonnaise *ferme-auberge*.
But a painting over the bar depicting a conga line of vintage brand
icons—the Morton Salt girl and Mr. Peanut among them—locates
you in pop-culture territory. This much-acclaimed yet somehow
low-profile bistro is, in short, highly idiosyncratic. And that's all
to the credit of Owner-Sommelier Aaron Forman and Chef Scott
Parker. As fearless as they are savvy, they revel in comfort food
gone wild paired with the cleverest of boutique wines—and so do
we. On no other menu in town will you find schmaltz juxtaposed
with seaweed, pork butt with duck eggs, pickled chanterelles with
Camembert "Cheez Whiz." That the dishes nearly always live up to
their delightful descriptions is no small wonder—and that they,
along with the wines, are fairly priced is an even rarer feat.

The Über Sausage, 2730 E. Colfax Ave., City Park, Denver, CO
80206; (303) 862-7894; http://theubersausage.com; Hot Dogs/
Sausages; $. Just a few blocks from the nostalgia trip that is
Steve's Snappin' Dogs (p. 157), this City Park upstart plays a
whole new ballgame. Though co-owner Alex Gschwend also looked
to the past for inspiration—namely his Swiss chef-grandfather's
recipe box—in launching the spiffy sausage stand, the results are

distinctly tailored to the here and now. Served on French bread and sporting everything from grilled apples and mango salsa to blue cheese, the selections sourced from **Continental Deli** (p. 167) include bison brats and chicken sausages as well as the Swiss-style signature made with veal. But the huge corndog is the dark horse in this race—chorizo dunked in a cornmeal batter that yields a golden-brown, almost fritter-like crunch. And the thick-cut, fried-to-order potato chips are too much fun: hit the condiment bar to sprinkle them with any—or all—of seven seasoning blends, including pumpkin pie spice (essentially cinnamon sugar, which is great on potatoes, as anyone who's ever had plum dumplings knows). It's a cute space, too, dotted with pendant lamps made from old jars and barrels and fronted by an umbrella-shaded deck.

WaterCourse Foods, 837 E. 17th Ave., Uptown, Denver, CO 80218; (303) 832-7313; www.watercoursefoods.com; Vegetarian; $$. Prime people-watching is just one quirky perk of any trip to this spacious and super-cool Uptown vegetarian haunt. At the epicenter of Denver's youthquake for well over a decade, it nonetheless attracts a diverse group of folks from sunup to sundown—hour-long waits are common—who are savvy enough to know that meatless eats don't have to be anemic. On the contrary, the fare here is as colorful and hearty as can be, from the NYC—cage-free eggs scrambled with brie, sundried tomatoes, and spinach—to the fat "Reuben," eschewing corned beef for smoky portobellos, to the intriguing, housemade vegan "cheeses" and the sweat-inducing buffalo seitan (hey, don't knock it 'til you've tried it). Throw in an order of some of the best thick-cut onion rings around as you toss back a local brew to the tunes of the best band you've never heard of. (Make it two—after all, the servers are in no hurry, so why should you be?)

Landmarks

Bastien's Restaurant, 3503 E. Colfax Ave., City Park, Denver, CO 80206; (303) 322-0363; www.bastiensrestaurant.com; American; $$$. The fortuitous pun on "bastion" will ring in your ears the moment you enter this delightful City Park throwback to the interwar era (1937, to be exact). So will Sinatra, whose tunes invariably clinch the mood that the distinctive architecture sets: pass the long mirrored bar inside the circular building to reach the split-level dining room, where strung lights and twigs bedeck the wooden beams supporting the peaked roof, and a curving staircase leads to a skylit mezzanine. Or don't pass the bar, for that matter: we're rather fond of bellying up for a stiff drink accompanied by complimentary breadsticks. The menu spans decades, but golden oldies are the kitchen's obvious forte. Stuffed mushroom caps, for instance, are almost comically over-the-top, crammed with crumbled veal and smothered in a sauce made of sweet cream, butter, and mozzarella. The signature steak is wonderful, sprinkled with a blend of brown and white sugar, then cooked to medium-rare and no further—that's a sticking point. Technically, it comes with your choice of potato, but practically speaking, you've got no choice—go for the twice-baked spud with cheddar, sour cream, and chives. For a final blast from the past, try skillet-baked apple pie.

Chada Thai, 2005 E. 17th Ave., City Park, Denver, CO 80206; (303) 320-8582; www.chadathaidenver.com; Thai; $$. Though the serene, earth-toned dining room dotted with folk art is pleasant enough, this low-key spot near City Park hardly appears to warrant landmark status. But here's what you can't tell by looking: it's the reincarnation of Denver's very first Thai restaurant, opened by the late Lily Chittivej way back in 1959. Now it belongs to her protégée and daughter-in-law, Nita, whose touch is seasoned and sure—which means that the food is dignified, not Disneyfied. Take curry puffs whose beef-and-potato filling and fruity, housemade sweet-and-sour sauce eclipse the usual stale wontons. Or the *phad ka prow* with mushrooms, just one of many stir-fries distinguished by their fresh ingredients and expert handling to yield saucy mélanges of satisfying depth (even slivered ginger is tender, not woody). Or the seafood custard known (although not as widely as it should be) as *hao moak*: it's among the most accomplished versions we've seen, a mosaic of delicately curried snapper chunks, shredded cabbage, and basil, steamed until set in banana leaves. Laughs Chittivej of the dish: "You've got to really love making it, because it takes forever." We're so glad she does.

Charlie Brown's Bar & Grill, 980 Grant St., Capitol Hill, Denver, CO 80203; (303) 860-1655; www.charliebrownsbarandgrill.com; Bar & Grill; $$. Now mellow, now rollicking, this legendary lounge in the endearingly seedy Colburn Hotel on Capitol Hill is as rich in local lore as it is awash in artifacts (check out the model ships and Elvis statuettes lining the shelves of the sunken bar). One-time patrons Jack Kerouac and Allen Ginsberg may well have knocked one back on the very spot where you now swivel about in your leather armchair; Bill Murray's been spotted at sing-alongs around the grand piano. And the regulars are no less colorful than the traces of visitations past. They're here first and foremost for the free-flowing booze—including two-for-one 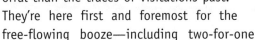 deals come happy hour. But when hunger strikes, the kitchen comes through with a gargantuan menu that runs the gamut from bar snacks and burgers to Greek, Italian, and Mexican platters (not to mention breakfast daily). How we heart the chopped steak smothered in onions and accompanied by a giant baked potato that's in turn accompanied by butter, sour cream, and bacon bits. Plentiful and cheap as it all is, however, nothing tops the whole pig roasts held weekly on the patio throughout the summer—they're free.

The Cherry Cricket, 2641 E. 2nd Ave., Cherry Creek, Denver, CO 80206; (303) 322-7666; http://cherrycricket.com; Bar & Grill; $.

The Cheesy Cricket is more like it—dark, rowdy, and chintzy from the main lounge to the billiards room in back. Of course, the regulars wouldn't have it any other way. After all, at well over 60 years old, this beloved burger bar is nothing if not a refreshingly ragtag departure from its yuppified surroundings. Besides, for all the grub on its long and flagrantly greasy menu, the signature item has garnered kudos from coast to coast—inspiring loyalty in average Joes and celebs alike—with good reason: it's cooked to order, it packs a wallop, and it's cheap by today's indie gourmet standards, even after you add on the à la carte toppings. And add them you must. The likes of fried eggs, cream cheese, green chile, and peanut butter are as integral to the overall experience as draft beer by the pitcher and classic rock on the loudspeakers. Carry on, ye wayward sons of Cherry Creek.

Mercury Cafe, 2199 California St., Downtown, Denver, CO 80205; (303) 294-9281; www.mercurycafe.com; Organic; $$. You simply have to see it to believe it. The Merc, as this Curtis Park institution is affectionately known, is the most eye-popping, jaw-dropping asylum of bohemia this side of the Milky Way. Bordello-red from top to bottom, the main room turns on a kaleidoscope of strung lights, stained glass, bamboo, carved wood, fringe, painted roses, and vintage sculpture lamps. Live music, dance classes, film screenings, poetry readings, and astrology meetings fill the equally wacky event spaces on a daily basis. It's all so entertainingly chaotic that food's practically an afterthought. But not to Chef Tofu (yep, that's what they call him), who oversees a 100 percent organic kitchen that whips up elk nachos, shish kebabs over quinoa, gluten-free linguine, vegan desserts like the maple-sweetened torte, and more. The full bar is entirely stocked with organic products, too. Come for the tempeh eating, stay for the tarot reading.

Pete's Kitchen, 1962 E. Colfax Ave., City Park, Denver, CO 80206; (303) 321-3139; www.petesrestaurants.com; American; $. Back in 2007, the *New York Times* published a profile of Colfax Avenue titled "A Notorious Main Drag, in Line for Big Changes." At the center of the photo used to illustrate the 'Fax's "hardscrabble soul" sat this septuagenarian greasy spoon, in all its neon-trimmed glory. As well it should have. This is the epitome of a Denver diner, where the aroma of hashbrowns permanently fills the air above the creaky booths, which flank a long counter lined with chrome stools, an ever-turning spit, and a griddle manned 24/7. Even the youngest waitresses seem world-weary as they sling plates laden with the usual, no more and no less: huge omelets, sandwiches, gyros, and the green chile–smothered breakfast burritos that are to us what bagels with cream cheese are to New Yorkers. Of course, it all comes with a splash of local color (if not a downright dousing, especially in the wee hours). Greek-born restaurateur Pete Contos owns a slew of legendary dives, but this one takes the cake. Make that pancake.

Strings, 1700 Humboldt St., Uptown, Denver, CO 80218; (303) 831-7310; www.stringsrestaurant.com; Contemporary; $$$. The late Noel Cunningham put Uptown on the map when he opened Strings in 1986. A quarter-century later (and counting), it remains a bona fide dining destination. The Dublin-born owner was an indefatigable presence in the sprawling, high-ceilinged dining room, and the heartening loyalty his memory inspires in his employees rubs off on their customers. For all the upscale, white-cloth trappings, then, Strings' service is highly personal. Likewise, though the menu is contemporary and seasonal, it rests on a solid foundation, eschewing experimentation for attention to detail. Mediterranean influences meet thoughtful presentation in dishes like harissa-touched lamb ravioli with preserved lemon and green olives or the signature, vanilla-scented cashew-crusted seabass over saffron couscous. Lunch and brunch are slightly more casual, especially out on the bustling patio. But the best seat in the house may be at the bar come happy hour, when long-timer Kris Lykins makes you feel right at home over downright bargains like the terrific calamari tubes stuffed with goat cheese risotto or—get this—housemade corn nuts.

Specialty Stores, Markets & Producers

Argonaut Wine & Liquor, 760 E. Colfax Ave., Capitol Hill, Denver, CO 80203; (303) 831-7788; www.argonautliquor.com.

Although Argonaut isn't the biggest liquor retailer in metro Denver, it's close—and it's certainly the most established. No niche operation, the Capitol Hill institution simply stocks everything on aisle after aisle; when we're looking for wines from Uruguay, obscure Belgian beers, Dutch advocaat, Latvian bitters, or the latest in local craft vodkas, we come here first. And if we can't find what we seek, we ask; customer service is unusually fine-tuned for a store of this size.

Continental Deli, 250 Steele St., #112, Cherry Creek, Denver, CO 80206; (303) 388-3354; www.continentalsausage.com. Nationwide TV coverage of Biker Jim and his wild concoctions—above all that jalapeño-cheddar elk dog—might lead non-local audiences to assume that his supplier, Continental Sausage, is some radical upstart. But the Gutknechts have been in the sausage-making business for eight generations—and their long-standing retail outlet in Cherry Creek has the decidedly Old World flavor to show for it (right down to the selection of German-language crossword-puzzle books and serial romances). Here you'll find handmade *fleischekäse* and *leberwurst*, *cervelat* and *Thüringer* brats alongside all the cheeses and creamy deli salads they were made for; generous samples are served up with a smile at one counter, while sandwiches and strudel are assembled for a song (or yodel?) at another. Shelf upon shelf of imported pantry staples and European-style baked goods complete the picture—tins of smoked fish, spätzle and knödel mixes, jars of rosehip jam, and bags stuffed with huge Kaiser rolls and loaves of real-deal seeded rye. Additional location: Black Forest Deli, 9535 W. 58th Ave., Arvada, CO 80002; (303) 425-0859.

Liks Ice Cream, 2039 E. 13th Ave., Capitol Hill, Denver, CO 80206; (303) 321-2370; www.liksicecream.com. With literally hundreds of flavors in its portfolio, this bubblegum-colored corner shop on Capitol Hill has been churning out a daily batch of 32 for years. We're suckers for the pale, delicate rose sorbet and kicky, pecan-studded cayenne-caramel ice cream, but there's also frozen yogurt, sherbet, and custard for a change of pace. And speaking of changes of pace, a scoop of Sleepless—espresso ice cream studded with chocolate-covered coffee beans—is sure to put a spring, if not a leap, in your step.

Lovely Confections, 1489 Steele St., City Park, Denver, CO 80206; (720) 524-7770; www.lovelyconfectionsbakery.com. Even her name is delicious: the owner of this strawberry-and-chocolate-hued shop in City Park is one Porche Lovely, who's as sweet as her cupcakes are, yes, lovely. For the nonce, they're all she makes, in a select array of flavor combinations. But that's enough. We love the Bee's Knees—honey-lemon buttercream atop lavender-scented yellow cake—and the pure zing of the all-lemon cutie. Most of all, though, we seek out the inspired weekend specials: imagine rosemary with almond buttercream or sweet potato with sage–brown butter frosting. (That Lovely uses organic ingredients wherever possible—right down to the naturally colored sprinkles—is just the icing on the cake, so to speak.)

Marczyk Fine Foods, 5100 E. Colfax Ave., Park Hill, Denver, CO 80220; (303) 243-3355; www.marczykfinefoods.com. **Although their Uptown flagship (770 E. 17th Ave., Denver, CO 80203; 303-894-9499) continues to deliver the goods with flair, the Marczyks have really outdone themselves with this huge grocery and liquor shop on East Colfax. Gourmet imports and the products of nationally renowned purveyors like Niman Ranch and Cypress Grove abound on the shelves, at the butcher's block, and in the dairy case, while the seafood counter sparkles with sashimi-grade cuts—but the heart and soul of the store inheres in local finds. Think home-grown baby eggplants and Chioggia beets in the produce section. Ice cream pints hand-packed by Spuntino (p. 44) and Sweet Action (p. 204). Udi's breads (p. 46). Selections from Novo Coffee (p. 108), Savory Spice Shop (p. 109), and Justin's Nut Butters—all Colorado success stories. Of course, Marczyk's own deli is no slouch when it comes to prepared foods: the dips are fab, the whoopie pies famed, the entrees and sides fresh and fun (look for spuds stuffed with green chile and corn). And we've experienced reverse sticker shock while perusing the wines, with many boutique labels coming in at under $10.**

Oliver's Meat & Seafood Market, 1718 E. 6th Ave., Country Club, Denver, CO 80218; (303) 733-4629. **Tracing their meat-cutting roots back to 19th-century Virginia, five generations of the Oliver family have devoted their lives to this butcher shop and deli over the course**

of nearly nine decades. Established in 1923, its current Country Club location isn't the original—but it might as well be, boasting the well-worn look of a neighborhood staple and the easy banter of old hands behind the counter. "So many places you go, they don't know the product," says Jim Oliver by way of explaining the store's longevity; here, the expertise extends far beyond all the standard cuts of beef, pork, lamb, and poultry as well as fish to off-cuts, game, and delicacies: rabbit, alligator, duck and frog's legs, escargot in the shell, you name it. Oliver and company also make nearly 50 different sausages, including salmon-halibut, and they're quick to offer cooking tips.

Omonoia Greek Bakery, 2813 E. Colfax Ave., City Park, Denver, CO 80206; (303) 394-9333. The story of Greek food in Denver is like that of Jewish food: though the local communities are sizeable, their presence on the dining scene is unfortunately negligible. So while bakeries like Omonoia are a dime a dozen in some cities, here they're not to be taken for granted. For its *kourambiedes* alone, we're fans of this unassuming City Park pastry shop: reminiscent of Mexican wedding cookies, the shortbread mounds are incredibly light, crunchy with almonds, and covered in confectioner's sugar. But there's also *tsoureki* (sweet braided egg bread), *galaktoboureko* (creamy custard in phyllo), and of course baklava.

Pablo's Coffee, 630 E. 6th Ave., Denver, CO 80203; (303) 744-3323; www.pabloscoffee.com. A constant buzz—in every sense of the word—fills the air of this beloved corner coffeehouse. Though almost archetypally artsy with its mini-chandeliers and mounted display of hand-painted messenger bags, it stands out as a consummate roaster as well as retailer. Owner Craig Conner's trademark blends enjoy veritable cult followings; you'll see the Danger Monkey logo on counters across town, while the Two-Stroke Smoke draws kudos from connoisseurs. Even the standard baked goods seem fatter and fresher here—and if that's just the caffeine talking, who cares?

The Truffle Cheese Shop, 2906 E. 6th Ave., Country Club, Denver, CO 80206; (303) 322-7363; http://denvertruffle.com. Fresh-faced as they look, Robert and Karin Lawler are restaurant-biz veterans—and the inventory of their clever little 6th Avenue boutique reflects their community ties as well as their honed palates. Local products you won't find anywhere else are a strength ("Help Fruition Farm name this cheese!" reads one sign.) But so are uncommon gems from Europe, including the likes of ricotta cold-smoked over juniper wood, carried by hand from Abruzzi to the States, or rye-soaked, barley-coated Cuise al Malto d'Orto, or paprika-rubbed Basque Ardi Gasna. Charcuterie hails from New York's famed Salumeria Biellese. And as for the other browse-worthy sundries—crackers and shortbreads, preserves, Galician tinned seafood—they too tend toward the unusual; explains Karin, "We learn about so many products from our own customers." (Their Country Club neighbors are, to be sure, a well-traveled bunch.) The Lawlers return the favor by teaching in-store tutorials, above all the popular mozzarella-making sessions.

South Denver

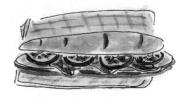

Baker District, Old South Pearl, Santa Fe Arts District, University, University Hills & Washington Park

Roughly due south of downtown Denver, a patchwork of neighborhoods emerges that, even well beyond the circumference of Denver University, possesses something of a college-town feel: old houses, big trees, young families, a steady stream of students. While Old South Pearl and Washington Park—known to locals as Wash Park—are well-established dining-and-shopping hubs, the Baker and Santa Fe Arts Districts have gone from gritty to gentrified in what feels like no time, and the area as a whole is scattered with long-standing ethnic joints and shabby-chic java huts (Stella's Coffeehaus [www.stellascoffee.com] and Buffalo Doughboy Bakery [on Facebook] come to mind) as well as increasingly boutique eateries, wine shops, and purveyors of eclectic mercantile goods (by way of example, check out the ultra-mod kitchenware at Hazel & Dewey [http://hazel-dewey.com] on South Broadway).

Amira Bakery & Deli, 4101 E. Evans Ave., University Hills, Denver, CO 80222; (303) 745-1766; www.amirabakery.com; Middle Eastern; $. You can tell this light, bright Lebanese counter joint is special from the moment you step inside to survey the neatly spaced, marble-topped tables—occupied almost entirely by the owners' compatriots—and beyond them to the kitchen with its turning spit and blazing ovens. Though the menu doesn't lack for staples—hummus and falafel, fettoush and tabbouleh, shawarma and baklava, as well as pita that arrives at your table hot and puffy—it specializes in the flatbreads known throughout the Eastern Mediterranean by various names (and spellings): *lahmacun, manaqish, lahmbajeen,* and so on. Never you mind the nomenclature—this pizzalike treat is the real mouthful in any case. The thin yet soft and chewy dough, glistening with olive oil, would be delicious plain, but it's even better with any of 21 possible topping combinations. Lamb and beef—minced to a near paste yet still juicy—is wonderfully spiced, speckled with finely chopped hot and bell peppers and onions, and sprinkled with pine nuts; add a squirt of lemon for an even sunnier kick. Or try the pie spread thinly with *lebni* (strained yogurt), then practically spackled with *za'atar,* the famed spice mixture redolent of thyme, sumac, and sesame.

Arada Restaurant, 750 Santa Fe Dr., Santa Fe Arts District, Denver, CO 80204; (303) 329-3344; http://aradarestaurant.com; Ethiopian; $$. Splashes of marigold and cherry-red notwithstanding, this Ethiopian storefront in the Santa Fe Arts District looks a little threadbare. But looks aren't everything—as the food itself proves. After all, those platters can get pretty messy, the chunky mounds of this and that leaking all over their spongy beds of *injera*—yet the flavors ring clear and true, right down to those last drenched bites of flatbread (truly the best part). Vegetables are the kitchen's strong suit—garlicky *gomen* (collard greens), juicy *fit-fit* (Ethiopia's minced answer to panzanella), comfy mashed *yater alitcha* (yellow split peas)—but the lamb stew (*yebeg siga alitcha*) is good, too. And although there's a full bar, we're smitten with the lemony, spiced sweet tea, leveling as it does the bumps of chili pepper we always manage to hit along the way. (It also takes the edge off kindly but sloooww service.)

Beatrice & Woodsley, 38 S. Broadway, Baker District, Denver, CO 80209; (303) 777-3505; www.beatriceandwoodsley.com; Contemporary; $$$. To step into this Baker District gem is to be wholly transported to another place and time: a rustic mountain cabin hidden among aspens, dotted with split logs and chainsaws—where tinted windows and gauze curtains suggest breezy sunsets and water flows into tin washbasins as if from a sparkling spring. And the strikingly whimsical, seasonal menu only enhances the far-away mood. Executive Chef Pete List's signature style is somehow both cutting-edge and quaint; to a dish, he turns out playfully named, gorgeously presented contemporary creations rich in heirloom ingredients and surprising touches—whether guinea fowl, yak, or Colorado goat (the "Kid's Plate"), freekeh, corona beans, or pinebud syrup. Crawfish beignets are a highlight among highlights, as is the pimiento cheesecake, and his pastas always sparkle. Nor does List's creative streak end with dinner; both weekday happy hour ("Nosh & 'Tails") and weekend brunch are equally delightful, enhanced by a well-edited wine list and superb craft cocktails. (Admittedly, your tab may be as breathtaking as the experience itself—but such is the way of 24-karat dining destinations.)

Bittersweet, 500 E. Alameda Ave., Denver, CO 80209; (303) 942-0320; www.bittersweetdenver.com; Contemporary; $$$. "We're at our best when we're not just doing the same thing; once we start a menu, we're almost working on the next one." So says Bittersweet Chef-Owner Olav Peterson of his uncompromisingly artisanal approach to contemporary cooking. Flanked by two organic gardens and a patio, the two-room space northwest of Wash Park is tranquil in warm gray tones accented by salvaged antiques; the subdued mood keeps the focus where it should be—on the food. In his allegiance to creativity, Peterson brooks no attachment to would-be signature dishes like the remarkable inaugural clam chowder or

SPOTLIGHT ON THE MIDDLE EAST

The Denver/Boulder area doesn't lack for Middle Eastern joints, particularly of the Lebanese, Syrian, and/or Persian persuasion, but the majority are interchangeable pita huts. Our painstaking efforts to suss out all exceptions to the rule (tough job, but someone had to do it) have led us to the following as well as to the other listings you'll find in Appendix A.

Arabesque, *1634 Walnut St., Boulder, CO 80302; (720) 242-8623; www.arabesqueboulder.com; Middle Eastern; $.* While the name plays on both the Palestinian heritage of Israeli-born owner Manal Jarrar and her former life as a ballerina, it also conveys the picturesque allure of her petite daytime eatery—a veritable front parlor amid blond wood planks, a wee fireplace, and almost visible swirls of aroma wafting from the kitchen. The brief menu's generic on paper (or, rather, blackboard), but Jarrar's technique has its roots in slow food, yielding the freshest of shawarma and sampler platters with lots of vegtables alongside lightly crusty, slightly puffed pockets of fresh-baked bread. Best bet: delicate baklava.

House of Kabob, *2246 S. Colorado Blvd., Denver, CO 80222; (303) 756-0744; Middle Eastern; $$.* Behind the strip-mall façade lies a genuine date-night surprise. Two small burgundy-walled dining rooms are dotted with bric-a-brac—urns, vases, platters; lively instrumental gypsy music wafts throughout; and plastic grapevines hang above the bar, which dispenses the anise spirit called *arak* as well as some truly decent wines from the homeland of Lebanese owner Ashraf

Saad. Meanwhile, despite the name, skewers aren't the half of a menu whose uncommon offerings shimmer with the likes of dried lime, pomegranate, and sumac. Best bets: ultra-crisp, kofta-stuffed, quesadilla-like *arayes*, served with a cooling yogurt dip, and funky lamb-tongue soup, which boasts huge, skin-on chunks of rich, tender meat in a brownish-green broth distinctly spiced with saffron.

Mecca Grill, *270 S. Downing St., Denver, CO 80209; (303) 722-4100; http://meccagrilldenver.com; Middle Eastern; $$.* We must have passed by this cute, comfy Lebanese storefront a thousand times before noticing it, a thousand more before venturing in. Now we're making up for lost time. For its beautifully seasoned, lovingly charbroiled kabobs, kofta, and shawarma paired with equally expert stuffed grape leaves; greaseless and nutty, herb-packed falafel; and vigorous tabbouleh, the aptly named Mecca's on our permanent rotation. Best bet: baba ghanoush we'd swear was hand-mashed, tinged with pomegranate and lemon.

Ya Hala Grill, *2100 S. Colorado Blvd., Denver, CO 80210; (303) 758-9376; www.yahalagrill.com; Middle Eastern; $$.* Anchoring the closest thing Denver has to a Middle Eastern restaurant row, this Syrian-owned long-timer makes hearty *kibbeh* (croquettes of lamb and cracked wheat); garlic dip that doesn't just bite but practically leaves toothmarks; and soothingly earthy *moujaddara* (lentils simmered with rice and onions). Best bet: the spunky jumble of chickpeas and toasted pita chips tossed with garlic, tahini, and olive oil known as *fatteh.*

the acclaimed sweetbread reuben; nor should you, because the repertoire, though small, bursts with exquisite one-offs. Stunning housemade sausages are only one example of Peterson's way with off-cuts, from pork cheeks to duck liver, but he lavishes just as much love on seasonal produce, home-grown, foraged, or otherwise. And a terrific wine list completes the picture of connoisseurship in its emphasis on lesser-known regions and varietals, tickling oenophiles pink (or white, or red) with the likes of Spanish Mencia and Lagrein from Alto Adige.

Black Pearl, 1529 S. Pearl St., Old South Pearl, Denver, CO 80210; (303) 777-0500; www.blackpearldenver.com; Contemporary; $$$. It's tempting to crack wise about the curse of the Black Pearl, since this suave neighborhood gathering place on Old South Pearl has been rocked by its share of kitchen kerfuffles and chef shuffles in the past couple of years. But it always seems to bounce back onto solid ground. Upscale yet homey from the warmly lit, split-level dining room to the bustling bar and firepit-graced patio, it dishes up contemporary fare with plenty of style and, at its best, substance too. Signatures like moules frites and the flash-fried calamari tossed with pistachios, scallions, and aged sweet soy never disappoint, while seasonal specials show multifaceted verve, be they melt-in-your-mouth jalapeño-carrot croquettes with gruyère fondue or piquillo peppers stuffed with duck confit over chili oil–spiked polenta. Owner-Sommelier Steve Whited's exploratory wine list is lots of fun, if a tad pricey—but come Sunday brunch, bottomless mimosas are a steal.

Budapest Bistro, 1585 S. Pearl St., Old South Pearl, Denver, CO 80210; (303) 744-2520; www.budapestbistro.com; Hungarian; $$. Though it's pretty enough for date night—a wee, glossy giftbox of a place in red and black—Budapest Bistro awakens sentiments perhaps too intimate and deep-rooted to share easily with strangers, calling out as it does to the humble, homesick Old World peasant in all of us. Founded by Hungarian native Anna Hellvig well over a decade ago, it's run by a staff that's as kind as the food is soulful—meaty, creamy, doughy, and tasting, you'll swear, of centuries of hardship soothed by gentle humor. The menu offers some concessions to modernity, but standbys are its pride and joy: meltingly tender chicken paprikash over spaetzle, thick goulash with potatoes, stuffed cabbage, and strudel. By all means start with the *lángos*—a sort of cross between naan and garlic bread, accompanied by sour cream sauce for dipping; tearing into the fried puffs, you can almost hear bygone ballads of love and loss playing in your head. It's that evocative.

cafe | bar, 295 S. Pennsylvania St., Washington Park, Denver, CO 80209; (303) 362-0227; www.cafebarcolorado.com; Contemporary; $$. Judging by the wall-to-wall crowds, this Alameda Street surprise hit has really filled a niche. From the knowingly generic name to the *au courant* gray-and-white decor—all marble, chrome, and subway tiles—its streamlined aesthetic belies a menu that pops with vivid color and funky accents. Spoon-tender wedges of caramelized onion–and-sage bread pudding and perfectly crisped sweet potato fries smothered in whiskey cheddar with bite-size pieces of Black Forest ham are musts; the smoked goose-breast salad with goat cheese, fennel, and almonds in blueberry-sage vinaigrette proves a true original. You have to give the *strozzapreti* (a type of rolled noodle) and veggies a good toss with your fork so it's coated evenly in porcini butter, but a little effort goes a long way; reward it doubly with the perfect pairing—a glass of Infinite Monkey Theorem's peachy Black Muscat, poured straight from the can (you read that right). From scotch-infused pear pancakes for brunch to elk sausage–wild rice stew at lunch, the kitchen shows all the chutzpah the name ironically demurs.

Crimson Canary, 141 S. Broadway, Baker District, Denver, CO 80223; (303) 284-9026; www.crimsoncanarydenver.com; Italian; $$. Just as its older sib, **Interstate** (p. 186), revels in the trappings of the mid-century truckstop, so this Baker District joint writes its love letter to shady, old-school red-sauce parlors large on velvet-flocked wallpaper and booths beneath period mug shots of mobsters. If it's no less corny for being wink-wink, the end justifies the means as the kitchen, a class act, delivers retro-inspired but cannily executed eats. A dish of large veal scaloppini in mushroom ragù, succulent and perfectly seasoned, puts the very throwbacks it's imitating to shame, as does the accompanying fettuccine, finished in the pan with butter, herbs, and parmesan; giant ravioli with ricotta and sliced portobellos bubble with earthy flavor and painterly flair; pickled red onions, thin-sliced pear, and crumbled gorgonzola stand up to the panzanella's meaty bread cubes. And the drink menu's pitch perfect too, making merry with comebacks like Lambrusco and Rusty Nails as well as swell spritzers based on house-infused fruit liqueurs—the grapefruit is as fleetingly bitter as the 1945 film noir the Crimson Canary is named for.

Deluxe, 30 S. Broadway, Baker District, Denver, CO 80209; (303) 722-1550; www.deluxedenver.com; Contemporary; $$$. A bellwether for the rejuvenation of the Baker District, this stylishly snug boîte is a date-night favorite, full of two-tops and comfy yet intimate nooks like the chef's counter and tiny back bar. Chef-Owner Dylan Moore is the grandson of a local legend in the biz—namely Lucile Richards, the cofounder of Cajun/Creole franchise **Lucile's** (see pp. 197, 246)—but his own sensibilities skew contemporary; if the menu doesn't change much, it's only because he's created so many memorable signatures, from the cornmeal-fried oyster shooters and five-spice baby-back ribs to bouillabaisse and the smoked pork chop. And even so, Moore's always evolving. His retro-themed cocktail and small-plates lounge next door, Delite, turns out killer tidbits like bacon-and-pesto-topped deviled eggs and potato skins filled with smoked salmon and caviar; meanwhile, Deluxe itself has recently launched lunch service, featuring sandwiches that come with some of the best potato chips in town.

Devil's Food Bakery & Cookery, 1020 S. Gaylord St., Washington Park, Denver, CO 80209; (303) 733-7448; http://devilsfoodbakery .com; Bakery/Cafe; $. Diningwise, Old South Gaylord is no Old South Pearl; most of its eateries lack vigor. Not so this funky, lively bakery/cafe decorated with antique bric-a-brac in a style you might call country kitschen, right out to the lattice-trellised back patio strung with lights. As the name suggests, luscious, generously sized baked goods are its primary stock in trade—not only the eponymous mini-cakes but tartlets, cookies, scones, candies, and then some. (If the red-velvet-and-cream-cheese hedgehogs don't stop you in your tracks, the chocolate-and-peanut-butter buckeyes will.) But the Wash Park spot also does brisk business in full-service fare all day long. Think homestyle comfort food with a cheeky twist: housemade granola or skirt steak hash (preferably with a side of corn bread) for eye-openers, chicken potpie with sweet potatoes and biscuits or a spunky salad of grilled zucchini, feta, and pistachios in green goddess dressing come lunch and suppertime—when a small roster of beers and wines supplements the sizeable selection of teas and coffee drinks.

East Asia Garden, 1156 S. Broadway, Denver, CO 80210; (720) 259-7141; Chinese/Taiwanese; $$. All the way from the province of Liaoning, Chef-Owner Lee Qingrong has come bearing gifts. In a nondescript space on traffic-snarled South Broadway, she dishes up such hard-to-find but easy-to-adore Dongbei specialties as Three Earth Fresh (sliced potatoes fried with peppers and tomatoes) and braised hairtail, a white-fleshed yet strong-flavored fish cooked on the bone in a sweet soy gravy. Her *jiaozi* and *baozi* (dumplings and buns, that is) boast expertly glossy, silken skins and a side of black vinegar for dipping, and the Cross Bridge Rice Noodles she perfected under the tutelage of Yunnanese chefs are rightly a point of pride. But we're craziest about the traditional cold appetizers. From slivered cucumber, seaweed, and potato (raw "silk") to sliced beef and almost cabbage-like tofu skin doused in a marinade of ground chilies, sesame oil, and vinegar, we love the rough-and-tumble texture and sweat-breaking spice of them all, our very favorite being the mixture of creamy tofu and chopped black eggs with the fruity saltiness of olives. Running the front of the house, Qingrong's lovable family is the sugar on top.

El Diablo, 101 Broadway, Baker District, Denver, CO 80203; (303) 954-0324; www.eldiablorestaurant.com; Mexican; $$. From the Diego Rivera-esque murals to the mariachi music to the brain-blasting margaritas, this gonzo homage to the down-and-dirty cantinas of Guadalajara is so spot-on in terms of ambiance—evoking the opening sequence in *Touch of Evil*—that it feels as though it's anchored the Baker District forever. Almost always open (from 7 a.m. to 2 a.m. daily, with taco service until 4 a.m.) and almost always hopping, partners Jesse Morreale and Sean Yontz have built, more than a Mexican restaurant and huge, high-end tequila bar, a second home for its neighbors. Even so, when the food from the open kitchen is good, which is more often than not, it's *muy, muy bueño*. Highlights of the menu—as dizzyingly outsize as the space—include lamb tacos; enchiladas stuffed with beef cheeks, spinach, and potatoes; and slow-cooked, banana-leaf-wrapped pork shoulder. But time and again, it's the little things—smoky frijoles, myriad salsas, cocktail glasses rimmed with Oaxacan *sal de gusano* (*sí, sí,* worm salt)—that add up to ensure an experience that's more than the sum of its most obvious parts.

Gaia Bistro + Rustic Bakery, 1551 S. Pearl St., Old South Pearl, Denver, CO 80210; (303) 777-5699; www.gaiabistro.com; Bakery/Cafe; $$. Housed in a gingerbread Victorian that dates back to 1884 and fronted by a shady garden patio, this low-key daytime sanctuary on Old South Pearl is best-known for stuffed crêpes of all kinds—the heartier the better (try roast chicken, creamed spinach, blue cheese, and bacon on for size). But the organically minded, vegetarian-friendly kitchen doesn't stop there, presenting a goodly variety of egg dishes and sandwiches with the singular advantage of seeming healthful even when they're not (some of us, after all, can't resist the combination of duck sausage, caramelized onions, and green-chile cream on ciabatta). Wednesday through Saturday, Gaia's warren of tiny, earth-toned dining rooms transforms into a romantic hideaway in which to canoodle (discreetly) over a more eclectic, oft-updated menu; the likes of pumpkin ravioli in brown butter with candied walnuts are made for sharing—although so, for that matter, are the glazed sweet rolls in the bakery case at the cafe's entrance, ready to go for the morning after.

GB Fish and Chips, 1311 S. Broadway, Denver, CO 80210; (720) 570-5103; www.gbfishandchips.com; Seafood; $$. Technically, GB stands for "Get Battered," but the monogrammatic nod to the motherland can't be lost on owner Alex Stokeld. Not only has he jazzed up a rusty, dusty parcel of land on South Broadway with Union Jacks, soccer jerseys, and a mural of the Stones in lieu of actual scenery out on the back patio, but he's also mastered the art of proportion that defines the British fish fry—balancing firm-fleshed yet delicate strips of cod against smooth and thick, but not doughy, batter. On the thinner, tarter side, a side of curry sauce does for the chips what good old malt vinegar does for the cod and its shellfish alternatives (which also come with tartar sauce). Rounding out the menu are Cornish pasties, bangers, and a shepherd's pie whose mashed-potato topping is a bit stiff, but the gravied ground beef with peas and carrots beneath proves right proper—as do the obligatory bottles of English ale, providing yet another way to get battered. Additional locations: 5325 E. Colfax Ave., Denver, CO 80220; (303) 333-4551; 2175 Sheridan Blvd., Edgewater, CO 80214; (303) 232-2128.

Interstate Kitchen & Bar, 801 W. 10th Ave., Baker District, Denver, CO 80204; (720) 479-8829; www.interstaterestaurant.com; American; $. Evoking, in co-owner Joey Newman's words, "the Jack Kerouackian romance of road travel, when you threw a suitcase in the trunk and took off," this Santa Fe Arts District hot spot is a throwback to vintage Americana, from the "T-bird blue" walls to the antique pickup cab (which serves as a popular two-top), the pendant lamps made of stacked Bundt cake pans to the roadside memorabilia—and, of course, the eats and drinks. Like that of any self-respecting truckstop, the menu is rife with homestyle (albeit locally sourced) heavies: batter-fried chicken livers with hot sauce and brunchtime corned beef hash, carrot cake and root beer floats. We could make a meal of the green beans studded with pork-belly shards that accompany the fried chicken; the Cobb salad revamped with roast chicken thighs and hot bacon dressing flat-out rocks. In keeping with the theme, the bar puts most of its (deviled) eggs into the basket of domestic craft beer and small-batch bourbon; swigging a mint julep from a camper tin, you'll half-steel yourself to clamber back behind the wheel of your 18-wheeler and hit the long, lonely highway.

Izakaya Den, 1518 S. Pearl St., Old South Pearl, Denver, CO 80210; (303) 777-0691; www.izakayaden.net; Small Plates/Tapas; $$. It's hard—and unpleasant, and probably pointless—to imagine Old South Pearl without Midas-fingered pioneers Toshi and Yasu Kizaki. With the 2008 opening of this self-styled "sake house with tapas," the fraternal masterminds behind **Sushi Den** (see p. 197) struck hard-earned gold for the second time. Rough-hewn wood and glowing lanterns, high ceilings and tall windows, lacquer and rice paper combine to create a space that feels warm and cozy even when it's crazy busy (which is often). While the sushi largely duplicates the repertoire at the flagship steps away, the seasonal array of Asian-Mediterranean small plates are all its own. Potstickers are a sure thing, be they stuffed with lamb and lotus roots or pork and apples; so is the panzanella reimagined with crab, pistachios, and plum wine vinigrette. Sake served the old-fashioned way, in a small wooden box (or *masu*), only enhances the come-what-may mood. (By contrast, weekend lunch service is chill—and the Kyushu-style ramen noodles piping-hot.) At press time, the Kizakis were preparing to relocate Izakaya Den across the street next to Sushi Den; the concept, they say, will remain in place.

Jaya Asian Grill, 1699 S. Colorado Blvd., Denver, CO 80222; (303) 757-7887; www.jayagrill.com; Southeast Asian; $. Strip-mall setting notwithstanding, Jaya's an oasis in the desert that Denver unfortunately resembles when it comes to Southeast Asian food.

In a trim, red-walled space a few steps below street level, Chef-Owner David Yea—a native Singaporean with a quick smile—offers up a wide array of favorites from his homeland as well as Malaysia and Indonesia, rarely executed with less than aplomb. What isn't handled with surprising delicacy—be it *nasi goreng* (fried rice) with bits of salted fish and egg, street-style curried noodles with plump shrimp or fragrant curry *laksa* (mixed seafood soup)—is, on the contrary, lusty as can be: duck fried to a crackling lacquer, say, or heady chicken- or tofu-based *malacca* tossed with red chilies and peanuts, or tender, crêpe-like *roti canai* accompanied by aromatic dipping broth. Though the menu never changes, it somehow seems endless; every time we come, we spot something we're gung-ho to try—with Singapore's own Tiger beer in hand, of course.

Kaos Pizzeria, 1439 S. Pearl St., Old South Pearl, Denver, CO 80210; (303) 733-5267; www.kaospizza.com; Pizza; $$. Housed in an adorable little bungalow—complete with greenery-laced patio—on Old South Pearl, this pizzeria from the owners of **Gaia Bistro** (see p. 184) pulls out all the stops to yield wood-fired pies worthy of their Neapolitan influence. Growing what they can and importing what they should, the Kaos crew keeps the menu—far from chaotic—relatively short and sweet; the emphasis is on quality, not variety. Which isn't to say you'll be bored by your options. The sopressata pizza, for instance, warrants the hype it enjoys, topped with not only the namesake dry-cured salami but also thin-sliced potato, spunky pesto, and a locally sourced egg as well as two cheeses; also pesto-smeared, the wild mushroom pie with caramelized onions is equally snazzy. Of course, toppings are only as good as their base—in this case a thin, chewy crust charred in all the right places. (A selection of salads, oven-baked pastas, and panini, as well as wine and beer, seals the deal.)

KiKi's Japanese Casual Dining, 2440 S. Colorado Blvd., University Hills, Denver, CO 80222; (303) 504-4043; www.kikis japaneserestaurant.com; Japanese/Sushi; $. Talk about your hidden gems. Located in a strip mall on an unprepossessing stretch of South Colorado Boulevard in University Hills, KiKi's appears at a glance to be one of those cut-rate sushi bars you can pass on without a second thought. Not so, as it turns out. Cheerfully homey in mellow yellow hues, dotted with colorful knickknacks, the tiny dining room fills up quick with devotees of Tokyo native Michi Kikuchi's belly-warming, country-style Japanese cooking. Steaming noodle bowls and hot pots abound; deep-frying is expertly handled, as are pungent mackerel and smelt, grilled whole. But for sheer heart and soul, our two cents are on the gravy-drenched beef *hayashi* and rich curried *tonkatsu*. Washed down with sake, they smooth all the ragged edges the daily grind leaves behind.

Larkburger, 340 E. Alameda Ave., Denver, CO 80209; (303) 963-5357; www.larkburger.com; Burgers; $. He's studied under Wolfgang Puck and Paul Bocuse, he's an undimming star on Vail's posh dining scene—and, wouldn't you know it, Thomas Salamunovich makes a mean burger. Mean and green, that is. Like all the branches of Salamunovich's cherished mini-franchise, this strip-mall hot spot is a cypress wood–reclaiming, canola oil–recycling, wind-powered exemplar of eco-practice. Not that all that would matter much if the namesake items weren't so consistently satisfying. The menu's no bigger than it needs to be—a handful of simply dressed burgers, another of sides and beverages—and while we're generally suckers for novelty, a plain old Black Angus beef patty on a fluffy buttered bun with zesty house sauce and otherwise standard trimmings suits us just fine here (accompanied, of course, by long, slender, crisp-tender fries). That said, the beef chili—chunky with hominy and red onion, laced with cilantro—makes for a swell change of pace. Additional locations: 8770 Wadsworth Blvd., Unit B, Arvada, CO 80003; (720) 583-1582; 2525 Arapahoe Ave., Boulder, CO 80302; (303) 444-1487; 8000 E. Belleview Ave., Greenwood Village, CO 80111; (303) 779-0093.

Oshima Ramen, 7800 E. Hampden Ave., Unit 48, Denver, CO 80231; (720) 482-0264; Japanese/Sushi; $$. Eliciting chills in the prissy, grins and hand rubs from the chowhounds, this Tiffany Plaza soup shop is, not to mince words, rather a mess. The front counter seems to serve as a desk, strewn with paperwork; graffiti-scrawled marker boards and weird cartoons (one titled "Garlic and Boots") cover the Pepto Bismol–colored walls; smudged cruets and jars filled with condiments and seasonings dot the bar and tables that flank the open kitchen willy-nilly. Wearing an expression somewhere between glowering and amused, the ever-present chef-owner wordlessly suggests you take it or leave it. We'll take it, of course: his ramen is simply superb. Loaded with scallions, bean sprouts, and bits of seaweed, the basic shoyu broth is wonderfully oniony, enhanced all the more by a sprinkle of sesame seeds and red pepper; within it bobs a raft of thin, square-cut, springy housemade egg noodles and paper-fine slices of pork as well as a whole, broth-stained egg with a compelling, slightly sweet savor. The gyoza aren't quite as good as they look, but no matter; paired with a bottle of marble soda or beer, the soup alone will sit you in good stead—as will that refreshing dose of attitude.

Pajama Baking Company, 1595 S. Pearl St., Old South Pearl, Denver, CO 80210; (303) 733-3622; www.pajamabakingcompany .com; Bakery/Cafe; $. Cheery and airy in pastel hues, former CU hoops guard Russ Tearney's one-stop goodie shop has fast become an Old South Pearl fixture for the neighborhood's laptop-packers and stroller-pushers. From the crack of dawn to well past dusk, the bakery/cafe's display cases are laden with dozens of breakfast and dessert pastries, quiches, pies, takeaway deli items, and crusty loaves of bread; specialty sandwiches, pizzas, and coffee drinks round out the menu. The savories are solid to be sure (keep your eyes peeled for the quiche with chicken, muenster, and sundried tomatoes as well as to-go containers of chunky artichoke dip)— but the sweets are hard to beat. PBC's peanut butter brownies are among the best around, while the house-churned ice cream and sorbet shine in catchy flavors like banana-chocolate swirl, avocado, coconut-lime, and even peanut butter curry.

Palais Casablanca, 2488 S. University Blvd., University, Denver, CO 80210; (303) 871-0494; www.palaiscasablanca.com; Moroccan; $$$. Swathed from floor to ceiling in scarlet, royal blue, and shimmering gold, this breathtakingly, almost palatially opulent Moroccan restaurant is no mere departure from the grungy University-area norm—it's an absolute escape. Remove your shoes, settle onto an embroidered cushion, and prepare to be cared for in lavish fashion—the irrepressible Chef-Owner Said Benjelloun, who hails from Fez, tends not to take no for an answer, whether he's hand-feeding you warm house-baked bread or wielding a silver pitcher to spritz your forehead and fingers with orange-flower water. In the kitchen, his touch is no less exuberant. The scent of sun-baked spices, dried fruits, and nuts wafts from his tagines; the stuffed phyllo pie known as *b'stella* is a flaky, meaty-sweet sensation dusted with powdered sugar. With a week's notice, Benjelloun will roast a whole lamb for special occasions; he also offers hookah service on the patio and hosts belly dancers on weekend nights, when the menu is prix-fixe. One word of warning to tipplers: Palais Casablanca does not serve alcohol—but the warm, sweet mint tea is good for a sugar high.

Park Burger, 1890 S. Pearl St., Old South Pearl, Denver, CO 80210; (720) 242-9951; www.parkburger.com; Burgers; $. Dominated by an open kitchen, this tight squeeze of a corner joint on Old South Pearl can get stuffy, loud, and, in a word, claustrophobic (even the patio's a bit snug). On the bright side, however, an expansion is in the works; in the meantime Park Burger's got character to spare—and, more to the point, damned good Black Angus burgers with all the trimmings. You can build your own, but you'd be hard-pressed to come up with better combinations than those of the owner, French Culinary Institute alum Jean-Philippe Failyau—be it the unapologetically Gallic Croque Burger topped with ham, swiss, and a fried egg or the sharp-dressed El Chilango, smothered in cheddar, guacamole, and jalapeños. The cherry on top, so to speak? *Comme-il-faut* sweet potato fries alongside orange-creamsicle milk shakes— and a small but smart selection of craft brews, cocktails, and wines by the glass. Actually, the Uptown offshoot, Park & Co. (439 E. 17th Ave., Denver, CO 80203; 720-328-6732), has an even better bar (and a slightly more varied menu), while the Highlands branch hews closely to the flagship brand (2643 W. 32nd Ave., Denver, CO 80211; 303-862-8641).

Vert Kitchen, 704 S. Pearl St., Washington Park, Denver, CO 80209; (303) 997-5941; www.vertkitchen.com; Sandwiches; $. Between his classical French training and his early work with CorePower Yoga, Noah Stevens—chef-owner of this lunch-only charmer in what's optimistically been dubbed Washington Park West—is all about cooking the old-fashioned-cum-newfangled way: locally, seasonally, and sustainably. His sandwich selection is petite but *très* gourmet, eschewing the usual for nifty surprises en baguette like house-roasted turkey with balsamic figs and chèvre or fluffy, golden tortilla española. The same goes for ever-changing sides and starters—here a pattypan squash soup with apples and walnuts, there a refreshing sesame-peanut slaw or quinoa salad studded with corn and scallions; even the bottled sodas are artisanal. The vibe, meanwhile, is no less sprightly, as the narrow, art-dotted space leads to a sun-dappled (and slightly more spacious) split-level back patio. But the overall aura of strapping good health stops at the right place: with soft, chewy white chocolate–cashew cookies.

The Village Cork, 1300 S. Pearl St., Old South Pearl, Denver, CO 80210; (303) 282-8399; http://www.villagecork.com; French; $$. As though for an impromptu dinner party in some sunny French farmhouse, the tables at The Village Cork are adorably set with quirky, mismatched finds from thrift stores, yard sales, even customers' own china cabinets. Think brightly painted ceramic plates, patterned juice glasses, and old wooden bowls; the embossed slats of broken-down wine crates serve as cheese and charcuterie boards. Amid blackboard menus and cork-lined bartops, such details only enhance the cozy mood of this tiny corner wine bar; they're reflected further in the eclectic pours and plates. The wine list is small but intriguing, while

Chef Samir Mohammad's seasonal menu is a locally sourced yet French-inflected delight: pâtés, escargot, and beautifully realized entrees like bison au poivre with cauliflower gratin and blue-cheese streusel are nothing short of wondrous given that the service bar smack in the middle of the dining room doubles as the barely-there "kitchen."

Landmarks

Bonnie Brae Tavern, 740 S. University Blvd., Denver, CO 80209; (303) 777-2262; www.bonniebraetavern.com; Bar & Grill; $$. Since 1934, this neighborhood joint near Wash Park has been a home away from home for regulars in need of suds, grub, and the kind of comfort that can only come from neon memorabilia and creaky vinyl booths. Here the booze flows as liberally as ever, and the menu hasn't changed much over the decades either—you got your burgers and fries, your pot roast, burritos, and spaghetti. And then you've got your loaded pies, which the kitchen was slinging long before the pizzaiolos descended with their brick ovens and EVOO. This is unfussy, rib-sticking stuff served up by unfussy, wholly local folks. Take it or leave it.

El Taco de Mexico, 714 Santa Fe Dr., Santa Fe Arts District, Denver, CO 80204; (303) 623-3926; Mexican; $. The *mujeres* who've been running this buttercup-yellow but otherwise no-frills counter joint in the Santa Fe Arts District for ages are notorious for their brusque demeanor. They've earned it—along with their equally widespread reputation for some of the best Mexican eats in town, bar none. Curiously, regulars are hard-pressed to articulate what they love about the utterly simple tacos de carnitas and carne asada; the gut-busting, double-stuffed chile-relleno burritos; the

 chilaquiles with perfectly fried eggs and silken refried beans; spiced horchata; and above all the purest of pure green chiles. "El Tac just does everything right," they'll claim, using its affectionate nickname with a shrug. Enough said, really—along with a reminder to bring cash (cards not accepted).

Jerusalem Restaurant, 1890 E. Evans Ave., University, Denver, CO 80210; (303) 777-8828; www.jerusalemrestaurant.com; Middle Eastern; $. Open nearly 24/7 for going on four decades, this Denver University hangout has cured the hangovers of countless coeds day in and day out while easing the headaches of harried neighborhood households come dinnertime. In short, it's the default go-to for gyros, shawarma, and kabobs with all the trimmings. Truth be told, though, it owes much of its staying power to textbook vegetarian vittles: crunchy-smooth, earthy falafel; fragrant and juicy rice-stuffed grape leaves; expert, lemon-creamy hummus. (Flaccid french fries are an exception—but why rely on a Middle Eastern joint for your fix of spud sticks?) Though take-out orders go like gangbusters, the tiny dining area, flanked on three sides by patio seating and swathed in patterned fabric, is actually rather charming—not least for boasting a display case filled with all manner of honeyed, flaky, pistachio-flecked pastries.

Lucile's Creole Cafe, 275 S. Logan St., Denver, CO 80209; (303) 282-6258; www.luciles.com; Cajun/Creole; $. One can go on and on about the distinctions between Creole and Cajun cuisine. The former is essentially a refined, urban style of cooking that reflects the mutual influence of the Crescent City's numerous immigrant groups—French, Spanish, Italian, West African, Caribbean; the latter has its roots in the historically rural Acadian (French-Canadian) community. Or one can stress their present-day similarities—the ingredients and techniques they share, the broader elements of Southern cuisine they incorporate. Or, better still, one can just enjoy them. For some three decades, Chef Mickey Samuels has been honing a repertoire of such classics as gumbo, crawfish etouffée, eggs Sardou, fried oyster po'boys, and beaucoup beignets for cofounder Lucile Richards's beloved area franchise—including the bright, bustling Denver outpost (also see p. 246). But we're partial to the behemoth, dense, and crumbly buttermilk biscuit smothered in robust, paprika-spiked sausage gravy—as well as to the oh-so-hearty red beans, slow-cooked for 12 hours with smoked ham shank per the old wash-day custom of New Orleans's Afro-Caribbean populace.

Sushi Den, 1487 S. Pearl St., Old South Pearl, Denver, CO 80210; (303) 777-0826; www.sushiden.net; $$$. Stateside Japanese joints were few and far between when this Old South Pearl institution opened its doors in 1985—and judging by the throngs awaiting a table on the sidewalk nightly, you'd be forgiven for assuming that was still the case. That's how wildly popular Sushi Den remains to this day—with good reason. Fraternal *itamae*-owners Toshi and Yasu Kizaki rely on their youngest brother overseas, Koichi, to scour the fish markets of Fukuoka daily and ship his finds to Colorado overnight; they're no less rigorous about training their staff. The results, from both the bar and the kitchen, are rarely less than swoon-worthy. The emphasis is on pristine nigiri—from all the staples to sometime specials like ethereal needlefish and heady Spanish mackerel. But even the occasional concession to American palates is well handled (try the Rocky Mountain Roll with smoked trout, for instance). Sure, it's clamorous—you could call it Sushi Din—but it's all ours.

Specialty Stores, Markets & Producers

Bonnie Brae Ice Cream, 799 S. University Blvd., Denver, CO 80209; (303) 777-0808; www.bonniebraeicecream. It looks every bit the old-school sweets shoppe, complete with red-striped awning—and in many ways, it is, scooping up banana splits, ice cream floats, fresh-pressed waffle cones, and more. But at any given time, the quartet who owns this ever-swarming favorite near Wash Park use their noggins to whip up a few quirky flavors alongside the classics—brown banana, flan, deep-dish apple pie, or orange-cranberry, for instance—for a grand total of 28 tongue-ticklers.

Dietrich's Chocolate & Espresso, 1734 S. Evans Ave., University, Denver, CO 80210; (303) 777-3358; www.dietrichschocolate.com. It's all too easy to overlook this unassuming little storefront near Denver University, but there's a reason it's remained in business for more than three decades—namely the quiet dedication of its owner, Bavarian-born chocolatier Erich Dietrich, to his craft. His quaint little shop is jam-packed with all manner of sweet treats, some imported but most made on-site: nut clusters and nonpareils, marzipan and marshmallows, chocolate-covered pretzels and prunes, boxed assortments and truffles in flavors ranging from honey and pomegranate to mango-chili. (Dietrich's is also the only carrier of Marañon, the recently rediscovered white cocoa bean of Ecuador, in the state of Colorado.) A small breakfast and lunch menu is speckled with specialties from Dietrich's native Germany, but we could make a meal of the rose-infused dark-chocolate medallions alone.

Divino Wine & Spirits, 1240 S. Broadway, Denver, CO 80210; (303) 778-1800; www.divinowine.com. Run by the hippest, scruffiest, smartest band of geeks around, Divino is a bastion of sophistication amid the creaky antiques shops and medical marijuana dispensaries that line this stretch of South Broadway. For boutique wines you've never heard of, beers you've never seen before, and artisanal spirits so handsomely bottled they double as *objets d'art*, Dave Moore's sleek space is the place to be. Nearly 100 different grappas line the shelves, for instance, along with dozens of rosés; the wines of Germany, Greece, and Portugal get more than token nods, as do world-class sherries and dessert wines. Prove you're a true brew connoisseur, and you might be treated to a taste of the backroom stash—where rare ales from the likes of New Zealand and Norway are kept. If it all sounds cooler-than-thou, rest assured that the vibe here is playful, not brooding; free Saturday tastings and a monthly changing selection of "10 for $10" welcome one and all.

The Duffeyroll Cafe, 1290 S. Pearl St., Old South Pearl, Denver, CO 80210; (303) 953-6890; www.duffeyrolls.com. Though this Old South Pearl fixture is a full-service cafe and coffeehouse hawking sandwiches and such, it's notable after a quarter-century in business for one thing and one thing only: cinnamon rolls. Come early to get them at their most tender and delectable, glazed in any of six flavors—orange, maple, toffee, pecan crunch, and the guilty pleasure that is Irish cream, as well as plain. Additional locations: 4994 E. Hampden Dr., Denver, CO 80222; (303) 753-9177; 5198 S. Broadway, Englewood, CO 80113; (303) 996-5922.

East Side Kosher Deli, 499 S. Elm St., Denver, CO 80246; (303) 322-9862; www.eastsidekosherdeli.com. Given Denver's thriving Jewish community, the dearth of decent delis is a *shanda*. An extra cheer, then, for this glatt kosher mainstay. Flanking the aisles of dry goods and pantry staples, the display cases overflow with oniony latkes and *borekas,* myriad salads, briskets and veal chops, pickled herring and smoked salmon, loaves of pumpernickel and challah, trays of halvah and *mandelbrot,* and more (including *sufganyiot,* or jelly doughnuts, come Hanukkah). The sit-down restaurant in back, meanwhile, serves up all the corned beef and chopped liver, gefilte fish and matzoh balls, borscht and chicken soup with *kreplach* (mini-dumplings) to make a homesick New Yorker positively plotz. You can skip right over large sections of the menu devoted to Americanized Chinese, Mexican, and Italian fare— far better places for that—but don't you dare deny yourself a square of browned-to-a-crisp, savory-sweet Yerushalmi kugel or a chewy, nutty, soulful kasha knish. (How's that for kibitzing?)

Kaladi Brothers Coffee, 1730 E. Evans Ave., University, Denver, CO 80210; (720) 570-2166; www.kaladicoffee.com. In many ways, this coffeehouse near Denver University fits the mold of the classic collegiate hang—funky in feel and packed with hippies and hipsters alike debating current affairs over steaming mugs and vegan muf- fins. But Kaladi itself doesn't just talk the coffee talk; it also walks the walk. Owners Mark Overly and Andy Melnick, along with their highly trained staff, air-roast as many as 12 varietals as well as a few blends on-site; organic, fair-trade products are a secondary focus, but their main concern is connoisseurship, from light, bright Rwanda Abakunda to rich, full-bodied Peru Andes Gold (which Melnick compares, respectively, to Gewürztraminer and Cabernet Sauvignon, suggesting the importance of terroir to beans as much as grapes). If you get the jitters just thinking about it, make the switch to Xococatl—hot chocolate spiked with red chilies.

Les Delices de Paris, 600 S. Holly St., #101, Denver, CO (80246); (303) 320-7596; www.lesdelicesdenver.com. Christelle and Gerard Donat came all the way from Lille, France, to run this cheerful pâtisserie, which hews to tradition in all but its strip-mall setting. The display cases are stuffed silly with tender, butter-licked croissants and cream puffs, quiches and cakes, lunettes and lemon tarts—except when they're not; the goods tend to go fast, so rise and shine.

r + d Wine, 1080 S. Gaylord St., Washington Park, Denver, CO 80209; (303) 722-2129; www.rdwineshop.com. Between the name of his shop and the title on his business card—"unexpected sommelier"— it's clear that Jesse Bopp is on a mission to make oenology easy. It's even clearer once you set foot inside this Wash Park boutique. So that their customers can, indeed, conduct research on the world of wine and develop their palates without fear of the intimidation for which so many experts are infamous, Bopp and his partners have designed it to be as user-friendly as it is chic. Marked by cheeky signs that evoke the periodic table, the shelves are stocked not by region but by varietal, encouraging experimentation among those who, for instance, might be surprised to find a bottle of white Burgundy next to their favorite Napa Chardonnay. In the back room, there's even a display devoted to pairings: wines for barbecue, for spicy food, and so on. To further your education, the shop hosts tastings on Thursday and Saturday—but if you'd just as soon grab a six-pack or a bottle of bourbon, it sells microbrews and craft spirits, too.

Salumeria Cinque Soldi, 1284 S. Pearl St., Old South Pearl, Denver, CO 80210; (303) 996-6400; www.cinquesoldi.com; Deli. Growing up in an Italian family in Worcester, Massachusetts, master sausage-maker Mark DeNittis laughs that he "didn't realize that everybody didn't make salami in their basement." We Denverites are very lucky to have him doing it for us. Operating **Il Mondo Vecchio** in a sleepy storehouse district just off I-25, the former meat-cutting instructor for Johnson & Wales has developed a local cult following for the salumi he almost single-handedly churns out according to Old World tradition, using nothing but "meat, sea salt, spices, wine"—and the sweet time dry-curing takes. Though he does booming wholesale business with the likes of duck prosciutto, the Calabrian-style sopressata he was raised on, and what he calls the "twelve-second" taste sensation that is *lap cheong* (flavored with sweet soy, sake, ginger, and pomegranate, among other things), DeNittis, with partner Gennaro DeSantis, is also proud papa to this East Coast–style deli counter. They serve up panini and "wicked grindahs" to his acolytes on Old South Pearl.

Sugar Bakeshop, 277 Broadway, Baker District, Denver, CO 80203; (720) 458-5432; www.sugar-bakeshop.com. But for the old black-and-white episodes of Julia Child's *The French Chef* screening on one wall, this bakery/cafe on the ground floor of a Baker District office building keeps the decor to a minimum. All the better to showcase owner Natalie Slevin's gorgeous, seasonally themed cakes (think autumnal pumpkin cream cheese–maple)—and much, much more. The counter is strewn from end to end with irresistibles: caramel-walnut bread pudding. Puffy, colorfully iced pop tarts (try the scrumptious cinnamon). Mini-cupcakes and fat scones. Round and bar cookies, muffins and tea breads (some vegan, others gluten-free). Even the plain old brownies shine. As Julia herself would have said with a chuckle: *Bon appétit*!

Sweet Action, 52 Broadway, Baker District, Denver, CO 80203; (303) 282-4645; www.sweetactionicecream.com. Jam-packed year-round with locals from the moment it opens until closing time, this nationally lauded creamery has made an indelible mark on the Baker District with its hand-crafted scoops in ever-changing, often unheard-of flavors. In summer, you might encounter slow-burning green chile or soothing honey-corn bread; come winter, caramelized pear and Colorado whiskey brickle beckon. (And at any given time, if you spy a batch of baklava or horchata behind the counter, go for the gusto and get a whole pint.) Owners Sam Kopicko and Chia Basinger keep vegans in the loop too, always offering at least a couple of dairy-free options.

Boulder

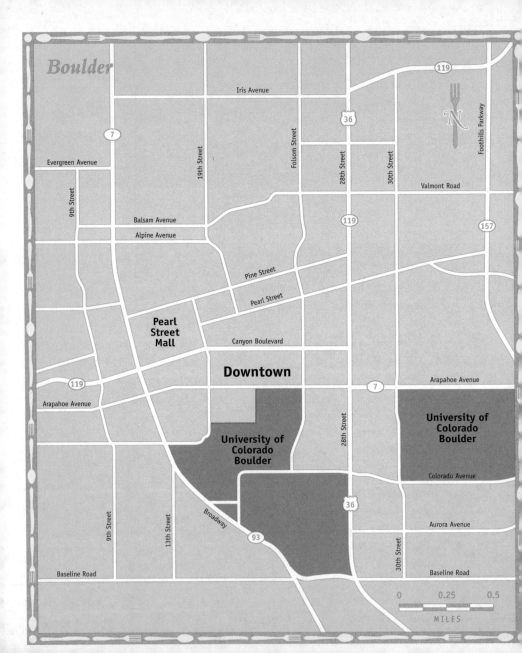

Boulder

Could this be the same town in which Mork from Ork once fit right in? Well, the short answer's yes. In many ways Boulder remains a combination of hippie enclave, rugged outdoorsman's paradise, and last refuge of scruffy trustafarians—as well, of course, as the ultimate college town (in 2011, *Playboy* ranked the University of Colorado number one among party schools). But it's also become a foodie magnet par excellence, swarming with master sommeliers and celebrated chefs whose every move gets tracked by the national press. So while Himalayan holes in the wall still elicit cheers from the spirit chasers ("Free Tibet!") and homegrown sub-shop chains like Snarf's (http://eatsnarfs.com) still churn out handheld hangover helpers day in and day out, the current dining scene is far too dynamic and sophisticated to stereotype with ease. Downtown, the Pearl Street Mall and environs teem with acclaimed eateries of all kinds, but there's really no neighborhood that doesn't contain a gem or two; these days, even The Hill, also known as CU's campus corner, claims a few. Welcome, then, to a bolder Boulder—or, as Mork would say, *nanu nanu*.

Agave Mexico Bistro & Tequila House, 2845 28th St., Boulder, CO 80301; (303) 444-2922; http://agavecolorado.com; Mexican; $$. Your first glimpse at Agave will leave you agog: how did they squeeze such a handsome, two-story space—its adobe walls, log ceilings, and copper and wrought-iron accents evoking a colonial plaza—into the corner of an old strip mall? We can't answer that question, not being architectural engineers, nor can we explain how this upscale casa is flying so steadily under the radar. But it is, and we think it's worth your while for the sort of regionally inflected fare—vibrant with seafood and produce—that remains hard to come by in the Rockies, awash as they are in Southwestern Mexican traditions. Shrimp and octopus, cactus and epazote (a type of herb), jicama and papaya all make appearances on a large menu whose linchpin, in our view, is the array of *molcajetes,* or earthy mélanges of meat, vegetables, cheese, and tomato or tomatillo sauces served in stone mortars. But with a Puebla native heading up the kitchen, you can bet the *chiles rellenos en nogada* are spot-on, like the carefully assembled *enchiladas verdes* with chicken (popular as far north as New Mexico yet inexplicably uncommon around here). It's all accompanied by fresh—indeed, made-to-order—corn tortillas and a decent if not exhaustive selection of premium tequilas. Really, this is quite the pleasant oasis in Boulder's sea of hype.

Arugula Bar e Ristorante, 2785 Iris Ave., Boulder, CO 80304; (303) 443-5100; www.arugularistorante.com; Italian; $$. To step into Alec Schuler's spruce, serene flagship, dominated by a rustic chandelier and dotted with ceramic tiles from Tunisia, is to become instantly smarter and more stylish. As you peruse the cork-covered wine list, assessing the novelty of a Swiss Chasselas or a Colorado Syrah against the dashing array of regional Italian pours, you'll relish the validation of your own good taste. And ordering a dish that's no less warm and approachable for being so elegant naturally reflects well on you. At least that's how we feel while sipping Corvina out of Stölzle stemware and nibbling on the likes of calamari scampi—the strips of flesh browned and buttery, the sauce ultra-lemony and sharp with lots of garlic and parsley—and precisely grained risotto plush with local mushrooms. Even dessert sets us afloat rather than weighing us down, be it lavender-infused crema catalana or Indian-spiced mascarpone. We don't know how Schuler does it, but we're convinced we're classier for the experience he provides.

Black Cat Bistro, 1964 13th St., Boulder, CO 80302; (303) 444-5500; http://blackcatboulder.com; Contemporary; $$$. Few, if any, Colorado chef-owners personify the locavore movement as fully as Eric Skokan. One of the first to operate his own farm—no vanity project but a 70-acre plot devoted to heirloom produce and heritage breeds—he showcases the fruits of his labor at this twinkling downtown bistro with an aptitude as seasoned as his attitude is seasonal. We'd tell you to splurge on the seven-course tasting menu, but at $80, it's a marvelous bargain rather than a bender, dish after beautifully realized dish. The gentle tang of chèvre hovers over a terrine of lightly pickled, diced carrots; white-radish soup touched with black truffle folds earthy notes into a creamy whole. Gnocchi, slightly crusted, takes a rustic turn via grilled chicken livers, sauteed greens, and a lingering trace of mustard and nutmeg; a tiny flute of apple-thyme tisane cleanses the palate before, perhaps, a scoop of gorgonzola acts as savory ice cream to another of beet granite. Adept pairing suggestions are a breeze for servers who know the outstanding, several-page wine list inside and out—but Skokan's bar program deserves far more attention than it receives; an aperitif cocktail will kick off your evening with no less sparkle than a half-bottle of Grower Champagne. See Eric Skokan's recipe for **Grilled Beef Ribeye with Beet Greens and Horseradish Aioli** on p. 332.

Brasserie Ten Ten, 1011 Walnut St., Boulder, CO 80302; (303) 998-1010; www.brasserietenten.com; French; $$. Frosted glass and mosaic tiles, marble and wrought iron, the lilt of piped-in jazz and conversation that, in an atmosphere like this, seems witty and engaging even if you can't actually make it out: this downtowner appears the very picture of a timeless brasserie—one that a confident kitchen brings into even sharper focus. Smart starts include oysters from the raw bar and steak tartare (along with a glass of Champagne, *bîen sur*); while classics like bouillabaise and coq au vin present themselves as the natural next step, we lean toward accomplished salads like the *poulet de pistou*—a punchy mixture of pesto-roasted, crème fraîche–drizzled shreds of chicken over vinaigrette-slicked wilted arugula, perfectly ripe slices of roast tomato, and rings of red onion. It's accompanied by a toasted bialy courtesy of the bakery at its older sibling across the street, **The Med**—which also produces the huge, airy croissants that shine come brunchtime. Unbeatable prices make happy hour here truly *heureux*, too.

Breadworks, 2644 Broadway, Boulder, CO 80304; (303) 444-5667; www.breadworks.net; Bakery/Cafe; $. It's a decent coffeehouse; it's an adequate deli; it's a fine place to fritter away a lunch hour (provided you don't require Wi-Fi). But this spacious, bustling long-timer is primarily a bakery, and in that department it shines, especially when it comes to savory breads. Bouncy popovers, cracklingly chewy ficelle studded with green olives, and two-cheese Italian rounds we like to sprinkle with balsamic vinegar take our top slots, but on any given day the display cases are filled with loaves of all shapes, sizes, and types; you could come here for two weeks straight without quite sampling them all.

Cafe Aion, 1235 Pennsylvania Ave., Boulder, CO 80302; (303) 993-8131; http://cafeaion.com; Small Plates/Tapas; $$. Behind an entrance no wider than a closet lies the charming surprise of a stairway-accessed dining room in which sunlight glints off brick walls and scuffed wood floors; two fireplaces and a couch near the bar give it the feel of an old loft (in fact, nearly a century ago, it was part of a CU fraternity). Likewise putting the "city" in "rusticity," Chef Dakota Soifer's seasonal repertoire blends with ease the foodways of the farmhouse and the tapería alike, as locally raised meat and produce—lamb, oxtail, squash, mushrooms—take on Mediterranean tones in the guise of dried fruits, nuts, and warm spices. (Take the stellar, if homely, example of the signature fried cauliflower—deeply browned, salt-dusted florets gaining tangy contrast from saffron-infused yogurt and a squirt of lemon.) We're equally delighted by the offer of chilled fino sherry as an accompaniment to house-cured salumi and the opportunity to order the doughnut holes served at breakfast right through lunch; such thoughtful details reveal the widely inclusive appeal that Aion— named for a defunct bookshop whose logo still marks the spot— aims to foster. And did we mention the fine sangria?

Caffe, 1720 Pearl St., Boulder, CO 80302; (303) 442-9464; http://frascacaffe.com; Bakery/Cafe; $. With three tiny tables, a couple of barstools, and all the standing room of an elevator, this slip of a cafe barely registers as a blip on the radar screen—unless you happen to know it's owned by Bobby Stuckey and Lachlan Mackinnon-Patterson of the adjacent **Frasca** (p. 215) and **Pizzeria Locale** (p. 230), in which case it looms large. Of course, the goods speak for themselves. While exclusive imports like fresh-pressed Umbrian olive oil and 30-year-aged balsamic vinegar beckon from the shelves behind the counter, the made-from-scratch pastries, salads, and sandwiches take priority, dazzling in variety for a place this size as well as quality. If pasta salads circa 1985 left you cold, Caffe's will put them back on heavy rotation with its hearty confetti of salami, provolone, marinated artichoke hearts, and peppers. Pressed on the grill to a uniformly dark gold, the popular panino with roast pork and truffle butter hardly needs our endorsement, but the bubbly open-faced tartines do deserve special mention. Even the chestnut-brown, sea salt–spangled, extra-chewy pretzel sticks sparkle—as do dense-crumbed, maple-glazed *bomboloni* that put most other doughnuts to shame.

Centro Latin Kitchen & Refreshment Palace, 950 Pearl St., Boulder, CO 80302; (303) 442-7771; http://centrolatinkitchen.com; Pan-Latin; $$. Though we frankly prefer its more focused sibling **Lola Coastal Mexican** (p. 39), Centro's hardly doling out sloppy seconds. No less cool for being colorful, with its sunflower motif, cement-topped bar, and long communal tables inside and out on the year-round patio, it's worth a trip for the menu of "passport cocktails" alone, which plays on libations from across Central and South America (don't get us started on the Colombian Corpse, blending both *aguardiente* and tequila with a splash of Lillet Blanc). And we share with the kitchen an abiding fondness for daring protein combinations, be it grilled tuna with white-anchovy chimichurri over roasted purple potatoes or nachos topped with lobster and pork green chile. When the crew pulls them off, they're tough to beat; otherwise, we do a 180° toward thoughtful vegetarian dishes like spiced butternut squash soup with candied pumpkin seeds and tomatillo–green apple relish or griddled goat-cheese sopes with black beans and avocado—thereby leaving room for fried bananas with rum-and-coke ice cream and a sprinkling of crushed, sugared peanuts (*ay yi yi*).

Cuba Cuba Sandwicheria, 2525 Arapahoe Ave., Boulder, CO 80302; (303) 442-1143; Cuban; $. We grappled with the classification of this Miami-colored **Cuba Cuba** (p. 73) sibling—love those patchwork ceiling tiles—before finally settling on Cuban rather than Sandwiches. Our reasoning: the rice bowls are not to be dismissed, especially the soupy picadillo with raisin-and-potato-studded ground beef and black beans. Still, for the vibrant mojo aioli on the *pan con lechon* (shredded roast pork) alone, it was a tough call, made all the tougher by the *minuta de pescado* featuring lightly batter-fried mahimahi with cabbage, onion, and cilantro on a baguette. Hmm . . . perhaps you'll have to judge for yourself whether we made the right decision; better gather your wits about you first by knocking back an eye-opening *colada* (three shots of traditionally sweetened espresso).

Dish Gourmet, 1918 Pearl St., Boulder, CO 80304; (720) 565-5933; http://dishgourmet.com; Sandwiches; $. It's a tight squeeze from the entrance—where an antique wooden pantry bearing imported tinned seafood, local preserves, and other sundries stands guard—around the crammed tables to the order counter laden with deli salads and daily specials. Even the lettering on the mounted chalkboards is cramped, making for a tough read—but a fun one, spanning some 30 sandwiches, one of which you'll eventually sport in your hot little hands. In a town as spoiled by choice as Boulder, the badge of creativity's hard-won, but Dish earns it with oners like the Whittier—which layers creamy duck-liver pâté, speck (basically smokier prosciutto), and brie on a baguette spread with honey mustard and apple chutney—and the scallion-speckled, cream cheese-enriched smoked whitefish on pumpernickel. Of course, it shares its gold star with a number of local producers, not least Ozo Coffee and **Bhakti Chai** (p. 250).

Frasca Food and Wine, 1738 Pearl St., Boulder, CO 80302; (303) 442-6966; www.frascafoodandwine.com; Italian; $$$. After all the prestigious awards, the national coverage, the celebrity guests, the sheer hype surrounding it from its beginnings in 2004 through its 2010 expansion right up to today, there remains the startling fact of Frasca itself: no imperial temple of gastronomic excess but a serene, sincere homage to the namesake taverns of Friuli. That Master Sommelier Bobby Stuckey and Chef Lachlan Mackinnon-Patterson have remained true to their original vision is evident at every turn: in the elegantly simple setting, the unflappably gracious service, and of course the ever-changing menu, marked by soulfulness and finesse in equal measure. To recommend anything in particular would be to defeat the purpose of the experience, which unfolds organically from moment to moment; we advise only that you set aside three hours for several courses, starting with superb cocktails and small plates before moving on to inspired, accomplished dish after dish of remarkably textured pastas, beautifully integrated entrees and desserts rendered with impressionistic agility—at least one of which you will, guaranteed, remember for life. Meanwhile, Stuckey's sweeping yet meticulously focused wine list is nothing short of extraordinary, and his eloquence in guiding novices and oenophiles alike to the bottle of their dreams unmatched. Enough, we think, said.

Izakaya Amu, 1221 Spruce St., Boulder, CO 80302; (303) 440-0807; www.izakayaamu.com; Japanese/Sushi; $$. To perch along the bar at **Sushi Zanmai's** (p. 237) tranquil alter ego—there's nowhere else to sit except for a lone window table and a low-slung, longer one in back for groups—is to be immediately and utterly transported. A traditional *izakaya* (or Japanese tavern) through and through, the air stirring with the graceful movements of both the smiling, kimono-clad servers and the deft-fingered chef before you, it presents a dazzling assortment—some 75 in all—of raw, pickled, grilled, fried, steamed, and simmered nibbles whose deceptively simple execution, one after another, is cause for sheer exultation. Choose a dish from every category for the full effect:

paper-thin yet velvet-rich slices of salmon sashimi dressed in egg yolk zing. Mild, fleshy, fried mackerel fillet basks in a lullingly perfumed broth bobbing with crisp-tender chunks of daikon, flower-cut carrot disks, and tiny enoki mushrooms. Spoonfuls of the exquisite custard known as *chawanmushi* dissipate on the tongue like clouds. And *kushikatsu* yields no fewer than 10 impeccable tempura skewers, each different (the salmon and lotus root stand out). At $20 for five courses, the tasting menu's almost unfair to the house; sake service is faultless; and leaving is a little like waking from a dream.

Jax Fish House & Oyster Bar, 928 Pearl St., Boulder, CO 80302; (303) 444-1811; www.jaxboulder.com; Seafood; $$$. When the long, narrow space that contains this Pearl Street fixture fills to the gills—which it often does from happy hour onward—you can feel as though you're an extra in the trash-compactor scene from *Star Wars*. So long as you get your own fill of the goods before the graffiti-covered brick walls close in, you won't mind a bit—in fact, you'll be happy as a clam. Overseen by the talented Sheila Lucero, the seasonal menu largely resembles that of its younger Denver sibling; suffice it to say here that her seafood's awash in flash and funk, be it a hot dog topped with Andouille sausage and crabmeat or grilled salmon over a wild rice cake with curried cauliflower and pickled cherries. Meanwhile, the Bloody Mary with horseradish-infused vodka and a shrimp garnish is practically a meal in itself. (Also see Denver listing on p. 80.) See Sheila Lucero's recipe for **Whole Grilled Trout with Autumn Vegetables in Brown Butter** on p. 333.

Jimmy & Drew's 28th Street Deli, 2855 28th St., Boulder, CO 80301; (303) 447-3354; www.jimmyanddrews.net; Deli; $. We know, we know: the notion that an old-school deli could thrive in the land of granola and tempeh—under the watch of guys named not, say, Saul and Levi but Jimmy and Drew—is just too improbable. But you'll trust it's not impossible as you take in the checkerboard floors, the red vinyl booths—and above all the fully loaded sandwich menu. It's all here—the pastrami and Italian cold cuts, the roast beef and turkey and egg salad, supplemented by chicken soup with matzoh balls and zingy, caraway-speckled coleslaw. While buckets of ink have been spilled over Jimmy's Favorite, essentially a Reuben slapped between two latkes, our own favorite's the Flatiron: on a soft onion bun layered with creamed horseradish, melted cheddar, and browned onions as well as lettuce and tomato are perched enormous chunks of the literally mouthwatering, achingly tender, just-pink house brisket. It's such an honest jawful.

The Kitchen, 1039 Pearl St., Boulder, CO 80302; (303) 544-5973; http://thekitchencommunity.com; Contemporary; $$$. A pioneer among pioneers, this mainstay on the mall deserves the countless kudos it has nabbed over the years for its unwavering commitment to the Boulder community and the ethicurean lifestyle. In their relaxed, if crowded, townhouse-like two-story space, owners Hugo Matheson and Kimbal Musk have long abided by the "recycle, reuse, reduce" mantra at every turn, just as their wind-powered kitchen has excelled at hyperlocal farm-to-table cookery since day one—well before the concept gained nationwide traction. The menu is, of course, mostly seasonal, though a couple of signatures have been granted permanent status—namely the purest and freshest of tomato soups; the fat, succulent lamb sausage; and the addictive, pecan-sprinkled sticky toffee pudding. If you're lucky, there'll be roasted mussels in chorizo cream or supreme salmon rillettes with pickled onions; if not, you'll still be lucky thanks to creamed mushrooms on toast or perfectly grilled pork chops. Employing both a beer and a wine director, The Kitchen also offers an unassailably tasteful, well-annotated selection of boutique pours; Colorado microbrews and sustainable wines flow from the taps at its slightly more rustic, gastropubby adjacent sibling, **The Kitchen [Next Door]** (1035 Pearl St., Boulder, CO 80302; 720-542-8159), well-matched to beet burgers and kale chips. (See also **The Kitchen** in Denver, p. 81.)

L'Atelier, 1739 Pearl St., Boulder, CO 80302; (303) 442-7233; www.latelierboulder.com; French; $$$. Yes, the name (which translates as The Studio), coupled with a banner that reads "The Artistry of Radek R. Cerny," is a tad precious; so is the posh dining room, with its elaborate table settings, papier-mâché mobiles that turn the ceiling into an upside-down koi pond, and display cases illuminating porcelain figurines. But hey, if you've got it, flaunt it; the Prague-born Cerny's cooking warrants a little pomp and circumstance. Intricate, sometimes gravity-defying, presentations herald his post-nouvelle approach to luxury ingredients: lobster and *foie* *gras*, chanterelles and Champagne—the latter of which, *naturelle-ment*, also kicks off a wine list that covers all the special-occasion bases (and then some). Of course, every occasion's rendered instantly special by the famed chocolate bag filled with ice cream and seasonal fruit for dessert; it's like a party favor you take home in your stomach.

Laudisio, 1710 29th St., Ste. 1076, Boulder, CO 80301; (303) 442-1300; http://laudisio.com; Italian; $$. Not everyone applauded Antonio Laudisio's 2006 move to this sprawling outlet in the 29th Street Mall. But when the staff is on the ball, we think there's still plenty to be said for the place. The seasonal menu, like the jazzy space, is large and appealingly sophisticated; at their best, *besciamella*-topped cannelloni filled with braised beef, pork, and chicken or seared sea scallops with cannellini, butternut squash, and chanterelles in brown butter vinaigrette live up to their rich descriptions. Fresh produce, often organic and locally sourced, is a strong suit, be it in the form of flash-fried zucchini chips with bright lemon aioli or roasted beets with housemade ricotta, their sweetness accented by a sprinkle of toasted hazelnuts and grape syrup. Laudisio's pan-Italian wine cellar is another: though we appreciate the selection of bottles for $35 and under, we covet the reserve list, with its numerous vintages of Barbaresco, Barolo, and Amarone. And the proportionately extensive happy-hour menu makes determining whether the kitchen's up to snuff that day a snap: come for a nibble (carpaccio, insalata caprese, mini-arancini), stay; maybe, for the whole enchilada (or raviolo, as the case may be).

Leaf Vegetarian Restaurant, 2010 16th St., Boulder, CO 80302; (303) 442-1485; www.leafvegetarianrestaurant.com; Vegetarian; $$. Making no bones (so to speak) about its green orientation, this serene spot off Pearl is designed to half-convince us we're sitting in a treehouse—a sleek, brick treehouse, perhaps, but a treehouse nonetheless, where filigreed globe pendants shine like moons on streaming foliage. That the kitchen concentrates on not only seasonal, contemporary vegetarian fare but also its vegan and raw offshoots—much of it sourced from the owners' nearby farm—goes virtually without saying; that it also emphasizes artistic presentation, however, does bear noting. In short, Leaf caters to today's ethicureans, not their tie-dyed throwbacks, with at least interesting and sometimes scintillating results. While soups stand out—from zingy pineapple gazpacho to robust white bean and spinach—salads, contrary to expectation, are the least of a menu that bursts with creativity: guacamole, sloppy joes, General Tso's, carrot cake, and even Thanksgiving dinner take on a whole new slant with the use of lentils, cashews, cranberries, kale, seitan, soy cream, and much more, especially paired with biodynamic wines and organic vodka–based cocktails. Sunday's vegan pizza night: how cute is that?

Mateo, 1837 Pearl St., Boulder, CO 80302; (303) 443-7766; www.mateorestaurant.com; French; $$. After 10 years and counting, the

Colorado's a Mexican marketplace first and foremost, but it's not without other outposts of Latin Americana; Peruvian ceviche, Brazilian *feijoada,* and Argentine asada all have their place here (see Appendix A for further listings).

El Chalate, *8119 E. Colfax Ave., Denver, CO 80220; (303) 333-0818; Salvadoran; $.* Even over the blare of the soccer games on the flat-screen TV, you'll be able to hear the cooks in the kitchen of this bright-orange, primarily Salvadoran joint slapping the *pupusa* dough into shape all the way from the dining room. Though the menu's crammed with homestyle specialties like stewed *pollo guisado* and *sopa de pata* with cow's feet and tripe, that sound functions as the Pavlovian bell for us cravers of the just-griddled, stuffed, savory, and super-cheap (at $1.35 apiece) corn pancakes. Best bet: Besides *pupusas,* the fresh banana bread to go, of all things, warms the cockles—it's virtually pudding in a crust.

Empanada Express Grill, *2600 East St., Unit G, Golden, CO 80401; (720) 226-8362; Venezuelan; $.* Originating in Golden, this unassuming, family-owned Venezuelan trio is just that—golden, at least

luster on Matthew Jansen's Provençal pearl hasn't dimmed a bit. Brick-warm yet linen-crisp, it tends toward quietude at lunchtime, lively clamor in the evening; the kitchen keeps a steady pace either way. The contents of its bouillabaisse, for instance, vary based on market availability, but its quality does not; nor does its smart in the eyes of the urban prospectors who flock here en masse to stake their claims on the signature arepas and empanadas. Simultaneously crisp and fluffy, they spill with fillings as lush and colorful as the tropics. Best bet: the sweet-savory Criolla with beef, black beans, white cheese, fried plantains, and a splash of chimichurri. Additional locations: 4301 44th Ave., Denver, CO 80212; (303) 955-8362; 4122 E. Colfax Ave., Denver, CO 80220; (720) 226-4701.

Zudaka, *4457 N. Broadway, Boulder, CO 80304; (303) 442-2717; www.zudakarestaurant.com; Vegetarian; $.* With its vivid red-and-yellow brick storefront and down-to-earth interior, this looks like any other far-south-of-the-border kitchen. Surprise! The mostly Venezuelan cheap eats just so happen to be wholly vegetarian. Arepas, with or without meat substitutes, comprise the bulk of the menu, but most dishes come with intriguing *guasacaca,* or guacamole sharpened with vinegar rather than citrus juice. Best bet: *agua de panela*—soothing sugar cane–sweetened water with lemon.

presentation in a cast-iron pot complete with melted gruyère-topped crouton. As at its sibling **Radda** (p. 232), pastas are a strong point, especially gnocchi as plump as pincushions, draped in béchamel with swiss chard or dunked in mushroom fumet with chanterelles. Gratins, too, are a sometime specialty; bubbling in a ramekin of garlicky parmesan cream under breadcrumbs, green beans still count as a vegetable. And wine from the mostly French list still counts as a fruit, we think, so you'll have earned an after-dinner bite of *pot au chocolat*.

The Mediterranean Restaurant, 1002 Walnut St., Boulder, CO 80302; (303) 444-5335; www.themedboulder.com; Mediterranean; $$. While the Boulder dining scene has spread like wildfire all around it, this considerable long-timer has held its ground. Entering the Med, as it's familiarly known, is like finding yourself inside a giant piece of majolica pottery, gleaming and ultra-colorful; the sprawling main space leads to a sunny patio and a smaller dining room in cooler hues—all buzzing steadily from open to close, but especially during a rip-roaring happy hour. The convivial momentum builds largely on a huge menu of tapas, pizzas, pastas, paellas, and other dishes that run the gamut of inspiration from Spanish and Italian to Greek and Provençal; though execution varies, it's rarely less than enjoyable. That's especially true of the small plates, which change subtly with the seasons. Hummus might contain curry here, black beans there; meatballs in vibrant marinara could be made with pork or lamb; goat cheese or slow-cooked wild boar may fill empanadas. We're just as happy, however, that the mushrooms in garlic sauce never change—and that the bar doesn't rest on its sangria-splashed laurels, with an extensive wine list that takes chances on lesser-known regions and varietals: Kerner and Schioppettino from northern Italy, blends from Portugal and Slovenia.

Modmarket, 1600 28th St., #1212, Boulder, CO 80301; (720) 440-0476; www.modmarket.com; American; $. Coolly minimalist as a space capsule, the flagship of this quickly expanding local franchise was bound to hit it big in Boulder: the cycling-and-climbing set falls for the healthful fast-food schtick every time. Then again, so do their cubicle-dwelling counterparts—and not because they've confused the place with a Mac outlet (at least not primarily). Rather, it's because the seasonally tweaked offerings are generally more fun—and tastier—than their listed calorie counts would suggest, especially when it comes to salads. Take the Superfood, a spunky mix of spinach, kale, quinoa, feta, blackberries, carrots, and almonds in champagne vinaigrette that's even better topped with locally made tofu; the mint- and orange-spiked Mongolian with edamame and soynuts; or the Thai Coconut with chicken and sweet potato. But there are soups, sandwiches, and pizzas, too—some vegan and/or gluten-free—as well as cane-sugar sodas, local beers, and more. This is pedal-pushing, cliff-facing, head-clearing fuel. Additional locations: 1000 S. Colorado Ave., Glendale, CO 80246; (303) 757-1772; 8575 E. Arapahoe Rd., Ste. F, Greenwood Village, CO 80112; (303) 220-9963.

OAK at Fourteenth, 1400 Pearl St., Boulder, CO 80302; (303) 444-3622; www.oakatfourteenth.com; Contemporary; $$$. Just months after opening in late 2010, this Boulder hit proved a little too white-hot for its own good, shuttering for the better part of a year after a fire caused extensive damage. But its owners, fellow **Frasca Food and Wine** (p. 215) alums Bryan Dayton and Steven Redzikowski, have finally returned with a vengeance. Aside from an expansion, the new space, sleek in light woods and warm gray tones, looks a lot like the (not very) old one, as does the locally and seasonally oriented menu—after all, why fix what wasn't broken (just charred)? Inaugural signatures like the fried pickles with green goddess aioli and braised meatballs have made triumphant comebacks, especially the latter, now served over burrata grits. And while Chef Redzikowski has a way with grilled pork, we're partial to his vegetarian dishes, be it luscious heirloom bean-and-root vegetable gratin or a nifty take on pierogi featuring winter squash, chestnuts, and pumpkin seeds. Similarly, beverage director Dayton's mocktails hold as much fresh appeal as his cocktails—think house-made kumquat-tarragon soda (which can, however, be kicked up with Campari). See Bryan Dayton's recipe for the **Aspen Highland** on p. 342.

PastaVino, 1043 Pearl St., Boulder, CO 80302; (303) 955-8791; http://pastavino.com; Italian; $$. Occupying the sort of long, narrow space one associates with the dining neighborhoods of coastal cities, this Pearl Street eatery comes by its worldliness honestly. Both chef Fabio Flagiello and wine director Corrado Fasano hail from Italy (Trieste and Torino, respectively), and the imprint of the Boot on their shared aesthetic is clear from the sleek yet brightly accented dining room to the intensely multi-regional character of both the glass-and-bottle selection and the extensive menu. Lombardian *braesola*, Ligurian *trenette al pesto*, and Florentine *bistecca* are just a sampling of the classics between which Flagiello works all manner of specialties, be it Alpine-style beet-stuffed ravioli with poppy-seed brown butter and beef ragù or braised pheasant agnolotti. Yet there's one way in which PastaVino is clearly community oriented: The list of beers and cocktails is aimed squarely and smartly at Boulder's critical mass of connoisseurs.

Pearl Street Steak Room, 1035 Pearl St., Boulder, CO 80302; (303) 938-9604; Steak House; $$$. Finally, a chophouse for the cool kids. With all of 32 seats (including a five-top bar) in a swish, marble-and-ebony-hued hideaway, says Mara Soutiere (who with husband, Peter, also owns **Sushi Tora**, p. 236), "we're not trying to do the volume of a Morton's; we wanted to source the best beef we can find—and we found it." Eschewing the standard breeds for Australian Wagyu and Holstein—whose genetics, she says, "haven't been altered the way Black Angus have"—their kitchen's otherwise sticking to the traditional model of classic cuts and sauces, à la carte sides, and a smattering of hors d'oeuvres like mini-lobster rolls and chicken-fried sweetbreads with apple butter. The wine list, too, is tried-and-true: Champagne, big-house Burgundies, meaty Cabs. But what style the goods possesses: pumpkin bisque pops with gingerbread, walnuts, fried sage, and a flourish of spiced cream;

the plate-spanning, 32-ounce tomahawk chop is a wonder to behold; and the skillet-baked fig-apple cobbler sprinkled with sea salt and topped with praline ice cream warms from the tummy to the toes. True to form, a meal here will take a chunk out of your wallet—but think of it as a donation to the anti-granola cause.

Pickled Lemon, 1155 13th St., Boulder, CO 80302; (720) 353-4442; www.pickledlemon.com; Middle Eastern; $. The brainchild of the quick-casual biz whizzes behind **Udi's Bread Cafe** (p. 46)—Udi Baron himself is an Israeli-born former economist—this colorfully mod counter joint on the Hill puts the fixings at the forefront, right where we like them. On a fairly simple foundation of stuffed pitas and platters—falafel, shawarma, kabobs—rests a slew of jazzy condiments: sumac-marinated onions, horseradish-spiked roasted beets, and tabouli jeweled with pomegranate seeds, for instance—as well as a variety of pickles, including cauliflower and turnip as well as the eponymous lemons, at the self-serve bar, where a quintet of sauces flavored with roast garlic, mango, and more also await. At least half the fun in here is in customizing your order; good old piña coladas provide no small kick, too.

Pizzeria Basta, 3601 Arapahoe Ave., Boulder, CO 80303; (303) 997-8775; www.pizzeriabasta.com; Pizza; $$. You can get as lost as a mouse in a maze looking for this pizzeria in the midst of a mixed-use complex on the east side of town; when you finally locate it, you'll be rewarded like one, too—with cheese. Of course, that house-pulled mozzarella isn't all you'll get, but it shines on uncompromising wood-fired pies that—from the dusty, buckled crust to the minimalist topping combos—convey simplicity itself. With daily specials, Chef Kelly Whitaker caters a bit more liberally to the fickle palate, adding fingerling potatoes here, butternut squash there; the rest of his menu, meanwhile, proves an admirable mix of the painstakingly conceived and effortlessly executed. One day lasagna with sous vide pork belly and burrata may call your name; another, peppery celeriac soup garnished with a fennel cracker and polenta bolognese, invigorated by the presence of figs, beckons. And while the wine list sparkles with obscure gems to catch the eye of Italophiles (Cesanese from Lazio, Calabrian Magliocco), a quartet of Colorado wines on tap are a gesture of goodwill we respond to with feeling.

Pizzeria da Lupo, 2525 Arapahoe Ave., Boulder, CO 80302; (303) 396-6366; www.pizzeriadalupo.com; Pizza; $$. **Empire Lounge and Restaurant**'s (p. 268) younger sibling couldn't be more inviting; vintage fixtures, snazzy tiled floors, and old framed photos put the "parlor" in "pizza parlor." But what puts the "pizza" in the phrase is a wood-burning oven that fires up pies boasting the last word in crusts. They look thick, but they practically float on air while supporting a delicate balance of toppings—the tomato sauce seemingly stroked on with a brush, the cheeses like gently dolloped cream, the wispy white of a cracked egg nearly dissipating on contact. *Cecine*—chickpea pancakes—are more than a gluten-free alternative, they're crisp-soft and delicious in their own right; in fact, we'd just as soon order a round, topped with nothing but a drizzle of olive oil and a sprinkling of sea salt, as an appetizer. Not to knock the small plates; a warm salad of borlotti beans with radicchio and pancetta, for instance, balances beautifully its earthy, salty, and bitter notes. The wine list is small but pizza-friendly, and the bar keeps hard-to-find brews from Boulder's own **Upslope** (p. 301) on draft—cheers to that.

Pizzeria Locale, 1730 Pearl St., Boulder, CO 80302; (303) 442-3003; www.pizzerialocale.com; Pizza; $$. Like its celebrated sibling next door, **Frasca Food and Wine** (p. 215), this coolly sleek pizzeria is pitch- and picture-perfect down to the last facet (ask about the provenance of the hand-built, tile-covered oven in back and the gleaming prosciutto slicer in front). Along the gray walls and marble-topped bars, elaborate floral arrangments and photographer Dave Woody's vivid Neapolitan street scenes add bursts of color—but the rainbow effect comes straight from the seasonal menu. Master Sommelier Bobby Stuckey and his wine team tailor their selection of wines by the glass to complement pies while opening Frasca's enormous cellar up to customers; meanwhile, the bar crew delivers the most delicately fragrant of spritzers (the cantaloupe's dreamy). True to Campagnese style, the pizzas are deceptively simple—the *mais,* for instance, is at once luscious and borderline light, spread with crème fraîche and buffalo mozzarella, then dotted with rosettes of prosciutto cotto and corn kernels. But if you never got past the stellar salads and *contorni* (technically sides, doubling as antipasti), you'd still be in the pink. True story: This is the best *insalata ai frutti di mare* we've had anywhere, Italy included.

Pupusas Sabor Hispano, 4550 N. Broadway, Unit 3E, Boulder, CO 80304; (303) 444-1729; Salvadoran; $. *Es muy lindo,* this bright spot in the characterless sprawl of North Boulder, its dining room bridged by a hacienda-style façade and dotted with artifacts—a painted bench here, an old stone fountain filled with candies there. Though the menu's dominated by Mexican staples—enchiladas, tostadas, *mariscos*—the name serves as a big fat clue to the kitchen's much-ballyhooed specialty: equally big, fat Salvadoran *pupusas.* More expensive than most, they're also larger—practically the size of small pizzas—and just that much better too: the dough smoother, springier, and oozing with *queso blanco* mixed with refried beans, *chicharrónes,* roasted chiles, chicken, or even fiddle-head ferns (you can also customize them with other meats, like carnitas and barbacoa). A splash of tomato sauce and a dollop of *curtido* (slaw) accompany them, but we like to throw in a side of *pacaya*—essentially a palm-flower fritter reminiscent of a fried zucchini blossom. Better still, unlike the majority of its ilk, this place has a full bar, slinging *micheladas,* guava-mango mojitos, and margaritas that come two-for-one during happy hour.

Radda Trattoria, 1265 Alpine Ave., Boulder, CO 80304; (303) 442-6100; www.raddatrattoria.com; Italian; $$. **Mateo**'s (p. 221) younger sibling does most things well; it does some things very, very well—and it does them in a clean, sophisticated space whose ochre hues cast a Tuscan glow, while shimmering white bricks frame the wood-fired oven in the open kitchen. Salads radiate refinement; the signature is our go-to, blending julienned endive with chopped hazelnuts and shaved *grana padano* in a sunny emulsion of truffle oil and lemon juice. Seasonal pastas, too, are handled with grace—the gnocchi satiny, the bolognese light and fresh without skimping on the veal, never mind the beef, pork, and lamb (whew!). And the just-so wine list brims with Italophilic finds. Though we'd give the edge to Mateo if we had to, we're really glad we don't.

Ras Kassa's Ethiopian Restaurant, 2111 30th St., Boulder, CO 80302; (303) 447-2919; www.raskassas.com; Ethiopian; $$. Thatched fringe and woven *mesobs*, bright yellow walls, and an enchanting back patio right on the bank of a burbling creek set a festive mood enhanced by welcoming service—but the jubilance that suffuses its unusual menu ultimately earns this Ethiopian spot a star on our map. The kitchen supplements standards like *tibs* and *doro wot* with delights we've not encountered elsewhere—trout pan-fried to a golden crisp, for one, and vegetarian stews incorporating beets, sweet potatoes, and butternut squash along with the more common split peas and lentils. Likewise, the wine selection is just that—no token pair of house pours but an array of bottles from

South Africa; even the requisite imported honey wine is rounded out by locally produced mead. It all adds up to a swirlingly heady experience.

Riffs Urban Fare, 1115 Pearl St., Boulder, CO 80304; (303) 440-6699; http://riffsboulder.com; Small Plates/Tapas; $$. Ciao, cappuccinos and Wi-Fi; hello, cocktails and human connections. What was once a bustling bookstore cafe is now a no-less-lively small-plates lounge decorated with eclectic conversation pieces—and flanked by a long banquette and bar that make for just the relaxing spots to discuss them; the super-friendly staff may even join in while slinging spirits from a Colorado-proud shelf (try anything made with liqueur from Dancing Pines or Leopold Bros.). Meanwhile, the tidbits streaming from the open kitchen run by **Q's Restaurant** (p. 246) Chef-Partner John Platt garner plenty of chatter in their own right for their juxtapositional flair, pairing sea scallops with corned beef hash or duck confit with a splash of maple syrup; whipped ham may not sound ethereal, but mortadella *spuma* does—and is, dusted with parmesan flakes and accompanied by crostini, balsamic-poached figs, and toasted pistachios. Seems whiling away an afternoon's as easy here as it ever was.

Rueben's Burger Bistro, 1800 Broadway, Boulder, CO 80302; (303) 443-5000; http://ruebensburgerbistro.com; Burgers; $$. The layout strikes us as a bit odd—open and bare but for a smattering of cycling memorabilia. And for no particular reason we can discern, the theme carries over to the menu via allusions to the pro-racing circuit. What we get at gut level, however, are the punch-packing burgers. The patties alone stand out: flagrantly pink inside and seasoned to release the juices that mingle with a good, honest touch of grease on the surface—all the more when they're stuffed with a little mozzarella and pancetta, as in our favorite combo, the Vuelta. The soft, shiny, flavorful pretzel bun supports a good 2-inch layer of toppings—in this case nuggets of deep-fried onion, thick pickle chips, fresh butter lettuce, and a schmear of ponzu aioli, but in others, toasted pumpkin seeds contrast with mashed avocado or bourbon-poached green apples with melted brie (there's also a monthly special, for instance a riff off Hawaiian pizza with ham, pineapple, and pepper jack). Meanwhile, design-your-own loaded mac-and-cheese is like trail mix for us nonathletes—and the deep Belgian beer list, supplemented by a few locals, needs no explanation either.

SALT the Bistro, 1047 Pearl St., Boulder, CO 80302; (303) 444-7258; http://saltthebistro.com; Contemporary; $$$. Though it pays homage to its former occupant, the Boulder institution that was Tom's Tavern, in decorative flourishes—the logo remains on the brick façade, the old tin ceilings are original, and the sculpture at the entrance glints with glass from the old windows—SALT is no hangover hut. The interior now possesses a business-day–to-date-night appeal via a stylish combination of mod and rustic elements that reflects acclaimed Chef-Owner Bradford Heap's farm-to-table flair (which he began developing at his Niwot flagship, **Colterra**, well before the trend went household). The smartly conceived menu revolves around produce from start to finish: lively, bountiful salads tumble with, say, cubes of roasted butternut squash, caramelized onions, sauteed wild mushrooms, goat-cheese crumbles, and toasted pumpkin seeds; a swoony vegetable tasting plate includes everything from black-quinoa fritters and Indian-spiced chickpeas and cauliflower to chowder sips; fruit desserts such as the oversize apple-cheddar crostata with buttermilk-caramel ice cream prove positively toothsome. (Then again, Heap's take on Tom's beloved burger is, we dare say, better than the original, accompanied by world's crispiest fries.) Topped off with the region's biggest selection of Colorado wines and a cool customized cocktail menu composed of mix-and-match ingredients, a meal at SALT is oh-so *au courant*.

Salvaggio's Deli, 2609 Pearl St., Boulder, CO 80302; (303) 938-1981; Sandwiches; $. Boar's Head cold cuts (capicola, mortadella, salami, and all) piled high on house-baked rolls are this straightforward sub-shop trio's bread and butter (so to speak). But at this branch alone, the crowning glory involves those gorgeous brown hunks of prime rib turning slowly on the countertop rotisserie (no wonder they showcase it in the window). It comes with your choice of cheese, veggie garnishes (pepperoncini are a must), and condiments, but you can trust that crust on the surface of the medium-rare meat—it doesn't need much enhancement beyond a schmear of horseradish mayo plus a drizzle of olive oil and vinegar. It does, however, require a few napkins. Additional locations: 1309 Pearl St., Boulder, CO 80302; (303) 545-6800; 1107 13th St., Boulder, CO 80302; (303) 448-1200.

Sushi Tora, 2014 10th St., Boulder, CO 80302; (303) 444-2280; http://sushitora.net; Japanese/Sushi; $$. Upon taking over this airy, streamlined, buff-and-bamboo downtowner from the original owners, Peter and Mara Soutiere were determined to prove that, in Mara's words, a sushi restaurant "can be non-Japanese run and still maintain [a commensurate] level of respect for the cuisine"—and so they have, importing fresh fish directly from markets around the globe and serving it with housemade soy sauce and root, not powdered, wasabi. That's not to say they're strict traditionalists; on the contrary, we've been mesmerized by specials like mysteriously delicate smoked hamachi sashimi—meticulously plated with strips of fried yucca, sliced Asian pea, and sprinklings of orange oil, golden raisins, and smelt roe—as well as by seashell-intricate mixed-mushroom and shiso-leaf tempura, garnished with a pleasantly bitter green-tea salt. Still, some of the most adventurous choices, at least by American standards, are categorically Japanese. Until you've tried it, don't knock downing the deep-fried head, shell and all, of an otherwise raw shrimp or biting into the flesh of an eel that not moments prior was wriggling in its skin right before your eyes. It may not be a pretty experience, but it's a poetic one, intensified by sips of cedar-aged sake.

Sushi Zanmai, 1221 Spruce St., Boulder, CO 80302; (303) 440-0733; www.sushizanmai.com; Japanese/Sushi; $$. As boisterous as its next-door sibling, **Izakaya Amu** (p. 216), is subdued—we did the macarena here once practically unnoticed, if that tells you anything—this old favorite is still rocking and maki-rolling. Amid turquoise ceramic roof tiles, red paper lanterns, masks, dragons, and vintage Japanese beer ads, you'll be treated to a sprawling menu that caters to sushi purists, mavericks, ambivalent newbies, pisciphobes, and vegetarians alike; for our part, we're tickled by the use of real crab, baby smelt, and pickled garlic, but as mileage varies the sushi and kitchen chefs fashion everything from the simplest nigiri to the Death Roll with grilled salmon skin and *shichimi togarashi* (aka "seven-flavor chili pepper"), from tempura and teriyaki to udon and rice bowls. After a quarter century in business, Zanmai can have the occasional off night, but it's still got more spunk than some restaurants 1/25th its age.

Tangerine, 2777 Iris Ave., Boulder, CO 80304; (303) 443-2333; http://tangerineboulder.com; American; $$. Adjacent to its sibling **Arugula** (p. 209), this peppy, poppy daytime spot puts every savvy spin on diner fare you could hope for and then some. Alec Schuler's crew doesn't just pour coffee, they pour a signature blend of organic coffee—French- or cold-pressed if you like. They don't just make Benedicts, they make Benedicts with nearly spherical poached eggs smartly topped with, say, hickory-smoked trout plus caramelized onions and apples or handsome crab cakes, which also pop up in a fennel-laced salad and a brioche sandwich under white cheddar.

Alongside buttermilk pancakes or their dense, earthy multigrain counterparts made with whole wheat, corn, and oats, they don't just offer pure maple syrup but also house pours infused with figs or blueberries. And the pastries change daily: think pumpkin-ginger scones and pear-almond muffins. We're not sure where the actual tangerines come in, but we'll keep returning to find out.

Tangier Moroccan Cuisine, 3070 28th St., Boulder, CO 80301; (303) 443-3676; www.tangiermoroccancuisine.com; Moroccan; $$. From the strip mall to the souk in seconds flat: such is the experience of entering this dim-lit, sumptuous den strewn with woven rugs and tapestries, embroidered cushions and ottomans around low tables. Memorably elaborate as an evening here can be amid multi-course feasts and, sometimes, belly dancers, we're not wholly sold on the rigmarole, so we'd just as soon stop by for a quiet à la carte lunch. In nearly 30 combinations, the tagines are usually solid, our picks being the tangy chicken *m'qualli* with preserved lemons and olives and lamb with apples and prunes or dried apricots.

Thai Avenue, 1310 College Ave., #220, Boulder, CO 80302; (303) 443-1737; www.thaiavenueboulder.com; Thai; $. In a town that should by rights be teeming with Thai joints catering to its mixed population of world travelers and college students, this is the unlikeliest of notables. Located in a food court on the Hill, it looks every bit the purveyor of greasy, sugary, interchangeable Americanized grub; in fact, it's more an ambassador of no less greasy but far more distinctive hawker-style comforts. So if the menu doesn't deviate from the norm in kind—curries, noodles, stir-fries, fried rice—it nonetheless delivers in its well-balanced execution. We're partial to the rice noodles with egg, though the eggplant with basil gets high marks; check for sometime specials as well.

Tiffin's, 2416 Arapahoe St., Boulder, CO 80302; (303) 442-2500; www.tiffinsrestaurant.com; Indian/Himalayan; $. In this stark white counter joint, decor is nil—but what your eyes can't discern, your nose will. The scent of pickling spices hangs like a curtain at the entrance; part the folds to discover an array of hearty vegetarian southern Indian street classics based on rice, lentils, and potatoes. Crêpes (*dosas*), savory fried and stuffed pastries (*samosas*), steamed rice cakes (*idli*), and the mélange of puffed rice and noodles known as *bhel puri* are fast becoming as common to Coloradans as curry and tandoori, but *vada pav* deserve equal attention: essentially sliders, they come as a pair of soft potato fritters on griddled sandwich buns with chopped red onions and sinus-clearing dollops of mint and tamarind chutney (ask owner Justin Patel about the spice mix he uses, and he'll gladly interrupt his cooking to proffer a spoonful of ground peanuts, sesame seeds, chilies, garlic, and cumin). On the sweet side, there's milk-shake-thick mango lassi and *shrikhund,* a Gujarati specialty of saffron-tinged, sweetened yogurt, as well as better-known *kheer* and syrup-submerged *gulab jamun*; might as well throw in an order or two with the rest, seeing as how you could literally ask for one of everything on the menu and still spend less than you would at Tiffin's full-service counterparts.

Walnut Cafe, 3073 Walnut St., Boulder, CO 80301; (303) 447-2315; www.walnutcafe.com; American; $. Like **Dot's** (p. 245) and **The Buff** (p. 243), this is the kind of casual, cheery neighborhood joint that might get taken for granted elsewhere—but in ever-more-exclusive Boulder, it stands the antidote to a preciousness that can sometimes feel suffocating. No micro this or heirloom that here—just the basics served up with an extra-special helping of funk: goofy flavored lattes, omelets and sammies, nutty waffles, and the sentimental fave that is pancake-battered French toast. Better still, owners Julia Buonanno and Dana Derichsweiler were serving up honestly gooey pies by the wedge well ahead of the retro curve—and at the South Side branch (673 S. Broadway, Boulder, CO 80305; 720-304-8118), they're setting a whole new trend with slices of birthday cake–cum–everyday treat. Additional location: 2770 Arapahoe Rd., Ste. 116, Lafayette, CO 80026; (720) 328-9208.

West End Tavern, 926 Pearl St., Boulder, CO 80302; (303) 444-3535; http://thewestendtavern.com; Bar & Grill; $$. Of all the ever-popular siblings in the Big Red F family, this one's the least concept-driven, the most content to fill the niche of the casual local hang—which is just what's it's done for a quarter of a century in a comfy, taproom–esque two-story space best known for its upstairs deck overlooking the Flatirons, strung with lights and warmed by heat lamps. Our rule of thumb is to stick with simple food and complex drinks—which is easy enough to do. Just look no further than the cheeseburger deluxe topped with grilled folds of pastrami that nearly double it in size (and, happily enough, sodium content) and the skin-on fries smothered in cheddar, sour cream, guacamole, bacon, and chives; if you're set on mixing it up, however, the barbecued ribs are surprisingly skillful (note the telltale smoke ring). Meanwhile, a serious collection of whiskies and a number of well-handled cocktails round out the centerpiece beer list; the West End serves, after all, as the headquarters of the seasonal Boulder Brew Bus tour—not that connoisseurs need budge from their barstools to hop onboard the rotation of craft drafts and dozens of limited-release bombers.

Zoe Ma Ma, 2010 10th St., Boulder, CO 80302; (303) 545-6262; www.zoemama.com; Chinese/Taiwanese; $. Upmarket downtown Boulder is the last place you'd expect to encounter homestyle dim sum and noodle bowls cooked by a real live Taiwanese mama. But in this cute-as-a-dumpling storefront, with celery-green walls and all of eight tables (plus an outdoor counter lined with cool wooden stools), that's exactly what you'll find. Made with organic flour, the *bao* stuffed with marinated, simmered diced pork are slightly denser and more richly textured than most. Huge, fork-tender chunks of stewed chicken and potato over rice and the weekly special that is wonton noodle soup with roast duck have all the steamy, evocative vigor of Proust's madeleine. And we're equally fond of the sticky rice cakes whose understated sweetness derives primarily from the raisins and goji berries they're studded with, plus just a pinch of brown sugar. It's all tummy-patting (and, okay, -padding) stuff.

Zolo Grill, 2525 Arapahoe Ave., Boulder, CO 80302; (303) 449-0444; www.zologrill.com; Southwestern; $$. Back when it opened in the mid-1990s, this shopping-center fixture was quite the oasis in a foodie desert—somewhat ironically, since the actual desert was the source of its inspiration. Now Boulder's one of the hottest dining destinations in the nation, while Zolo's hardly changed a whit—and that, in our book, is a good thing. It still rocks a look that's no less urbane for being as colorful as a kachina doll collection; more important, the food's as good as ever, sharing with its Big Red F sibling **Lola Coastal Mexican** (p. 39) a knack for big flavors in bold combinations that here recall the heyday of Santa Fe–style cookery without sentimentalizing it. Encrusted in blue cornmeal, topped with buttered crabmeat, and accompanied by a mushroom tamale, fried catfish proves at once funky and elegant, for instance, while red chile–braised, shredded pork shoulder over a jack cheese biscuit with sweet potato fries and greens puts the "South" in "Southwestern." Zolo also joins Lola in maintaining a goodly collection of tequilas, which are showcased in margaritas free of cloying frippery.

Boulder Dushanbe Teahouse, 1770 13th St., Boulder, CO 80302; (303) 442-4993; www.boulderteahouse.com; Middle Eastern; $$. Dushanbe is the capital of Tajikstan, Boulder's sister city—and, apparently, the giver of the world's most lavish gifts. Commissioned by its mayor in 1987, this *choyhona*, or teahouse, finally opened to the public in 1998—and it's been dropping jaws and setting hearts aflutter ever since. To say it's one of the most beautiful places you'll ever set foot in is no exaggeration; indeed, it's essentially a Persian cultural museum devoted to the one-of-a-kind handiwork of Tajik craftsmen—elaborate ceramic tiles, carved cedarwood columns, kaleidoscopic ceiling panels, copper sculptures, and woven rugs and pillows all come together to create a magical realm in turquoise and rose, jade and ochre. In any other setting, the selection of nearly 150 teas might impress; the eclectic, competently executed bill of Persian, Himalayan, American, and other breakfast, lunch, and dinner fare would warrant more than a passing mention. But here, what you drink and eat barely matters—the atmosphere provides rejuvenation enough.

The Buff Restaurant, 1725 28th St., Boulder, CO 80302; (303) 442-9150; www.buffrestaurant.com; American; $. Flip sides of the same coin largely define American cuisine in Boulder: the hippy-dippy health food of yore and its trendy ethicurean counterpart. In between, there's little room, even on the Hill, for the sort of strapping chow that puts the twinkle back in the bloodshot eyes of students in college towns everywhere. In one incarnation or another, The Buff has filled that niche for decades—and netted legions of loyalists in the process. On Sunday mornings in particular, you'll spy knots of them huddled around the motel parking lot in which this homey, clattering three-room diner is situated, waiting for their turn to tuck in to the famous saddlebags—fried egg–topped pancakes whose batter contains your choice of crumbled breakfast meat; Western-style skillet-fried potatoes with all the trimmings; or the over-the-top caramel-pecan quesadilla. Such hangover helpers have assistants of their own, of course, in the form of bargain Bloodies and mimosas ($1 apiece with an entree) and coffee drinks topped with foam art; judging by the happy chatter of the gathering hordes, they do their job well.

Chautauqua Dining Hall, 900 Baseline Rd., Boulder, CO 80302; (303) 442-3282; http://chautauqua.com; American; $$$. One word: panorama. Make it two: veranda. You can make out every crag of the Flatirons from the porch of this turn-of-the-century land-mark; for that reason alone, it's well worth a visit. That it operates on a seasonal schedule, serving dinner only in the warm months, is no matter; given the caliber of Boulder's current dining scene, you can frankly do better come evening in any case. But when the sun's shining on those blue-violet peaks, there's no reason a simple omelet or old-fashioned club sandwich served al fresco can't hit the spot.

Dot's Diner, 1333 Broadway, Boulder, CO 80302; (303) 447-9184; American; $. Return to the Boulder of old, when hippies outnumbered the hipsters and yuppies, through the door of this endearingly dingy, creaky, scuffmarked greasy spoon on the Hill. Along the counter in front, regulars chat up the dreadlocked line cooks while digging into oatcakes; couples linger over omelets and organic coffee at the handful of tables in back. The short-order grub's mostly functional, a sort of edible alarm clock—eggy, toasty, smothered in cheese or gravy. But the peppery home fries shine with the patina of a well-used griddle—and the knobby, crumbly buttermilk biscuits satisfy to the core. Additional location: 2716 28th St., Boulder, CO 80301; (303) 449-1323.

Flagstaff House, 1138 Flagstaff Rd., Boulder, CO 80302; (303) 442-4640; Contemporary; $$$. The views through the floor-to-ceiling windows of this historic property nestled in the foothills (or for that matter from its almost vertiginous terrace) will take your breath away. So will service that's as fluid as it is kid-glove from the moment you take your seat in the peak-roofed dining room, tastefully done in hues that blend with the scenery. Naturally, your inner cynic will grumble, the setup is too good to be true; this must be a surf-and-turf tourist trap—until a peek at the menu silences all skepticism. The daily-tweaked repertoire is as rarified as the mountain air in some ways, intimately earthy in others, yoking wild mushrooms, bitter greens, and humble roots to delicate shellfish, rich fowl, and royal chops with bravura. And when you glimpse that iPad wine list, you'll wonder if the whole mountainside wasn't excavated to house Flagstaff's cellar. So sit back, suspend all disbelief, and surrender to the pampered life for a spell.

Lucile's Creole Cafe, 2124 14th St., Boulder, CO 80302; (303) 442-4743; Cajun/Creole; $. The local institution that is this Louisianalicious Cajun-Creole franchise started right here way back in 1980. Though the south Denver branch (p. 197) boasts a larger lunch menu (and a license to pour great Bloodies), the flagship has history on its side, housed in a sweet yellow cottage just off the mall whose quaint rooms get packed to the rafters daily—just as they have for decades—with diners craving chicory coffee and the famous beignets dusted with powdered sugar, followed by pan-fried trout with grits, fried-eggplant Benedicts, and the like. The close quarters—and even the invariable wait to enter them—only contribute to the sense of community that makes a meal at Lucile's such a foolproof way to start a day in Boulder. Additional location: 2852 W. Bowles Ave., Littleton, CO 80120; (303) 797-1190.

Q's Restaurant, 2115 13th St., Boulder, CO 80302; (303) 442-4880; www.qsboulder.com; Contemporary; $$$. Located just off the grand lobby of the Hotel Boulderado, this long-established destination incorporates elements of its historic surroundings—columns, decorative moldings, stained-glass panels—into a genteel setting that nonetheless shows flashes of modernity in hammered copper and curving lines. Following suit, Chef John Platt builds seasonal, contemporary layers on a foundation of elegance. Breakfast, brunch, and lunch juxtapose the homey—batter-fried apple slices drenched in crème anglaise and the signature clam chowder accompanied by dill-flecked drop biscuits, say—with sophisticated creations like grilled asparagus over pan-fried polenta with bits of prosciutto and gorgonzola in wild-mushroom vinaigrette or seared crab cakes kicked up with salsa verde and hearts of palm. Dinner's an even more polished affair: think seared scal-lops perfumed with vanilla and grapefruit alongside parsnip frites or juniper-scented roast buffalo loin over chanterelle risotto, fol-lowed by a scrumptious pear-Camembert galette with rosemary honey. But at the Corner Bar across the lobby—a classy little haunt with mezzanine seating and sunlight streaming through two-story windows—the tireless Platt also offers well-thought-out snacks like cauliflower gratin and shrimp arancini. The wine list isn't huge, but it certainly fills the bill.

The Sink, 1165 13th St., Boulder, CO 80302; (303) 444-7465; www.thesink.com; Bar & Grill; $$. Every college town worth its pennant has one—that crusty old watering hole where generations of students have marked countless rites of passage. We'd say "if only walls could talk," but we don't have to—like the low ceil-ings, they're entirely covered with murals and graffiti, while the tables are laminated with news clippings; the story of this joint, established in 1923, unfolds in every nook and cranny. These days, the industrial lagers have largely been replaced by craft brews, but not much else has changed in decades: the kitchen's been flip-ping its legendary burgers since 1955, while the Colorado-style pizza pies—yes, there is such a thing—are a must for their thick whole-wheat "ugly crusts" memorably served with squeeze bottles of honey for dripping and dipping. You don't even have to like the place to love the place, if you catch our drift.

Specialty Stores, Markets & Producers

Boulder Wine Merchant, 2690 Broadway, Boulder, CO 80304; (303) 443-6761; www.boulderwine.com. With every bottle of wine you purchase here, you get a free gift—that of commanding knowledge. Owner Brett Zimmerman is a master sommelier, and his shop reflects his emphasis on education. In one corner, a reading table flanked by a small browsing library also serves as the sideboard for regular in-store tastings guest-hosted by winemakers and brewmasters from around the world; day to day, Zimmerman's staff ably works the floor, suggestions at the ready. We're especially impressed by the Austrian and Northern Italian finds here, as well as by the local representation and, less obviously, a fine array of craft bitters—but we'd be remiss to neglect the selection of well over 100 vintages from Burgundy.

Boxcar Coffee Roasters, 1825B Pearl St., Boulder, CO 80302; (303) 527-1300; http://boxcarcoffeeroasters.com. With a retail counter up front and a space in back for planned brewing and tasting classes, Vajra Rich enthuses, he and his wife, Cara, finally "have a place where people can come talk to us rather than just reading a bag." (They happen to share it with **Cured**; see next listing.) Enlightening as he is on the subject of coffee, you'd do well to take him up on his offer. He'll hold forth on his "highly coveted" antique German roaster, whose cast-iron construction "really holds the heat," a "big deal" for "fussy" beans—"and it looks like a cool old-school steam train." He'll explain how he rigged his "cult classic" La Marzocco espresso machine with the help of a Seattle designer to yield a higher-capacity, "one-of-a-kind hybrid." And of course he'll delve into the importance of seasonal roasts: "We don't have, say, Guatemalan coffee year-round because there's one annual harvest. Coffee sparkles when it's fresh, but it can really fade, especially at this altitude." Rich is, in short, an engaging, energetic (not to say caffeinated) spokesman for the perfect cup—which is exactly what he pours, be it a single-origin Sumatran or a signature blend.

Cured, 1825B Pearl St., Boulder, CO 80304; (720) 389-8096; www.curedboulder.com. Not just cured but curated: Will Frischkorn and Coral Ferguson's sunny, scrupulously maintained market is a truly special find. At the entrance, a display of pantry products sourced from near and far yields stunning discoveries—elegant fruit vinegars, funky pickles, exotic seasonings; alongside it stands a table laden with local breads and produce—"whatever the farmers have that they think is best that day," explains Frischkorn. In back, the

COLORADO MADE

Some, like IZZE Beverage Company and Fiona's Granola, have gone national (or at least regional); others are strictly local. Either way, indie food producers abound in Colorado, a DIY paradise if ever there was one. The following constitute a notable sample; for details on availability, visit their websites and Twitter feeds, as well as the specialty shops listed in each chapter.

Bhakti Chai, *(303) 484-8770; www.bhaktichai.com; Twitter: @ BhaktiChai.* Organic, fair trade and spiced, according to Ayurvedic principles, with ginger, cardamom, clove, fennel, and black pepper— if this isn't India, it must be Boulder. (Try the coffee-splashed variety for an extra kick.)

Denver Pretzel Co.; *(970) 481-0548; www.denverpretzelcompany .com; Twitter: @DenverPretzelCo.* That they're big, soft, and chewy goes without saying; that they're studded with everything from candied bacon and jalapeños to pumpkin seeds and chocolate sprinkles warrants exclamation points. Cart in tow, the owner pops up regularly at **Renegade Brewing Company** (p. 300).

Helliemae's Salt Caramels, *(303) 834-7048; www.saltcaramels.com; Twitter: @helliemaes.* The effervescent Ellen Daehnick makes her sea-salted block caramels the old-fashioned way—which means they're "just shy of scorched," in her words, giving them a more nuanced flavor to complement their compelling texture: not too rigid, not too yielding. Seasonal flavors like jasmine tea and green apple supplement the year-rounders (plain, coffee, and, our favorite, cardamom).

MM Local, *(720) 235-8346; http://mmlocalfoods.com; Twitter: @ mmlocal.* Area farms supply the produce for the juice-packed fruits, sauces, and pickles that just about burst from their beautiful jars with intensely pure flavor.

MouCo Cheese Company, *(970) 498-0107; www.mouco.com; Twitter: @moucocheese.* This Fort Collins–based cheesemaker's red-smear ColoRouge and Camembert, known for their pristine, practically deliquescent pastes, are near-ubiquitous on cheese platters around town.

Noosa, *(970) 493-0949; www.noosayoghurt.com; Twitter: @Noosa Yoghurt.* With the mouthfeel of pudding, this honey-sweetened, fruit-swirled yogurt made by Aussie expats has in no time built a bona fide cult following—among them many a chef who proudly lists the brand on their menus.

Polidori Sausage, *(303) 455-5701; http://polidorisausage.com; Twitter: @PolidoriSausage.* However trendy, it's the rare housemade salumi that stacks up to the Italian sausages this North Denver old-timer's been churning out since 1925; no wonder half the pizzerias in town use it.

34°, *(303) 861-4818; http://34-degrees.com; Twitter: @34Degrees.* As a complement to most cheeses, dry, dull water crackers pale in comparison to these ultra-thin, lacy-edged, subtly flavored "crispbreads."

focus is on handmade cheeses and charcuterie from domestic artisans like Washington's Kurtwood Farms, Vermont's Consider Bardwell Farm, and Denver's own **Fruition Farm**—there's even wild salmon caught and smoked by a Boulderite who spends his summers in Alaska—plus accoutrements like cultured butter, duck fat, goat's milk fudge, and condiments from the kitchen of nearby **Frasca Food and Wine** (p. 215). Behind that, off a small hallway, a boutique collection of some 85 wines—"everyday bottles we pick to go with what's up front," Frischkorn says—is supplemented by an all-Colorado lineup of craft spirits and microbrews from such up-and-comers as Crooked Stave and Crystal Springs. Finally, Frischkorn and Ferguson share their space with the equally uncompromising **Boxcar Coffee Roasters** (p. 248) and run it with the help of a staff as eager to serve as they are.

Glacier Homemade Ice Cream & Gelato, 3133 28th St., Boulder, CO 80301; (303) 440-6542; www.glaciericecream.com. A whopping 70 to 80 flavors—from a portfolio of hundreds—rotate constantly at Mark Mallen's flagship jackpot, splashed with the very hues of the ice cream (and gelato, and sorbet, and frozen yogurt) it serves. Novelties like brightly sprinkled birthday cake, root-beer float, and chunky Rice Krispie treat round out customer favorites such as chocolate mousse and intense Colorado peach (for which Mallen uses up to 2,000 pounds of fruit a year); as long as there are scoops of our own top pick, moon pie, to be had, we'll never grow up. Additional locations: 4760 Baseline Rd., Boulder, CO 80303; (303) 499-4760;

1387 S. Boulder Rd., Louisville, CO 80027; (720) 890-5992; 421D W. 104th St., Northglenn, CO 80234; (303) 452-6560.

Kim & Jake's Cakes, 641 S. Broadway, Boulder, CO 80305; (303) 499-9126; www.kimandjakescakes.com. "I'm from New Orleans, and we drink a lot," laughs Kim Rosenbarger, "and [husband-partner] Jake is a certified sommelier." That goes some way toward explaining their penchant for booze, but it doesn't begin to capture the whimsy and polish of their creations. For that you'll have to see (and taste) cakes like the Strawberry Margarita with lemon-lime icing or the cream cheese–frosted Vino Rosso, made with your choice of red wine—we'd suggest something Spanish to complement the curls of, get this, aged Manchego on top; the Rosenbargers also have a way with spices, blending curry and black sesame seeds, paprika and smoked salt with caramel and chocolate to complex effect. Working out of a tiny space containing all of one table, they don't run a full-service operation here—no coffee, no breakfast pastries or sandwiches—but they nonetheless welcome the everyday walk-in with open arms in the form of daily-changing cupcakes, citrus-avocado bars, "picnic cakes"—oversize whoopie pies in flavors like chocolate stout with malted-milk buttercream—and, on Friday, gluten-free goodies. Isn't that sweet, even when it's also savory? See Kim Rosenbarger's recipe for **Nut Brown Ale Cake with Caramel Icing** on p. 336.

Ku Cha, 1141 Pearl St., Boulder, CO 80302; (303) 443-3612; www .kuchatea.com. Though the name translates as "bitter tea," rest assured owner Qin Liu is no austere herbalist; on the contrary, his store forms a shelter for the senses in the midst of overstimulating Pearl Street Mall. Sunbeams and flute music fill the air, posh rugs deck the wood floors, and the shelves bear artful arrangements of more than 140 teas from the world over, with sample tins for sniffing your way to enlightenment. A small tray of mochi, cookies, and other sweets gleams at the brewing and purchase counter; in back, a section reserved for museum-worthy teaware leads to a tasting and seminar room. Fermented teas are a passion of Liu's for their digestive benefits; given the gastronomic bonanza awaiting just beyond his doors, it might behoove you to give one a test run.

Liquor Mart, 1750 15th St., Boulder, CO 80302; (303) 449-3374; www.liquormart.com. May as well wonder what the oldest and largest liquor store in Boulder by far doesn't carry as ask what it does. The answer is just about everything, what with some 13,000 products in stock. Ever heard of Bolivian coca-leaf liqueur or Alaska Distillery's smoked-salmon vodka? You have now. The wine department devotes half an aisle to organic, biodynamic, and otherwise sustainably produced wines alone. And as for beers, you name it, they carry it, from Russian porters to Norwegian live ales—not to mention some off-the-shelf limited releases into which regulars know to inquire; feel free to mix and match your own six-packs while you're at it. Barware, party supplies, and even some home-brewing helpers on the cheap make this a one-stop shop to top them all.

Piece, Love and Chocolate, 805 Pearl St., Boulder, CO 80302; (303) 449-4804; www.pieceloveandchocolate.com. This isn't just a shop, it's a slice of the sweet life. Owner Sarah Amorese wants her customers to not only enjoy chocolate but also explore it; to that end, she's created a space that celebrates its origins and showcases its many facets at every turn. Or, rather, two spaces: a back room for baking and tasting classes as well as the main floor, where dangling palm fronds and Brazilian beats evoke the equatorial Cocoa Belt and a bevy of tables, hutches, and display units stand, yes, chock-full of chocolate in every conceivable form. Imported and gift-packaged bars, nibs, powders, pastes, sauces, caramels, marshmallows, and pretzels are the least of it; the centerpiece is the long counter in which row upon row of truffles and cordials resemble jewels—some, indeed, are literally cut like gems, shimmering with edible gold paint. They're not all housemade—"The whole concept," Amorese says, "was to be kind of a co-op for local companies"—but they are all inspired, incorporating everything from savory herbs to craft beer. The gorgeous cakes, pies, and tortes, meanwhile, are wholly hers; the brownie-crusted white-chocolate cheesecake is as tangy and luscious as could be.

Rush, 1207 13th St., Boulder, CO 80302; (303) 546-9666; http://rushbowls.com. If this shop on the Hill—packed as tightly and colorfully as its to-go containers, sold in Whole Foods throughout the West—isn't on the fast track to retail franchisedom (despite owner Andrew Pudalov's current claims to the contrary), we'll eat our words. So long as they're blended into one of its signature concoctions, we won't really mind. First and foremost are the blended-fruit bowls in 16 more-or-less healthful combinations, all topped with granola and honey. On the svelter side, there's the yoga bowl with fat-free frozen yogurt, tropical fruit, and green tea; on the more decadent, the chocolate-covered strawberry combines strawberries and bananas with chocolate and frozen yogurt under a hard chocolate shell; and in between, ingredients range from açaí berries, peaches, and guava to almonds, coconut milk, and graham crackers. Double as many smoothies are basically taller, juicier bowls—with the occasional addition of vitamin supplements for an extra, yes, rush. Additional location: 4593 N. Broadway, Boulder, CO 80304; (303) 442-7874.

Spruce Confections, 767 Pearl St., Boulder, CO 80302; (303) 449-6773; www.spruceconfections.com. This toasty little joint at the far end of the mall set the bar for indie coffeehouse-style bakeries in Boulder years ago—and though the block's now jammed with newer kids, Spruce, true to its name, feels as fresh as ever. For that we credit owner David Cohen's slightly offbeat approach to the goods, paradoxically so old-fashioned it's new again. Fruit-layered scones have an unusually delicate crumb; so-called ugly muffins delight made with croissant dough scraps; trendy cupcakes give way to quaint mini-cakes, flat-topped and frosted as finely as their full-size counterparts (the golden almond with raspberry buttercream appears straight out of the pages of a 1950s women's magazine). And wholesome curios like hand-rolled rugelach, shortbreads the size of soap cakes, and agave-sweetened, walnut-studded millet bars abound. There's a small case packed with salads and sandwiches, too, but for lunch we'd just as soon hit up Spruce's sister shop, **Two Spoons** (p. 258), a few blocks away. Additional location: 4684 Broadway, Boulder, CO 80304; (303) 449-5819.

Tee & Cakes, 1932 14th St., Boulder, CO 80302; (720) 406-7548; www.teeandcakes.com. "Tee" as in shirt, "cakes" as in cup: Jointly owned by a baker and a graphic designer, this wee spot squeezes an eclectic assortment of apparel and hand-printed cards in with a display case whose daily selection of pastries and dainties is pretty well picked over by mid-afternoon. So come quick for the full range of goodies: not just specialty cupcakes in fun flavors like strawberry milk shake, gingerbread stout with cream cheese icing, and the

much-touted bacon-sprinkled chocolate but also whoopie pies, cake pops, and brownies—including our top pick, the dense, buttery toffee blondie with lots of chopped walnuts and just a whiff of espresso.

Two Spoons, 1021 Pearl St., Boulder, CO 80302; (303) 545-0027; www.twospoonsboulder.com. One for the soup, one for the gelato. The name of this sweet little nook reflects its whole-hearted devotion to the former in fall and winter, the latter in spring and summer (though both are served year-round, each has its seasons in the sun—or snow, as the case may be). In warm weather, the counter's stocked with more than 20 flavors of intensely pure hand-crafted gelato, including chocolate-banana, pistachio-lime, and pineapple-ginger; when the chill sets in, some eight soups dispel it like a charm. As appealing as the rotating options are—white bean–buffalo chili, Ethiopian spiced lentil, and chicken soup with pristine-white, velvety matzoh balls, for instance, all served in ceramic mugs for in-store patrons—it's the nifty array of toppings we can't resist: tamari-glazed walnuts, sunflower seeds, oyster crackers, grated cheddar, and more. An even bigger bonus, meanwhile, requires a third spoon: from December through February, the strikingly polite counter crew dishes up four organic hot cereals—oats, rice, corn, and cracked wheat—that, like everything else here, exude a disarming wholesomeness.

Suburbs

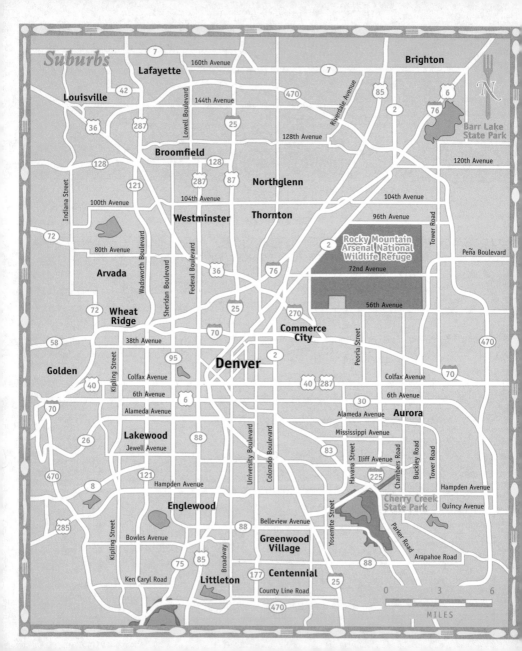

The Best of the 'Burbs

Here as elsewhere, strip malls and chain outlets define the sprawling suburbs of Denver and Boulder. But here as elsewhere, there's gold to be found in them there hills (okay, in the shadow of the Rockies). To the east, Aurora's particularly rich in holed-up gems of all ethnic bents; to the west, pickings are farther and fewer between—and all the sweeter for that. Still, better let your GPS rather than your instincts be your guide (see: sprawling).

Foodie Faves

African Grill & Bar, 1010 S. Peoria St., Aurora, CO 80012; (720) 949-0784; http://afrikangrill.com; Ghanian; $$. Next door to **Thai Flavor** (p. 278) is a whole other world of flavor—whose outgoing owners make for excellent tour guides thereto. Adwoa Ford-Wuo will not only walk you through the menu but also explain how this or that dish is eaten in Nigeria or Senegal as well as in her native Ghana; it's a fascinating primer for a hearty meal. Festive, nutty *jollof* rice is an obvious place to start, but fried plantains with beans or peanuts—*red red* and *kelewele,* respectively—come in a close second. Spheres of *fufu,* the staple starch paste, balance the salt-licked vigor of tomato-based "peanut butter soup," while a side of meat pie really sweetens the pot, its crumbly, buttery crust spilling forth perfectly spiced ground beef. Although the going can be slow, shooting the leisurely breeze over some cheap booze in the ultra-casual yet comfy, artifact-adorned dining room is half the fun.

Ali Baba Grill, 109 N. Rubey Dr., Unit F, Golden, CO 80403; (303) 279-2228; www.alibabagrill.com; Middle Eastern; $$. While the flagship of this Lebanese-Persian hybrid is stunningly bedecked—elaborate panels, draped fabrics, metalwork lanterns—its outpost to the south (5380 S. Greenwood Plaza Blvd., #110J, Greenwood Village, 80111; 303-779-0026) doesn't exactly pale by comparison, bathed in the light of a crystal chandelier that glances off golden walls. And excepting storebought pita, both kitchens rise to the pretty occasion of their settings. In lieu of the usual hummus, try *muhamara*, a grainy, red-brown dip of ground walnuts, bulgur, and red peppers; it's top-notch, tart up front and earthy on the finish. Likewise, although we prefer the gyros at **Athenian Restaurant** (see next listing), Ali Baba's almost braid-shaped lamb-based kafta kabobs are as juicy and judiciously seasoned as they come.

Athenian Restaurant, 15350 E. Iliff Rd., Aurora, CO 80013; (303) 578-6011; www.atheniangreekrestaurantco.com; Greek; $$. We guess the parking lot of an Aurora strip mall is as likely a place as any to encounter such a charmer. Diner by morning, taverna by afternoon, this Greek go-to is delightfully appointed—every nook and cranny from the enclosed, fountain-graced patio to the spacious, sunny dining rooms marked by columns, sculptures, mosaics, friezes, urns, and all the other things you read about in Classical Art and Architecture 101. And the exuberance of the decor mirrors that of the staff; the servers will hail you like dear friends, while Tom Stathopoulos, the apron-clad owner, may emerge from the kitchen to greet you—when, that is, he and his crew aren't cooking up a storm of old favorites: moussaka, spanakopita, you name it. The thick, cucumber-laced tzatziki alone is worth the price of admission (not that that's high), and it complements just about everything: oil-cured dolmades oozing with creamy rice, two-bite *tiropitas* (cheese-stuffed phyllo triangles), lightly breaded and fried calamari tubes. But the meats are the show-stoppers, tender and perfectly seasoned across the board: fat meatballs, glistening lamb-and-beef gyros, herb-flecked cubes of chicken and pork souvlaki. The baklava's homemade too; huge portions, however, may call for a shot of digestion-easing ouzo instead.

Azitra, 535 Zang St., Ste. C, Broomfield, CO 80021; (303) 465-4444; www.azitra.us; Indian; $$. Indian restaurants in greater Denver are, for the most part, interchangeable—bland of decor, limited of palate. Joining **Jai Ho** (p. 271) is this Broomfield exception to the rule, which announces its urbanity with a warm-lit, cleanly colorful, lounge-like space and, of all unexpected things, a sizeable and serious wine list (think Sicilian Grillo and Spanish Montrasell). The menu, too, bespeaks modern elegance, taking a chefly rather than home-cooked approach to regional dishes through the use of mussels, crab, and goat as well as carefully customized rather than one-size-fits-all spicing. So while tikka masala is here for the asking, why make the trek from D-town unless it's for the sake of adventure amid lesser-known dishes like highly aromatic but richly coconutty seafood *kerala* curry or *gobhi* Manchurian (cauliflower fritters in a tangy sauce)?

Bender's Brat Haus, 700 S. Buckley Rd., Aurora, CO 80017; (303) 872-3569; Deli; $. Sprouting from a bare patch of suburban pavement, this strip-mall sausage vendor sure doesn't gild the lily: the digs are sub-shop basic, unless you count the collection of college pennants lining one wall. But said lily is a beaut: the juice-squirting house brat on a bun barely needs a squiggle of mustard, especially when you factor in a side of warm, sweet-and-sour potato salad. So-called kraut burgers—beef-and-cabbage-stuffed buns better known in the Midwest as bierocks—are fluffy handfuls o' fun too.

Cafe Jordano, 11068 W. Jewell Ave., Lakewood, CO 80227; (303) 988-6863; http://cafejordano.com; Italian; $$. Lakewood's locals love this comfy, family-oriented red- (and white-) sauce joint beyond all measure. But even if we can't gauge it, we get it—home-style cooking soothes the weary soul, especially when drenched in cream or smothered in cheese (or both) and paired with rustic red wines. Look for the dishes justifiably labeled "favorites," including *pollo alla Roberts* and *pollo alla Gregorio*; on the slightly lighter side, there's *bucatini colorati* tossed with white beans, broccoli, and feta as well as a selection of classics—cacciatore, parmigiana, and so on—updated with buffalo loin. Of course they all come with trimmings: soup or salad, garlic bread, spaghetti on the side. When we say this place is all but critic-proof, we say it with affection.

Chef Liu's Authentic Chinese Cuisine, 562 S. Chambers Rd., Aurora, CO 80017; (303) 369-2220; Chinese/Taiwanese; $$. As upscale as it gets for a strip mall in Aurora, sedate in hues of forest and berry, and staffed by a reservedly polite crew, this white-cloth Sichuan specialist promises a tranquil evening out. And then, just when you've let your guard down over quiet conversation and a stemless glass of inexpensive wine, the kitchen sets off the fire alarm. Pearly and firm yet truly melting in your mouth, chunked fish fillet stir-fried in smoky "numbing chili oil" flecked with bean sprouts, scallions, and cilantro leaves is masterful but not that spicy—until, suddenly, it is, making you cough and sneeze and giggle all at the same time. The chili sauce accompanying the dim sum–style eggplant, shrimp-stuffed and deep-fried, likewise registers on the Scoville scale in a sudden. If you're blasted sufficiently awake to notice the Chinese-language menu, rest assured it's rife with all the offal you could ask for; ask away, because the more requests they get for something other than sesame chicken, the more likely they are to bring back nixed rarities like the chestnuts braised with cabbage.

China Jade, 12203 E. Iliff Ave. #D, Aurora, CO 80014; (303) 755-8518; Chinese/Taiwanese; $$. Blunt praise for a bare-bones place: this strip-mall Sichuan kitchen is the real deal. Though we favor the wontons at **Tao Tao Noodle Bar** (p. 277), the rest of the menu shines (and sometimes burns): marshal a crew to chow down family-style on the classic likes of electrifying dry-fried green beans that pop with minced chilies and pork; plush speared eggplant (and more pork) in velvety garlic sauce; soft cubes of ma po tofu illuminated by the reddish glow of their musky, fiery cooking medium; and comparatively subtle, stir-fried cumin (here called "ziran-flavored") lamb. That's what we do, anyway—but judging by the steady stream of pork-shoulder casseroles borne by the servers to surrounding tables, you might be just as well advised to do as the Joneses (by any other name) do instead.

Cracovia Restaurant and Bar, 8121 W. 94th Ave., Westminster, CO 80021; (303) 484-9388; www.cracoviarestaurant.com; Polish; $$. The story of how Lester Rodzen made his way from Communist-era Poland to run this handsome suburban go-to with wife Maria is the stuff of political thrillers. The food he serves, by contrast, amounts to pure comfort—dumplings, cabbage rolls, potato pancakes, and the like are all near and dear to regulars' hearts. But even those items that fall outside the comfort zone of most Americans prove easy to embrace. Topped with browned onions, the loose-grained, barley-speckled *kiszka*, or blood sausage, is wonderfully nutty and almost spoonably soft; firmer and saltier white kielbasa pairs to a T with honeyed housemade mustard. To cut through the lulling warmth of it all, meanwhile, there's soupy, caraway-laced sauerkraut and *zupa ogórkowa*, a light-textured potato soup speckled with bits of pickle. But if you're determined to leave here with your own wild tale to tell, call ahead to order the *golonka flambé*, a platter of roasted pork knuckles on the bone best served with copious vodka for you and a few gung-ho cohorts to knock down over the course of a memorable (or hazy, depending on your tolerance) evening.

Damascus Grill, 1339 W. Littleton Blvd., Littleton, CO 80120; (303) 797-6666; www.damascusgrill.com; Middle Eastern; $$. The turquoise façade cheers; the pink walls and beaded lanterns cast a warm glow about the small, casual dining room. And the food at this Syrian-owned Littleton staple has a similarly heartening effect. Hooray for housemade pita, boasting a papery, lavash-like texture to complement hummus with the consistency of whipped cream; both come with our favorite dish, *munazala*—a trio of silken, skin-less baby eggplants stuffed and roasted with browned ground lamb and onions. For an occasional switcheroo, though, we go for broiled trout or the lamb-and-okra stew brightened with pomegranate and cilantro. In any circumstance, a pot of sweet mint tea and a palate-cleansing dish of rose-water pudding soothe to the last.

Dolce Sicilia Italian Bakery, 3210 N. Wadsworth Blvd., Wheat Ridge, CO 80033; (303) 233-3755; www.sicilianbakeryco.com; Bakery/Cafe; $. Franco Spatola does his family, who hails from Marsala, proud at this sunny little strip-mall spot, which he runs *con molto gusto*. Adhering to Moorish-influenced Sicilian tradition, he offers tray after tray of delightful cookies and pastries flavored with dried, candied fruits and nuts, but he borrows the specialties of other regions as well. We're powerless to resist most of them, frankly, including the lacy, chocolate-dipped Florentines; the rainbow "cookies" (actually mini-slices of cake) so popular with the East Coast transplants who frequent the bakery, according to Spatola; the cannoli and Neapolitan *sfogliatelle;* and above all the simple, crunchy, almond-based Venetian amaretti. Yet they're not even what get us in the door; that honor goes to the huge yet delicately encased spinach calzones and square-cut slices of classic pan pizza (our pick's the Mediterranean with feta, artichoke hearts, and olives).

The Empire Lounge & Restaurant, 816 Main St., Louisville, CO 80027; (303) 665-2521; http://theempirerestaurant.com; Contemporary; $$. It's nothing we can put our fingers on, but we feel as though we're walking into a bowling alley every time we set foot in The Empire. Maybe it's the retro neon signage against a small-town backdrop, maybe it's the long, narrow space with its shiny wood floors—or maybe it's the fact that ordering off

Chef-Partner Jim Cohen's approachable yet interesting menu is invariably like rolling a strike. Odd on paper, a signature salad of frisée and radicchio with fried calamari rings and miso-balsamic vinaigrette is a 10 in the mouth, complex of both flavor and texture. And speaking of salads, we'd order the pulled-pork slider for the hot-and-cold jalapeño-pecan slaw alone. Cohen known his way around a crucifer too, so keep your eyes peeled for cauliflower and brussels sprouts amid bistro-style steak cuts and trattoria-worthy risotto. Finally, the fittingly edited list of cocktails and wines by the glass is as flirty as the good-natured crowd at the bar in back. In a word, score.

Guadalajara Authentic Mexican Buffet, 11385 E. Colfax Ave., Aurora, CO 80010; (303) 344-3862; www.mexbuffet.com; Mexican; $$. Sound the mental trumpets: to step into this fluorescent, mariachi-blasting Colfax cafeteria is to feel you've arrived at a heck of a fiesta. No fewer than five buffet tables gleam and steam with much too much *comida*: pork ribs in cactus sauce, shrimp in garlic sauce, barbecued beef, goat stew, chiles rellenos, enchiladas, two kinds of *posole*, *calabacitas*, a make-your-own taco bar, and more, as well as chicken nuggets and stewed corn for the kiddos, abundant fresh fruit for dessert, and beer by the bucketful to wash it all down with. What more could you want—besides a long, well-earned siesta afterward?

Hessini Roots International Cafe, 2044 Clinton St., Aurora, CO 80010; (303) 317-6531; www.hessiniroots.com; Nigerian; $. He didn't author a self-help romance book for nothing. Ifiok Etuk, the Nigerian-born owner of this humble Aurora hideaway, is a smoothie through and through—who nimbly finds the way to your heart through his cooking as well as his hospitality. Expertly fried, cornmeal-dusted catfish nuggets, for instance, reveal his firm grasp on American-style soul food, while the specialties of his homeland give new meaning to the term. You'll have to slap your own hands before you polish off a whole bowl of the snack called *chin chin*; essentially sugar cookies in the form of small fried nuggets, they're highly addictive. Equally stirring are traditional stews like *afang* and *egusi*; while the former is reminiscent of chopped collard greens, the latter resembles nothing we've ever tasted, and boy, are we hooked on the chunky paste of ground melon seeds cooked with onions and habañeros in palm oil. Sop up every last bite with hunks of *fufu*, a sort of mashed-yam bun, and pudding-creamy fried plantain slices. Pepper soup with goat is another delicious staple; as for cow's feet, if anyone can seduce us into trying them, Etuk can.

Jabo's Bar-Be-Q, 9682 Arapahoe Rd., Greenwood Village, CO 80112; (303) 799-4432; www.jabosbarbeq.com; Barbecue; $$. A native Oklahoman with an accent as low and slow as his 'cue, Dwight "Jabo" Lawson brought 50-year-old family recipes all the way from Shawnee to open this red-boothed strip-mall counter joint in the 'burbs—easy to miss but well worth the inevitable U-turns. First and foremost are those ribs—practically one-quarter bark (that's the

crust), beneath which the meat slides off the bone in tender shingles—but of course there's also pulled pork, beef brisket, smoked chicken, and hot links. Of 20-plus finishing sauces that rotate throughout the year, including cherry, habañero, and the ever-popular mango, we crave the seasonal, sweet-tart cranberry with just the right amount of peppery spice; among the sides, honey-maple baked beans may be the best we've ever had, perfume-sweet yet not cloying. Save some to use as a dip for chunks of the doughnut-like "Utah scone" topped with a melting pat of honey butter; if your eyes don't roll back in your head, you've done something wrong—better try again.

Jai Ho, 3055 S. Parker Rd., Aurora, CO 80014; (303) 751-5151; Indian/Himalayan; $$. An island of mood-lit contemporary style rising from Aurora's sea of holes in the wall—check out those cool, cream-cushioned benches lining the full bar and the elaborately wrought porch swing in back—Jai Ho stands out as well from the vast majority of metro Denver's interchangeable Punjabi restaurants. Specialties from India's southern regions dominate its lengthy repertoire, including *dosas* (crêpes) as thin and shiny as cellophane—yet somehow still fluffy—and dense, chewy, intriguingly aromatic *medhu vada* (savory lentil doughnuts) that we like to dip into the trio of excellent chutneys on offer (coconut, tomato, mint). The freshly spiced complexity of the kitchen's myriad curries belies slapdash, large-batch cookery, even on the lunch buffet, which flouts cliché via delectable discoveries like *ven ponghal*—a creamy, savory rice pudding typically eaten for breakfast—as well as superior takes on northern classics like unusually dark, nutty *biryani*. If the winningly cheeky but somewhat vague descriptions of unfamiliar dishes from Tamil Nadu and Andhra Pradesh leave you baffled, on-the-ball servers will fill you in—so you've got no good excuse for sticking with tikka masala. Additional location: 1915 28th St., Boulder, CO 80301; (303) 444-5151.

Korea House, 10293 Iliff Ave., Aurora, CO 80247; (303) 696-0011; Korean; $$. What may be the most atmospheric niche in Aurora's quasi-Koreatown, replete with cheesy-but-pleasing faux-rock walls and waterfalls, is certainly one of the most inexplicably underappreciated. We've yet to find better *panchan*, the varied selection ranging from crisp-edged tofu skin to glorious gravied *ddeokbokki* (glutinous rice tubes)—and that's just the beginning. The meats for the tabletop grill are of excellent quality; look for the combo with brisket (*chadol*), marinated short ribs (*kalbi*), and fresh bacon, which also comes, courtesy of smiling servers, with pungent sesame and soybean dips, salad, and soup—we heart the spicy beef and potato served bubbling-hot in a stone pot. The menu's endless, though, so if barbecue's not your thing, there's plenty more to fill your belly, from the familiar (*jap chae*, or glass noodles) to the funky (raw skate). A shot of soju supplies an extra dose of courage should you need it.

Maandeeq East African Cafe, 1535 S. Havana St., Unit C, Aurora, CO 80012; (303) 745-2355; Somali; $$. This place is a hoot. Upon taking over the former strip-mall home of a Chinese restaurant, Dahir Shire opted not to change a thing—so his two-room space is elaborately decorated with murals, tiles, and lanterns depicting imperial palaces and golden dragons. He runs his kitchen in the same, er, casual fashion, presenting a very basic printed menu but keeping a typed sheet of other specialties at the front counter; we suggest glancing around at what his Somali compatriots are eating before you order. One thing you're sure to see are huge platters of goat meat; the extra-tender bone-in chunks come with a puckeringly tart salsa verde–like dipping sauce, your choice of flavorful rice flecked with red and green food coloring or spaghetti (both traditional, believe it or not), goat-brothed veggie soup, salad, and, of all things, a banana, which Somalis eat with just about everything. Though it's supposed to, it may or may not also come with *chapeti*, a flatbread similar to its Indian namesake; golden-brown *sambusas*, piled high on the plate, likewise borrow from Indian samosas. Sometimes Shire serves the doughy, *fufu*-like mash, eaten with one's hands, called *ugali*; sometimes he doesn't. In short, it's all a bit of a crapshoot—but you win either way.

Masalaa, 3141 S. Parker Rd., Aurora, CO 80014; (303) 755-6272; www.masalaausa.com; Indian/Himalayan; $. Like **Jai Ho** (p. 271), this small, humble strip-mall joint specializes in southern Indian fare; unlike its admittedly fairer neighbor, Masalaa is strictly vegetarian. But the repertoire is no less hearty for that, based on a rib-sticking array of fritters, crêpes, pancakes, and rice cakes. Start with the fried lentil-spinach patties called *keerai vadai*; move on to *kashmiri uthappam*, a buttery (or rather ghee-y), vaguely pizza-like lentil flatbread topped with chopped dried fruits. Or check out the Mumbai specialties; the likes of *bhel puri*—a scrumptious snack of puffed rice, potatoes, onions, chutney, and tamarind sauce—and *pav bhaji*, a sort of deconstructed sandwich composed of veggie curry accompanied by a wheat bun, are a rare treat around here. And if *dosas* are your thing, you're in luck (or trouble, depending): on Wednesday nights, Masalaa hosts an all-you-can-eat "dosa festival."

Opus, 2575 W. Main St., Littleton, CO 80120; (303) 703-6787; www .littletondining.net; Contemporary; $$$. When this special-occasion suburbanite has all its brown-buttered ducks in a row, which is more often than not, it's a winner. An intimate dining room, with stone floors and a fireplace amid saffron and cinnamon hues, sets the mood for the unabashed luxuries that Michael Long (see **Aria**, p. 132) favored and that his protégé, Sean McGaughey, now presents with a painterly eye. Highlights tend to include anything involving *foie gras* or lamb, though fond memories of a sweetbread cannelloni we had long ago lead us to seek out the unusual, be it crisp-roasted brussels sprouts with bacon and coffee "soil" or sous vide filet mignon with pickled mushrooms. If we're feeling especially flush, we might spring for the five-course seafood tasting menu; wine pairings depart thoughtfully from the obvious (think a Piquepoul-Sauvignon blend from Languedoc with warm crab salad).

Seoul BBQ, 2080 S. Havana St., Aurora, CO 80014; (303) 632-7576; www.seoulkoreanbbq.com; Korean; $$. As bustling as though it were being filmed in time-lapse, this clean, well-lighted strip-mall joint overflows come lunchtime with extended families, crisp businessmen, and cadets from the nearby Air Force base clad in head-to-toe camo. Most are here for the tabletop barbecue, but we're always eyeballing the stuff we can't easily find elsewhere, like pan-fried kimchi, *sundae guk*—blood-sausage soup—and *mukbap*, or acorn jelly in cold beef broth with spicy red-pepper paste and crumbled seaweed. We're not saying we're gung-ho about every morsel, but for the opportunity to sample them unquestioned, we're indebted.

Shead's BBQ & Fish Hut, 12203 E. Iliff Ave., Unit H, Aurora, CO 80014; (303) 755-0818; www.sheadsbbqandfishhut.com; Barbecue; $$. A hut it ain't, unless you count the thatched fringe and wall-mounted fishnets this otherwise bare Aurora strip-mall outlet sports. But likeable it most certainly is. Ordering's a breeze: try the delectable burnt ends (rib tips), moist barbecued chicken, or fried catfish—and save room for dessert, be it banana pudding or sweet-potato pie. Done and done.

Sherpa House Restaurant and Cultural Center, 1518 Washington Ave., Golden, CO 80401; (303) 278-7931; www.us sherpahouse.com; Indian/Himalayan; $$. For its ambiance alone, this purveyor of Tibetan, Nepalese, and Indian cuisine is well worth the journey to Golden. One room of the old two-story it occupies re-creates a traditional sherpa kitchen, festooned with copper pots and ceramic flasks; in the space behind it, tapestries surround an elaborately carved and painted Buddhist shrine. And they lead in turn to a tree-shaded deck. Of course, the food only enhances the atmosphere. Start with *momos*, a half-dozen glossy steamed or unexpectedly delicate fried crescents served with a light, bright tomato sauce for dipping; move onto the novelty that is stewed yak—but get a side of *saag paneer* for good measure too; it's our surprise favorite, extremely fresh-tasting and scented with lemon and nutmeg.

Silla, 3005 S. Peoria St., Ste. F, Aurora, CO 80014; (303) 338-5070; Korean; $$. Empty this place of its tabletop grills and the largely Korean clientele gathered around them, and you could mistake it for a country-and-western bar: the interior has that wood-grained, beer-stained feel. But rest assured Silla ain't no honky-tonk—despite the fact that the excellent marinated *kalbi* come this close to good old cowboy prime rib. Served on a shallow platter rather than in a bowl, the superlative *bibimbap* has the best crust-to-fluff ratio we've ever seen, rice-wise; it's topped with a perfectly perky-yolked fried egg. And dumplings the size of calzones defy physics with translucent skins that somehow support whole fistfuls of of kimchi within. One or two, and you'll be stuffed silla—er, silly—but since the packed-tight dining room is sometimes understaffed, hence service slow, you'll have some time to digest before waddling out into the sunset.

Street Kitchen Asian Bistro, 10111 Inverness Main St., Ste. B, Englewood, CO 80112; (303) 799-8000; www.streetkitchenasian bistro.com; Southeast Asian; $. We wouldn't trust anyone featuring market stall–inspired pan-Asian fare in a glossy setting at the edge of a suburban golf course surrounded by condos and office parks. Anyone, that is, except Mary Nguyen of **Parallel 17** (p. 150). Accessible but not dumbed down, her menu interlocks Malaysian, Thai, and Vietnamese as well as Japanese and Chinese parts into a festive whole, complete with a rotating selection of dim sum. While the *char kway teow*—rice noodles fried with egg, sausage, and sprouts—hews admirably to the classic preparation, pinwheels of roasted pork-belly strips studded with garlic and chives are, equally admirably, all Nguyen's own. Best of all, though, is the Thai roast chicken: the skin a shimmering crisp, the meat beading with juices, the presence of coconut milk, lemongrass, and lime just perceptible. It happens to pair perfectly with the house-infused raspberry sake.

Tao Tao Noodle Bar, 10400 E. 6th Ave., Aurora, CO 80010; (303) 366-1761; Chinese/Taiwanese; $$. Name notwithstanding, noodles comprise only a small part of the menu at what we hope is David Lee's permanent home following the demise of the much-missed

Chopsticks. A lovely little spot—scattered with jade Buddha statues and cool light fixtures shaped like egg baskets and fronted by a semicircular, enclosed patio—it features a somewhat shorter but no less stellar Chinese and Taiwanese menu combining some of the old favorites with a few new notables. Lee's silk-petal wontons in red chili oil are as good to the last drop as ever, his street-style noodles fried with chunks of pork and bits of egg as slurpable as before. But the three-cup chicken is revelatory: bone- and skin-on chunks of dark meat smothered, along with basil and whole cloves of garlic, in a richly evocative, tangy sauce made of equal parts sesame oil, soy sauce, and rice wine. And the sesame hot pocket—a dense, slightly sweet, split bun with which you stuff accompanying ground pork or chicken—is superb, too. Lee himself recommends the harbor-style shrimp and the sweet-and-sour pork loin; we think you can trust his word.

Thai Flavor, 1014 S. Peoria St., Aurora, CO 80012; (720) 859-7648; Thai; $. Like most Thai restaurants in Denver, this one's in a strip mall; like most Thai restaurants in Denver (and beyond), the generic name offers no clue as to its quality—and neither does the vaguely pleasant interior, colored red and gold and dotted with the requisite elephant-print artwork. Unlike most Thai restaurants anywhere, however, this one makes an eggplant salad resembling nothing we've ever had before. Boasting an almost scallop-like texture, the peeled chunks are tossed with sliced red and green onions in a brothy dressing—or dressing-y broth—that's citrusy, spicy, sweet, and funky all at once, topped with slices of a fried omelet whose yolk oozes with each bite. Also excellent is the *pak boong*, or water spinach, stir-fried in bean sauce with garlic. But really, the whole menu is a gold mine, from the action-packed *tod mun pla* (fried fish patties) to soupy *rad na* that puts Thai Flavor's sugar-happy rivals to shame. We don't say "you can't go wrong" often, but by all means order freely here.

Trompeau Bakery, 2950 S. Broadway, Englewood, CO 80113; (303) 777-7222; http://trompeaubakery.com; Bakery/Cafe; $. On Sunday, the day we Americans most associate with leisurely breakfasts flanked by coffee mugs and crossword puzzles, French-born Pascal Trompeau's beloved pâtisserie et boulangerie is sadly closed. But the rest of the week, he and his lovely wife-partner, Barbara, are hard at work from the wee hours (they open at 6 a.m.) until mid-afternoon, turning out golden, puffy spheres of brioche; crackling baguettes and tender *chasseurs aux pommes* (essentially apple turnovers); fat croissants filled with everything from turkey and swiss cheese to almonds and peaches; and brown-blistered, individual quiches in a select array of flavors at any given time, including Louisana-style spicy sausage, asparagus-leek, and classic quiche Lorraine with bacon. They're all great, but we're partial to the mushroom-parmesan (or, sometimes, Swiss). Thin and crisp-edged as it is, the crust still gives off plenty of buttery flake; the interior is at once fluffy and gooey and bursting with juice from big chunks of white mushroom. At about 4 inches in diameter, it's the perfect size, leaving just enough room for, say, a raspberry danish to go.

US Thai Cafe, 5228 W. 25th Ave., Edgewater, CO 80214; (303) 233-3345; www.usthaicafe.com; Thai; $$. It would be fair to assume that, with a name like US Thai and a suburban address, this odd little spot—really just a kitchen flanked by a dozen or so tables—capitulates to American tastes. Certainly the menu hews to stateside staples like *som tam* (green papaya salad) and pad Thai. But glance around at the chalkboards lining the hot-orange walls of the back room, bearing translated phrases of which one stands out—"Too spicy! *Ped mak mak*"—and any fears of bland fare will begin to melt away. Mind you, the food actually isn't too spicy; rather, true to the tenets of Thai cookery, it balances Scoville heat with sweetness and sourness, fish-sauced funkiness, and freshness. We lean toward the light-textured but fairly glowing green curry, but as secondhand recommendations go, you can't beat the sight of an off-duty cook blowing through a bowl of *tom yum*.

Virgilio's Pizzeria & Wine Bar, 10025 W. San Juan Way, Littleton, CO 80127; (303) 972-1011; www.virgiliospizzeria.com; Pizza; $$. Way out in chainland, this ranch house–style behemoth resembles its corporate brethren in most every way—right down to the corny, cork-lined details: photos of goombah icons, Rat Pack–era jazz on the stereo, shakers of green-can Parm on the tables.

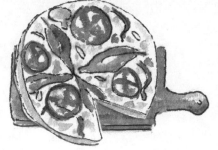

Skeptics will balk, rightly, at the silly candy-flavored "martinis" and novelty appetizers—knots, poppers, pinwheels—served in plastic baskets. But when the pie arrives, the smirks subside. Though founder Virgilio Mario Urbano hails from Campagna, this is the New York–style stuff: crunchy-thin but not flimsy crusts, quality toppings laid on thick. We adore the olive oil–brushed Dolce Diavolo, which packs a flurry of punches with neon-tangy peppadews, rich meatball slices, salty crumbled feta, and sharp garlic—preceded by a mess of warm, house-pulled mozzarella.

Yak and Yeti, 7803 Ralston Rd., Arvada, CO 80002; (303) 431-9000; www.theyakandyeti.com; Indian/Himalayan; $$. Now here's something you don't find every day: a combination Himalayan restaurant and microbrewery in a historic, yellow-brick Queen Anne two-story. With a cozy pub downstairs and a warren of folk art–dotted dining rooms above—get a load of the private room with a turret ceiling painted to resemble the starry night sky—it couldn't be quainter. But while atmosphere's enough to get you in the door, the food is what will bring you back, paired with a pint of unusual brew (chai stout, cocoa wheat, and brown rice–honey ale, oh my). Amid the mostly Indian repertoire, mild, creamy curries like *makhani* and *korma* stand out, but a few Tibetan and Nepalese specialties are worth a look-see, in particular the so-called soybean pickle—essentially a refreshing edamame salad made piquant with ginger, garlic, and cilantro. Additional location: 8665 N. Sheridan Blvd., Westminster, CO 80003; (303) 426-1976.

Yanni's, 5425 Landmark Place, #109D, Greenwood Village, CO 80111; (303) 692-0404; www.yannisdenver.com; Greek; $$. Take the taverna setting at face value: stone-tiled floors and clean white walls dotted with blue ceramics and seascapes serve as a memo to trade in the gyros for something a little more special. That includes pungent dips like *taramosalata*—an addictive puree of roe and olive oil—and garlicky, potato-based *skordalia*, followed by leg of lamb roasted with potatoes or grilled swordfish (better still is the snapper, when and if it's available; call ahead to confirm). Meanwhile, we winos are especially appreciative of the fact that the bar sometimes offers specials on overstocked bottles.

Landmarks

Casa Bonita, 6715 W. Colfax Ave., Lakewood, CO 80214; (303) 232-5115; Mexican; $$. This being a food lover's guide, Casa Bonita has no business appearing anywhere near it; *la comida es terrible*. But it was a landmark to end all landmarks even before the Colorado-raised creators of *South Park* immortalized the pink palace in a now-famous episode, and so it shall ever be. Combining elements of stuccoed *palacios,* palm groves, grottos, gold mines, and swashbucklers' caves into one giant bastion of unspeakable vulgarity, it features cliff divers, roving mariachis, fire jugglers, and all the grotesque tropical cocktails you'll need just to take it all in. Put this one on your bucket list—with an addendum to eat beforehand or afterward.

The Fort, 19192 Hwy. 8, Morrison, CO 80465; (303) 697-4771; www.thefort.com; Steak House; $$$. Built in 1961 up near Red Rocks to resemble a 19th-century fur-trading post, The Fort is now a valuable piece of property in its own right, listed on the National Register of Historic Places. Frontier chic is the hallmark of this adobe-walled beacon; though we can't wholeheartedly recommend it sheerly on the merits of the kitchen, we can do so on the strength of its kitsch. Come on the weekend when a Native American flutist works the room, setting the stage for braised bison tongue, batter-fried Rocky Mountain oysters, elk chops, cowboy steaks, lamb ribs, and, in short, more meat than you can possibly take in in one sitting—which could also be said of the views. Hilarity ensues in the attempt to pair peanut butter–stuffed, pickled jalapeños with trophy wines from the colossal list.

Specialty Stores, Markets & Producers

Arash International Market, 2720 Parker Rd., Aurora, CO 80014; (303) 752-9272. This cheerful, bustling market boasts a large produce section, a halal butcher counter, and a vast array of hard-to-find products from the the Arab Levant and the Balkans. It's your one-stop shop for Bulgarian cheeses and Iranian flatbreads, dried mulberries and watermelon seeds, fenugreek water and halvah, goat shoulder and lamb neck; goodness knows we all need one of those.

The Chocolate Therapist, 2560 W. Main St., Ste. 100, Littleton, CO 80120; (303) 795-7913; www.thechocolatetherapist.com. Owned by Julie Pech, author of *The Chocolate Therapist: A User's Guide to the Extraordinary Health Benefits of Chocolate*, this pretty little boutique itself resembles a gift-wrapped box of bon-bons, inside which rests an assortment of goodies that we personally doubt will improve our fitness but certainly lifts our spirits. Among our picks, made on-site, are the espresso-infused bars, the chili pepper–flecked meltaways, and the snappy, dark chocolate–enrobed toffee squares.

Dah Won Rice Cake, 2222 S. Havana St., Unit I, Aurora, CO 80014; (303) 369-7890. Next door to Paris Baguette Bakery, this miniscule storefront is cluttered up to here with rice cakes, rice cakes, and more glutinous rice cakes—the handiwork of the kindly gentleman who oversees it all. He can explain to you what the colorful packaged blocks and blobs are stuffed and topped with: our favorites are the sticky, savory-sweet red-bean mochi dusted in salty green-bean powder and the cake-like squares topped with dried fruit and nuts, but options abound. A few bucks will land you more sweets than you can chew through in a week.

The English Teacup, 1930 S. Havana St., Aurora, CO 80014; (303) 751-3032; www. englishteacup.com. It's the last thing you'd expect to find amid the Ethiopian markets and Korean kitchens of Aurora's strip malls, but this adorable tearoom, grocery, and souvenir shop is a treasure trove for Anglophiles. China cabinets, refrigerated cases, and tables draped with lace tablecloths line the bright space, laden with knickknacks commemorative of the royal wedding, cans of haggis and marrowmeat peas, bags of crisps and other imports, from treacle and Aero bars to blancmange and bitter shandy; a rack of quaint illustrated cookbooks stands at the entrance with titles like *Favourite Boating Recipes*. And while you're getting your fill of take-home treats, you can take the immediate edge off via a small menu of traditional eats: scones and crumpets, steak-and-kidney pie with baked beans or a simple bacon buttie make for a merrie olde afternoon.

Manneken Frites, 5616 Olde Wadsworth Blvd., Arvada, CO 80002; (303) 847-4357; http://mannekenfrites.squarespace.com. Ultra-thick-cut, extra-skin-on frites served in a paper-lined cone with your pick of nearly 20 dipping sauces: but for dogs, a few draft and bottled Belgian brews, and soda from Durango-based company

Zuberfizz, that's all this Olde Town Arvada outlet offers. You couldn't ask for more. Though the Ghent sauce flavored with shallots and chives is traditional, we're suckers for the curried ketchup and pesto mayo. Granted, when you get right down to it, our favorite flavor's choice, so here's to the flight that lets us throw in peanut and pomegranate-barbecue sauces, too.

Maria Empanada, 5209 W. Mississippi Ave., Lakewood, CO 80226; (303) 934-2221; www.mariaempanada.com. This sparklingly clean, modern empanada counter showcases the art of *repulgue*, or pastry folding, as practiced by warm, welcoming Buenos Aires–born owner Lorena Cantarovici; the crimped and braided edges of more than a dozen different types of crescents and buns serve as a clue to their fillings—from traditional beef, corn, and ham-and-mozzarella to eggplant parmesan and pear-walnut. (We can polish off the spinach and hard-cooked egg, mixed with nutmeg-touched béchamel in an impossibly delicate, tender casing, in three or four gluttonous bites.) Cantarovici also makes remarkable, magazine-pretty savory tarts served by the 2-inch-high slice, including confetti-colorful mixed veggie with cheese; she can advise you as to which of her four dipping sauces best accompany each item—but our own advice is to try all four, at a mere 35 cents an ounce. The sweet chili mayo is swell.

Paris Baguette Bakery, 2222 S. Havana St., Unit I, Aurora, CO 80014; (303) 755-2070. The Korean mom and pop who run this tiny, strictly take-out bakery in an Aurora strip mall are as sweet as pie—not that you'll be able to judge for yourself on the spot, since they don't make pie. Nor do they make tarts, elaborate cakes, croissants, or anything else that might explain the choice of name—not even baguettes. Indeed, the small, neatly displayed selection consists mainly of lookalike buns—round, sugar-dusted, and fried—whose differences you'll have to trust to the signage: cream, cheese, streusel, sweet potato, and so on. But will you ever be glad you did. Boasting a springy texture and rich flavor not unlike yeast dough-nuts, they're equally delightful whether savory—stuffed with a hearty mixture of mashed potatoes, chopped hard-cooked egg, and bits of sauteed red peppers and onions, say—or sweet and sticky with red-bean paste. Check out too the fluffy slices of herb angel cake, flavored with dropwort, and the shatteringly crisp four-sec cookies—like flat, square Florentines studded with sliced almonds.

Rancho Liborio, 10400 E. Colfax Ave., Aurora, CO 80010; (720) 343-1210; www.liborio.com. At this *supermercado*, doing the gro-ceries feels to us like going to a carnival—from the piñatas sus-pended from the ceiling near the entrance to the *agua fresca*, taco, and tortilla stands that beckon en route to the produce section. There we'll score the likes of huge, ochre-skinned *calabaza Cubana* and *xoconostle* (a type of prickly pear) before moving on to the bakery for giant round loaves of *pan de acámbaro* and sweet, color-fully iced *concha*. Behind the butcher's case, spiced meat loaves await alongside freshly pickled pork rinds and thick links of blood sausage; at the adjacent seafood counter, crawfish, baby octopus, and green mussels sparkle. Finds at phenomenal prices are every-where: guava and quince paste by the slab, packaged *quesillo,* and so much more. It's better than winning a stuffed teddy bear along the midway. Though this branch is superior, there are additional locations: 6040 E. 64th Ave., Commerce City, CO, 80022; (303) 339-1320; 850 E. 88th Ave., Thornton, CO 80229; (303) 287-3100.

Rheinlander Bakery, 5721 Olde Wadsworth Blvd., Arvada, CO 80202; (303) 467-1810; www.rheinlanderbakery.com. Since 1963, the Dimmer family has operated this cheery wonderland chock-full of German and other pastries—tortes and strudel, turnovers and fes-tive cookies as well as several gluten-free items—along Olde Town Arvada's cute main drag. But the place really shines at Yuletide, in the form of stollen laden with goodies—not only almonds, walnuts, and pecans but also raisins and bits of dried papaya, mango, and pineapple; you can go for the gusto by adding marzipan (almond candy) into the mix.

Sweet Cow Ice Cream, 637 Front St., Unit B, Louisville, CO 80027; (303) 666-4269; www.sweetcow icecream.com. Combining traditional creamery methods with a penchant for anything-goes pop cheek, Sweet Cow founder Drew Honness is one mean scooping machine. From Gatorade sorbet and the breakfast of champions—cornflakes and bourbon—to caramel-apple and cinnamon-sugar Pop Tart, his ice creams are at their most innovative when they're steeped in trademark nostalgia. Our own pet case in point: vanilla-based, red pepper–flaked Kung Pao cashew (whew!).

Taste of Denmark, 1901 S. Kipling St., Lakewood, CO 80227; (303) 987-8283; www.tasteofdenmark.net. We found this unassuming, out-of-the-way Danish bakery by accident, and we almost wish we hadn't. With a huge assortment of strudel, flaky pretzel-shaped kringles, icing-topped butter rings, waffle sandwich cookies, and, of course, danish, as well as fresh-baked breads, all with ridiculously low price tags, it wreaks a week's worth of havoc on our waistlines in mere minutes. That said, one of our favorite items practically counts as health food: the thick, crunchy, hearty sunflower-seed crackers.

Tres Jolie, 2399 W. Main St., Littleton, CO 80120; (303) 795-0156. The name fits. Billing itself as a tea and Champagne lounge and boutique, this Littleton downtowner is an unapologetically girlie, pastel-frothed wonderland of whimsical home accessories and dainty refreshments: flowery teas, locally roasted coffee, sparkling cocktails, good sandwiches, and even better sweets. A glass of lavender soda and a one-bite lemon shortbread cookie unleash our inner Holly Golightly in a flash.

Vinnola's Italian Market, 7750 W. 38th Ave., Wheat Ridge, CO 80033; (303) 421-3955; www.vinnolasitalianmarket.com. Vinnola's is not only one of the oldest Italian groceries in town; it's also the biggest and best-stocked. The same holds true of its bakery, featuring breads and pastries of all kinds, from biscotti and cannoli to twists and rolls; come Christmastime, it goes the extra mile with house-made rather than the usual imported, prepackaged *pannetone*, studded with apricots, cherries, cranberries, and decidedly untraditional but nonetheless fun chocolate chips. There's even a decent sit-down eatery on-site, painted with all the obligatory murals and serving up a slew of red-sauce comforts to a crowd of regulars whose tables you should turn to for ordering advice.

Booze Cruise

Local Breweries, Wineries, Distilleries & Bars

Oregonians may grumble, but to deny that Colorado's the epicenter of the American craft-beer movement is to deny not only our nearly 150-year-old history as a brewing hub (see: Adolph Coors) and our rampant growth—with new breweries opening up at the rate of several per year—but also our role as host of the nation's premier beer extravaganza, the Great American Beer Festival. Far younger, but no less dynamic, are the wine and spirits industries, which have boomed in recent years; the state's now home to some 100 wineries and dozens of microdistilleries.

Many producers, to be sure, reside beyond the geographical scope of this guidebook. To name just a few, the revered New Belgium Brewing Company and Odell Brewing Company are both in Fort Collins, as are Funkwerks and up-and-comer Crooked Stave; Oskar Blues is in Lyons, and Left Hand Brewing Company in nearby Longmont; outliers include Durango's Ska Brewing Company, Greeley's Crabtree Brewery and countless others. Meanwhile, several worthy startups lack tasting rooms, such as Boulder's Crystal Springs Brewing Company, Denver's Black Shirt Brewing Company, and CAUTION: Brewing Co. (although the latter was working to change that at press time). Most of our wineries are clustered in the western part of the state, around the vineyards of Mesa and Delta Counties. And as for microdistilleries, they're scattered just about every-where: some of our favorites (in no particular order) include Montanya Rum in Crested Butte, Downslope Distilling in Centennial, Peak Spirits in Hotchkiss, Peach Street Distillers in Palisade, Dancing Pines Distillery in Loveland, and Denver's own Leopold Bros. You'll spot these labels on many a local back bar. (For further listings, visit the websites of the Colorado Brewers Guild, http://coloradobeer.org; the Colorado Distillers Guild, http://colorado distillersguild.publishpath.com; and the Colorado Wine Industry Development Board, www.coloradowine.com.)

By the same token, we couldn't possibly include every watering hole in town—that would entail a guidebook in itself. What we have done is compile a number of our favorites; it's worth noting, of course, that many others appear throughout the book, categorized as Foodie Faves or Landmarks. Suffice it to say that, in Denver and Boulder alike, there aren't many places you can't kick back with a craft brew, a glass of local wine, or a killer cocktail. Cheers all around.

Avery Brewing Company, 5763 Arapahoe Ave., Unit E, Boulder, CO 80303; (303) 440-4324; www.averybrewing.com; $. If there's a bad boy in Colorado's pack of acclaimed craft breweries, it's Avery. A cult favorite for its potent seasonal series—the Dictators, the Demons of Ale, the barrel-aged one-offs—this envelope-pushing Boulder powerhouse, led by the visionary Adam Avery, shows no signs of mellowing; on the contrary, in observation of its 20th anniversary in 2013, it's planning what one principal half-jokingly calls "a palatial brewery," complete with full-service restaurant, in order to increase capacity on best-selling year-rounders like White Rascal and the signature IPA. In the meantime, though, its current taproom is open daily to pour a score of beers—some available here and here only—paired with a full menu of snacks and sandwiches from **Savory Cuisines Catering**. Put this one at the top of your to-do list.

Boulder Distillery & Clear Spirit Company, 2500 47th St., #10, Boulder, CO 80301; (303) 442-1244; http://303vodka.com. Filled with vintage bric-a-brac to resemble the lab of some bygone mad tinkerer, this quirky distillery and tasting room was in fact jerryrigged on the rediscovery of a long-lost family recipe for potato vodka. Four afternoons a week, Steve Viezbicke and wife Terri open to the public to pour not only their lovingly crafted version thereof, 303 Vodka, but also 303 Whiskey (likewise spud-based), Rob's

Mountain Gin, and wacky house infusions in flavors ranging from peanut to pickle to peppermint.

Breckenridge Brewery & BBQ, 471 Kalamath St., Denver, CO 80204; (303) 573-0431; www.breckbrew.com. The intoxicating scent of smoke and mash wafts through the air of this mountain-town beer pioneer's multiuse outpost just south of the Santa Fe Arts District. Part brewery, part bottling plant, part country-and-western-style pints-and-parts joint, it keeps 16 signatures and seasonals, from Agave Wheat to Autumn Ale, on tap at a bar that also show-cases Colorado spirits, including Montanya rum and 303 Vodka (see preceding review). Its older Ballpark sibling (2220 Blake St., Denver, CO 80205; 303-297-3644) may be bigger, with a larger menu—but only this branch  serves up "comfort bowls" of mashed potatoes and gravy topped with your choice of 'cue. Why ruin a good beer when you can cry into spuds instead?

Bull & Bush Pub & Brewery, 4700 Cherry Creek Dr. S., Denver, CO 80246; (303) 759-0333; www.bullandbush.com. As proud as we Denverites are to promote our brewing culture, we've got some fiercely local secrets to keep. This is one of them (shh). Resembling its 17th-century Hampstead namesake from the Tudor-style architecture to the cheerfully cluttered, amber-glowing interior, it differs in one key respect: an on-site brewery run by the founders' son. Among Erik Peterson's many award-winning year-rounders, the Tower ESB (extra-special bitter) is perhaps the kingpin, but we love the fruity Hail Brau Hefeweizen; seasonals include his much-ballyhooed Legend of the Liquid Brain Imperial Stout and the nearly black, wholly captivating Smoke on the Lager. In addition to his own cellared vintages, Peterson also collects rare aged beers by the dozens and offers whiskies literally by the hundreds—far more than any other place in town with the possible exception of **Pints Pub** (p. 299). Gotta love those mashed potatoes with green chile, too.

Colorado Winery Row, 4640 Pecos St., Denver, CO 80211; (303) 477-9463; www.coloradowineryrow.com. Three afternoons a week (Thursday through Saturday), representatives from four home-grown wineries open their adjacent showrooms to the public for a taste of a region on the rise. While sampling **Bonacquisti Wine Company**'s and **Garfield Estates'** Rhône Valley varietals, **Cottonwood Cellars'** uncommon Lemberger, and/or **Verso Cellars'** distinctive, multi-clone Cabernet Sauvignon, you'll learn a thing or two about the potential of Colorado's high-desert terroir—and the pioneers who are mining its vineyards as surely as the prospectors who preceded them.

Copper Kettle Brewing Company, 1338 S. Valentia St., Unit 100, Denver, CO 80247; (720) 443-2522; www.copperkettledenver.com.

Likening their taproom to a "coffeeshop that 75 percent of our customers walk or bike to," former home brewers Kristen Kozik and husband-partner Jeremy Gobien remain lay enthusiasts at heart—and they wear that heart on their sleeve in the form of a line devoted to the winner of their biannual amateur brewing competition. That they're pros in practice, however, the pair proved from the get-go by winning a gold medal for their Mexican Chocolate Stout at the GABF in 2011, when the paint was barely dry on the Kettle's walls. Two other seasonals supplement a quartet of "easy-drinking" perennials that, according to Kozik, "really fly off the handles," including the nicely balanced Copper Mezzina Ale.

Denver Beer Co., 1695 Platte St., Denver, CO 80202; (303) 433-2739; http://denverbeerco.com. "Craft-beer drinkers are promiscuous," laughs Charlie Berger. "They like to try what's new and different and interesting." He and partner Patrick Crawford are only too happy to oblige. Indefatigable experimenters with everything from rosebuds to lychee nuts, they brew only small-batch seasonals, mostly one-offs; with seven taps that rotate at the rate of two or three a week, even smash hits like Graham Cracker Porter and Kaffir Lime Wheat come and go in their spacious taproom, a former auto-body shop made airy and vibrant in orange and yellow, with garage doors opening onto a picnic table–lined deck. It's quite the party central: food trucks park on-site near-daily, firkin tappings take place every Friday, and live jams fill the air on Sunday afternoons.

Dry Dock Brewing Company, 15120 E. Hampden Ave., Aurora, CO 80014; (303) 400-5606; www.drydockbrewing.com. When it was named Small Brewing Company of the Year at the GABF in 2009, few Denverites, let alone out-of-staters, had heard of this brewery and taproom ensconced in an Aurora strip mall. Since then it's been full-steam ahead for founder Kevin DeLange—who also owns the adjacent Brew Hut, a homebrewing supply shop—and head brewer Bill Eye. Two expansions haven't diminished the grass-rootsy, off-the-cuff spirit of their venture, where the crowd's relaxed, the popcorn's free, and the Paragon Apricot Blonde is ever-flowing—along with seven other year-rounders and a half-dozen seasonals. Firkin Fridays at Dry Dock are, DeLange chuckles, "always an adventure," featuring every cask-conditioned thing from coffee stout to coconut porter to mango pale ale (but not, rest assured, the wasabi rice ale they tried once and once only).

Great Divide Brewing Co., 2201 Arapahoe St., Denver, CO 80205; (303) 296-9460; http://greatdivide.com. It's hard to believe that this small, bare-bones taproom situated on a gritty corner in Five Points is attached to one of Colorado's best-loved breweries. Until, that is, you eyeball the tap handles—16 in all—emblazoned with such famous names as Yeti Imperial Stout, Hibernation Ale, and Hoss Rye Lager. There's nary an offering that hasn't garnered more than one medal in competition, yet the vibe is as chill as if this were just some neighborhood upstart, complete with eats from the food trucks that park out front on a regular basis.

The Infinite Monkey Theorem, 931 W. 5th Ave., Denver, CO 80204; (303) 736-8376; http://theinfinitemonkeytheorem.com. Currently working out of a Quonset hut on a stark stretch of the Santa Fe Arts District (though at press time plans were in place to move to a larger facility), urban winemaker Ben Parsons has made a smash success of what would seem to be an ill-starred venture. Sourcing grapes few Coloradans dare use from both in and out of the state—Malbec, Petit Verdot, Albariño, Verdehlo—he's garnered unprecedented acclaim, even rock-star status, from day one, and you'll spot the hard-to-miss label on many a local list. But to taste the wines on-site, you've got to wait out the winter; Parsons opens to the public only during First Friday Art Walks, which run April through October. It's well worth the trouble to kick back on an alley patio while a DJ spins tunes and **Pizzeria Basta** (p. 228) slings slices to soak up your Syrah.

Mountain Sun Pub & Brewery, 1535 Pearl St., Boulder, CO 80302; (303) 546-0886; www.mountainsunpub.com. Boulder's long since outgrown its image as a hippie enclave, but some of us miss the shaggy, tie-dyed years; now entering its second decade, the flagship pub of this microbrewery offers a flashback locals continue to cherish. Still, the loosey-goosey vibe comes in second in their hearts to the mighty fine draft beers—from the clean, citrus-and-evergreen-tinged XXX Pale Ale to the creamy Belgian Dip Chocolate Stout. And speaking of stout, during the long-running extravaganza that is February's Stout Month, Mountain Sun and its siblings pour a slew of house variations on the theme—imperials, creams, fruit infusions—as well as guest brews of that ilk, including the winner of its annual home-brew competition. As for the kitchen, it's as friendly to kiddos as it is to vegetarians. Additional locations: Southern Sun Pub & Brewery, 627 S. Broadway, Boulder, CO 80305; (303) 543-0886; Vine Street Pub, 1700 Vine St., Denver, CO 80206; (303) 388-2337 (this location hosts Belgian Beer Month in September).

Pints Pub, 221 W. 13th Ave., Denver, CO 80204; (303) 534-7543; http://pintspub.com. The red phone booth parked out front beneath the Union Jacks flapping in the breeze alerts you to the queen-and-country theme of this over-the-top British pub. It serves as a clue to the beers produced on-site—traditional UK styles all, including a pair of hand-pumped live ales—as well as to the standard pub fare (much of which is hit or miss, but the loaded Bisto chips, doused in curried gravy and topped with melting swiss, are swell). What it may not prepare you for is an extraordinary collection of single malts: some 250 from not just Scotland but all over the world, many of them extremely rare (as their three-digit price tags would suggest). The list provides helpful tasting notes, nicely supplemented by the knowledge of the servers.

Renegade Brewing Company, 925 W. 9th Ave., Denver, CO 80204; (720) 401-4089; www.renegadebrewing.com. On a dreary Saturday afternoon, there are few places we'd rather be than Brian and Khara O'Connell's microbrewery and taproom just a hop and a skip from the Santa Fe Arts District. The adobe façade bids us welcome from without; within, high wood-beamed ceilings and exposed-brick walls frame what feels like a block party, where a cart vendor hawks bacon-jalapeño pretzels in one corner and a regular parks her obedient dog in another. With more than 100 IBUs, the flagship Ryeteous IPA is the O'Connells' ode to hopheads, but we discern poetry in the Breakfast Burrito, a beer cocktail that blends Uno Mas—a poblano-infused amber ale—with Sunday Morning Strong coffee ale. And there's plenty more where they came from to warm your cockles; the O'Connells pride themselves on potent, flavorful pours—a total of eight at any given time—that they swear will never dip below 5 percent ABV.

Stranahan's Colorado Whiskey, 200 S. Kalamath St., Denver, CO 80223; (303) 296-7440; www.stranahans.com. Meeting its manifest destiny, this towering pioneer of Colorado's microdistilling boom was sold to Proximo Spirits in 2010—and the changes in management have engendered concern in many a proud local for the company's future here. So get to this southside whiskey distillery while the getting's still good; educational tours are conducted several times a week, or you can learn by osmosis at the on-premises **Rackhouse Pub** (see p. 314).

Strange Brewing Company, 1330 Zuni St. Unit M, Denver, CO 80204; (720) 985-2337; www.strangebrewingco.com. "Take something Strange home tonight," read the T-shirts displayed behind the bar; growlers in hand, the brewhounds who frequent this warm buzz of a hideout, hidden among the warehouses and train tracks of west Denver, do just that. A labor of love for John Fletcher and Tim Myers, Strange features 10 microbrews at any given time, two on nitro; signatures include Paint It Black, a stout flavored with coffee and honey, and oak-aged Cherry Kriek, while seasonals range from pumpkin porters to saisons. A popcorn machine stands ready at the entrance, but many a regular brings in boxes of take-out pizza—and happily shares with strangers-turned-drinking buddies.

Twisted Pine Brewing Company, 3201 Walnut St., Ste. A, Boulder, CO 80301; (303) 786-9270; http://twistedpinebrewing.com. As easygoing as this commerce-park tasting room may be, it keeps one beer on rotation that's anything but: the Ghost Face Killah brewed with six different types of chile peppers, including the brutal *bhut jolokia*. Love it or hate it, you've got to try it—with a glass of peach lemonade on the side. (We're not saying it'll extinguish the flames, but at least it won't fan them.) There's a limited selection of eats to boot.

Upslope Brewing Company, 1501 Lee Hill Rd. #20, Boulder, CO 80304; (303) 449-2911; http://upslopebrewing.wordpress.com.

Canned beer is back, and this Boulder brewery is rocking it with its year-round quartet of eco-conscious portables: two pale ales, one brown, and a lager. All are on tap at its lively tasting room—which doubles as a typical stop on the food-truck route—but so are four other limited-release pours, from dunkelweizen to a seasonal pumpkin ale that took the gold at the 2011 GABF.

Wit's End Brewing Company, 2505 W. 2nd St., Unit 13, Denver, CO 80219; (303) 359-9119; http://witsendbrewing.com. Brewing single-barrel batches at a time in the out-of-the-way glorified storage unit he jokingly calls his "speakeasy," nanobrewer Scott Witsoe clearly has a ball chatting up the beer buffs at his 10-seat bar—and introducing them to his quintet of taps, among them light, highly refreshing Jean Claude van Blonde; Slam Dunkelweizen, with its creamy banana notes; and apple-nosed Green Man Ale. Playing with everything from roasted pumpkin seeds to nine malts at once, Witsoe puts style guidelines on the back burner, chefly inspiration on the front; to stop by on a Friday or Saturday afternoon is to feel you've wandered into your neighbor's garage to hang out as he tinkers with his latest project. In a way, you have.

Wynkoop Brewing Company, 1634 18th St., Denver, CO 80202; (303) 297-2700; www.wynkoop.com. Colorado's first brewpub—opened in LoDo in 1988 by, among others, current governor John Hickenlooper—remains one of its foremost. The look is classic:

exposed pipes crisscross high ceilings; copper and brass accents gleam dimly against brick and wood; tanks loom behind glass; and stairs lead to a sprawling pool hall in one direction, an aging cellar in the other. And the brews follow suit. On tap are a dozen or so signatures and seasonals—GABF medalists invariably among them, including Patty's Chile Beer, its vegetal tinge clear and pure but not spicy—as well as a few guest beers (He'brew here, Duvel there). Brewery tours are a given every Saturday, but the ultimate Wynkoop experience warrants a visit on select Friday evenings (call for details), when a horse-drawn carriage laden with orders of Rail Yard Ale departs the premises to make downtown deliveries.

Cocktail Lounges

See Appendix B for many other listings under Cocktails.

Amaro Drinkery Italia, 2785 Iris Ave., Boulder, CO 80304; (303) 443-5100. Literally the middle sibling, separating **Arugula** (p. 209) from **Tangerine** (p. 237), this stylish slice of the lush life doesn't fix on the booze of the Boot to the extent its name suggests, but it turns out some nifty cocktails nonetheless. We can overlook the partial reliance on big-name spirits just this once, since the Tipsy Garden is a patio party in a glass—blending pink-grapefruit vodka with Sauvignon Blanc and muddled arugula, plus lemon juice and soda—and the gin-based Sleepy Southpaw proves peculiar yet refreshing with chamomile grappa, coca-leaf liqueur and celery bitters. Still, the pièce de résistance is the assortment of small plates—including mackerel salad and mushroom-gorgonzola ragù over polenta—from Chef-Owner Alec Schuler (who also uses the space, which is open only Wednesday through Saturday nights, to host brilliant wine dinners).

The Bitter Bar, 835 Walnut St., Boulder, CO 80302; (303) 442-3050; http://thebitterbar.com. Speakeasy-esque (see: discreet alley entrance) yet ultimately welcoming (think fireplace, cool couches), this snazzy lounge has hit its stride with a revamped menu of spirited savories and sweets—from caramel-bacon popcorn to delicata-squash gnocchi and s'mores to apple clafoutis with fig ice cream. But lots of venues in the vicinity of downtown Boulder serve such savvy stuff. What sweetens the pot for bettors on The Bitter is the presence of star mixologist Mark Stoddard, whose seasonal work with craft spirits and housemade products is simply exquisite. For instance, we're enamored with the Hokkaido Highball—a blend of Japanese single malt, elderflower liqueur, and apple drinking vinegar—and the sparkling Savory Sudds with cucumber and celery bitters. Meanwhile, everyone loves the so-called flasks, actually classic cocktails by the pitcher to inspire a vast improvement on the coffee klatch.

The Cruise Room, The Oxford Hotel, 1600 17th St., Denver, CO 80202; (303) 825-1107; www.theoxfordhotel.com. Excepting the stellar roster of oysters on the half-shell, the food here is only so-so (it comes from the kitchen of the seafood franchise next door). And other than classic martinis, the cocktails lack gravitas in the era of craft bartending. Wherefore, then, the legendary status of this hotel hideaway? You'll know at a glance. It opened the day after Prohibition was repealed and hasn't changed since; the long, narrow, softly glowing space is a testament to the enduring glamour of Art Deco, from the etched wall panels and chrome detailing to the marble tiles and working neon jukebox. Moreover, the bartenders are lovely, their feathers unruffled no matter the crush come happy hour. Now if only they'd put the kibosh on chocolate vodka.

Green Russell, 1422 Larimer St., Denver, CO 80202; (303) 893-6505; www.greenrussell.com. Located a flight below Larimer Square at the back of Wednesday's Pie (p. 111) and Russell's Smokehouse (p. 90), Frank Bonanno's homage to the Prohibition-era speakeasy is the whole jazzy package. Curved booths abut cool rock walls and red-cushioned stools line the bar, where nattily dressed pros led by beverage director Adam Hodak are less inclined to work from a script than they are to customize cocktails according to patrons' tastes, using the numerous house infusions, flavorings, and grow-room herbs at their disposal—think oak-aged bitters, black truffle-sea salt vodka, and fresh bay leaf—as well as chips off the old ice block.

Mario's Double Daughters Salotto, 1632 Market St., Denver, CO 80202; (303) 623-3523; www.doubledaughters.com. Behind the strange name of **Beatrice & Woodsley**'s (p. 174) LoDo sibling lies a dreamscape as wondrous as the myth that inspired it. Glowing, backlit red-and-blue stripes; booths that to many an eye loom like giant drops of blood; doves circling the branches of bare trees—all allude to the mysterious tale of an old carnival barker and his conjoined twin girls. So, more or less, do garish cocktails with Gothic monikers like Severed Goat's Head and Descent into the Maelstrom (never mind the blasphemous blend of 17 liquors that is the Succo Vaffanculo di Mario). Speaking of maelstroms, Mario's spell can all too easily be broken by overcrowding, so we come early and leave early, grabbing a slice from the adjoining pizzeria, Two-Fisted Mario's, if we're feeling particularly peckish.

Peaks Lounge, Hyatt Regency Denver at Colorado Convention Center, 650 15th St., Denver, CO 80202; (303) 486-4433; http://denverregency.hyatt.com. Penthouse panoramas being inexplicably scarce in downtown Denver, we hightail it to the 27th floor of the Hyatt when we've got guests to impress. There they can ooh and aah over the majesty of the Rockies on the near horizon—while we settle into the upholstery, survey the swank scene, and snack on mixed nuts (there's also a limited menu of appetizers and sweets). The wine list is ordinary, the cocktails unmemorable, the markup noticeable—but coming as they do from gracious servers against an unparalleled backdrop, we're content to shell out time and again nonetheless.

Williams & Graham, 3160 Tejon St., Denver, CO 80220; (303) 997-8886; http://williamsandgraham.com. "This is very personal for me, as a third-generation barman," says the renowned Sean Kenyon of his LoHi neo-speakeasy. Every stunning detail marks his words. Upon entering what seems to be a tiny old bookstore (and is—those cocktail primers are for sale), you'll be led by the hostess through a hidden door to the period piece that is his dark, tin-ceilinged, leather-boothed bar, woody with reclaimed boxcar flooring. Each page of the hand-bound menu bears an epigraph expressly written for Kenyon by some of the nation's best-known drink experts—but the meticulously curated collection of spirits and array of cocktails, classic and signature, speaks for itself with booming authority. It could all be rather intimidating were Kenyon not such a consummate host—cultivating a genuine rapport with his guests that, he hopes, will allow him to "take them places they haven't been before." Scotch diehards, for instance, might be inspired to try the Lowlands Dagger—a compelling blend of single malt, sherry, and gentian aperitif—but we've seen this gentleman scholar pour club soda with equal dignity. Superbly crafted small plates (think boar bacon with wild mushroom fricasee) only enhance the remarkably intimate experience.

Don's Club Tavern, 723 E. 6th Ave., Denver, CO 80218; (303) 683-3303; www.donsclubtavern.com. Most dives thrive on their grit, their bloodied-but-unbowed attitude. Not this 60-something Alamo Placita fixture, also known as Don's Mixed Drinks in deference to its beloved neon signage; here, the door and bar crews are as friendly as though they were running a spiffy country kitchen rather than a slightly tattered watering hole—and their pours are as generous as their welcomes. No wonder oldsters, youngsters, barflies, and beauties alike congregate at Don's—whether to relax over a round of pool or video poker, sneak a smoke on the back patio, or just kick back in a creaky booth until closing time, humming along to the classic-rock soundtrack.

Lost Lake Lounge, 3602 E. Colfax Ave., Denver, CO 80206; (303) 333-4345. Leave it to the owners of **Sputnik** (p. 310) to transform a former dive into another, better dive. This nightly scene on the 'Fax resembles a fishing lodge in *Twin Peaks*: the dim lights flickering against the wood panels slightly eerie, the scattered paintings and figurines seemingly salvaged from somebody's garage, the music lineup mesmerizingly schizophrenic (live piano one night, DJs another; vintage R&B here, hardcore punk there). If the fireplace at the entrance doesn't warm you to the bone, the $5 Happy Meal—a shot and a chaser—surely will. Good times, kids—which the photo booth will capture for posterity.

Pete's Satire Lounge, 1920 E. Colfax Ave., Denver, CO 80206; (303) 322-2227; www.petesrestaurants.com. There are few more enduring or beloved symbols of the Colfax Avenue of old, in all its vice-ridden glory, than the Googie-era neon signage that points, literally, to this mid-century institution, now owned by Pete Contos of the equally legendary **Pete's Kitchen** next door (p. 165). Though these days it's looking better for the wear thanks to renovations that have sadly erased most traces of its historic grime, the case remains that you will be hard-pressed to find a more cartoonish bunch of misfits, young and old, gathered in one place at one time—and you'll thrill to fit right in. Besides, nothing can change the fact that no lesser giants of 1960s counterculture than the Smothers Brothers and Bob Dylan once lurked here before hitting the big time. In that light, cheapo booze and bad Mexican food are just a "bonus."

PS Lounge, 3416 E. Colfax Ave., Denver, CO 80206; (303) 320-1200. If this Colfax classic looks a little sketchy, that's because it is. Three cheers to that. Chock-full of mismatched tchotchkes, it's also packed with every kind of character from geezers straight out of a Cassavetes flick to hipsters in hot pants. They come partly for the stiff pours, sure—but more than partly for the anachronistic brand of hospitality with which they're served: not only do the barkeeps sling shots gratis with your first round of drinks, but they proffer every lady a single rose. True story.

(And one that happens to have a neat twist: the adjacent pizzeria, **Enzo's End**, will deliver surprisingly fine pies right to your bar table.)

Sputnik, 3 S. Broadway, Denver, CO 80229; (720) 570-4503; www .sputnikdenver.com. On the cool kids' permanent rotation, this Baker District hang is your one-stop shop for kitsch of the ornamental and ingestible kind: vintage photo booth and turntables set against pink and orange stripes, check; lawnmower beers like Olympia, Lost Lake, and of course PBR, check; sweet potato fries with your choice of 17 dipping sauces, including the house blend of peanut butter and mayo, check. Goofy cocktails supplement the classic Bloodies and mimosas that flow on the cheap during weekend brunch, when the vibe is relatively mellow, but come showtime at the hi-dive, the adjacent music venue, claustrophobes beware: it's SRO in here.

The Thin Man Tavern, 2015 E. 17th Ave., Denver, CO 80206; (303) 320-7814; www.thinmantavern.com. Like its Dashiell Hammett–penned namesake, The Thin Man cuts an ineffably magnetic figure. Nothing in particular and everything at once stands out in the long, narrow space strung with pink lights: one wall's covered in medieval religious iconography, the other in disarming local artworks, and between them stands a marble-topped bar lined with an eclectic mix of high-end spirits, 16 taps, and 10 jars filled with house-infused spirits in flavors like cantaloupe and tomato-jalapeño. It's also lined, of course, with an appealingly diverse but uniformly laid-back crowd—among them sure to be cinephiles awaiting the Wednesday-night screenings of arthouse fare in the Persian rug–draped Ubisububi Room downstairs (nothing like a little Jim Jarmusch or Wong Kar-wai to go with a pint of Denver's own Glider Cider).

Pubs

See also Appendix B under Beer.

Ale House at Amato's, 2501 16th St., Denver, CO 80211; (303) 433-9734; http://alehousedenver.com. Jointly owned by two local giants—Breckenridge Brewery and Wynkoop Brewing Company— this LoHi hot spot is itself a giant joint, with 400 seats scattered throughout the warm, woody three-story space (which includes a rooftop deck overlooking the downtown skyline). Its 42 taps are devoted almost entirely to Colorado craft beers (with one reserved for cask-conditioned ale); rotation at least twice weekly ensures that there's always something new to try, not only from the principals but also Left Hand, Oskar Blues, Ska, and many more. That the wine and cocktail lists are nothing to sniff at themselves is a pleasant surprise, as is the presence of game on a menu with something for everyone: smoked, ale-steamed elk sausage with goat-cheese mustard and wild-boar burgers with brie? Yes, please.

The British Bulldog, 2052 Stout St., Denver, CO 80205; (303) 295-7974; www.britishbulldogdenver.com. Situated at the edge of downtown, this terrific little pub has nothing to prove in terms of authenticity. Snug and woody yet strikingly detailed—note the copper ceiling tiles, the stained-glass inlays, and the painted booths and wall panels—it's naturally a soccer follower's haven, opening as early as the overseas matches begin on weekends for viewing parties. But no matter when you wander in, you'll be treated to proper pints of ale from across the pond and solid Paki-Anglo pub fare (with or without mash, the juicy bangers are delish, but the spicy *chapli* kebabs are a rarer treat).

The Cheeky Monk Belgian Beer Cafe, 534 E. Colfax Ave., Denver, CO 80203; (303) 861-0347; http://thecheekymonk.com. Saucy moniker notwithstanding, this is a rather distinguished refuge from one of the 'Fax's grittier corners. Spacious and warm in red and brown and dotted with reproductions of Flemish Renaissance masterworks, it specializes in the venerated beers of Belgium, offering roughly 75 in the bottle and 30 on tap—all served in the proper glassware, of course. Owners James and Tina Pachorek are known for acquiring releases like St. Feuillien Blonde and Lindeman's Faro before anyone else in the country, while lining up brewers in the flesh for special events. As an added bonus, the grub is quite good. (Try the mussels in creamy curried broth, sweetened with orange juice and roasted apple slices; the accompanying thin-cut fries come with a delightfully garlicky aioli.) Better still, at the time of this writing, the Pachoreks were finalizing plans to open a brewery of their own next door. Additional locations: 14694 Orchard Pkwy., #700, Westminster, CO 80023; (303) 450-0789; Royal Hilltop, 18581 E. Hampden Ave., Aurora, CO 80013; (303) 690-7738; http://royalhilltop.com.

Falling Rock Tap House, 1919 Blake St., Denver, CO 80202; (303) 293-8338; http://fallingrocktaphouse.com. As the well-known face of what's long been dubbed the unofficial headquarters of the GABF, Chris Black credits "very long relationships with a lot of brewers" for his virtually unmatched ability to "get things that are only available in limited quantities." Once your eyes adjust to the blinding array of some 80 tap handles over the bar and the 2,000-plus beer bottles lining the walls, you'll see for yourself the "affordable luxuries" of which he speaks. Specializing in "extremely hoppy" domestics as well as Belgian imports, Black supplements his enormous, ever-changing selection of craft brews with a reserve list of rare vintages and one-offs. So long as you observe the rules for which he has an infamous (if somewhat tongue-in-cheek) penchant—"no whining, sit up straight, play nice"—there's no telling what liquid wonders you might be privy to.

Freshcraft, 1530 Blake St., Ste. A, Denver, CO 80202; (303) 758-9608; http://freshcraft.com. In a microbrewing mecca like ours, jumping on the craft-beer bandwagon is as easy as sticking your landing is hard. With Freshcraft, three brothers from Iowa have nailed it—and in the jaded market that is LoDo, no less. Offering some 20 beers on tap and more than 100 in the bottle, including a couple dozen on reserve, Jason, Lucas, and Aaron Forgy proudly represent what Jason calls "the renaissance in American artisanal products" (with a few European greats thrown in for good measure). Yet their legions of fans are here as much for the convivality as the connoisseurship. Join them at the ever-hopping bar for a half-pint of Odell's Bourbon Barrel Stout, say, and another of Crabtree's orange blossom–tinged Cezanne Saison. Or take a seat in the back room to watch the big game with a mystery brown bagger: it's on sale if you're willing to take one for the team. Throw in a breaded, fried pork-tenderloin sammy with a lusty "Go, Hawkeyes!" while you're at it.

Rackhouse Pub, 208 S. Kalamath St., Denver, CO 80223; (720) 570-7824; www.rackhousepub.com. Though it's attached to **Stranahan's** (p. 300), Rackhouse is no one-note tasting room. Welcoming the competition, it serves dozens of bourbons, single malts, straight whiskeys, and blends from around the world; locally made products dominate the selection in other spirit categories as well (including two of our favorites, Cap Rock gin and Downslope rum). Likewise, but for one line reserved for out-of-staters, the nearly 20 taps are dedicated strictly to Colorado craft brews, the majority connossieurs' curveballs—think sours and barleywines. At its best, the pub grub's as good as it gets—try the white pizza rustica or the ingenious corned-beef-hash burger. And the warehouse atmosphere's swell too: what co-owner Chris Rippe calls steampunk decor, we just call irreverently comfy. (The *Big Lebowski*–themed portrait of The Dude and Walter Sobchak at the entrance will assure you of that much.)

Wine Bars

See also Appendix B under Wine.

Caveau Wine Bar, 450 E. 17th Ave., Ste. 110, Denver, CO 80203; (303) 861-3747; http://caveauwinebar.com. Don't be deterred by the office-suite setting: this Uptowner is plenty warm and cozy on the inside, done up in rusts and browns and flanked by a brick-arched bar on one side, a fireplace on the other. It's a fine place to linger over a list of about 70 wines, most of which come by the glass—and though the emphasis is on California, lesser-known regions and grapes don't get short shrift: think Slovenian Pinot Grigio, Hondarribi Zuria from Txakoli, or Piedmontese Ruché. Come evening, small plates are served à la carte, but at lunch, they're set up along the bar tapéria-style; $10 will get you your fill of surprisingly good and varied snacks, including tuna-stuffed piquillo peppers, white bean–green apple salad, tomato sauce–glazed meatballs, panini by the wedge, and more.

Cellar Wine Bar, 2556 15th St., Denver, CO 80211; (303) 455-9463; www.cwbon15th.com. The epitome of a modern wine bar, this LoHi looker is sleek as could be in brown and white, gleaming from its marble and blown-glass fixtures to its picture windows to the smiles of its polished staff. And its selection is equally suave: neither too obvious for oenophiles or too obscure for newbies, it hits a sweet spot that's only enhanced by its kicky wine cocktails (Pinot Noir and ginger ale?!) and entrancing infused sakes. Even the small menu of cheeses, salumi, bruschetta, and other nibbles is smartly presented if not unpredictable (at press time, however, a more substantial menu was in the works).

Cork House Wine Restaurant, 4900 E. Colfax Ave., Denver, CO 80220; (303) 355-4488; www.corkhousedenver.com. Except for the occasional Greek white or Bulgarian red, the roughly 50-bottle wine list is only moderately stimulating. Ditto the Med-lite contemporary menu. Why come, then? Because the adequate glasses and plates are set against a beyond-charming backdrop. Two conjoined old houses have been renovated into one quaint stunner composed of several small rooms replete with fireplaces, stained-glass windows, pretty rugs, and bouquets on every table. If nothing else, it's a date-night test: if you can't make intimate conversation here, you can't make it anywhere.

Corridor 44, 1433 Larimer St., Denver, CO 80202; (303) 893-0044; www.corridor44.com. A friend of ours offered the best description we've ever heard of this LoDo Champagne lounge: "very Carol Channing's townhouse." Hello, Dolly! indeed: the long, narrow space, bedecked with chandeliers, plush ivory upholstery, and zebra-print accents, invites misbehavior of the most glamorous kind—and the bubbly all but guarantees it. The several-page list covers everything from Grower Champagnes and prestige cuvées to proseccos, cavas, and other sparklers from around the globe; supplementing some 16 pours by the glass and a handful of Champagne cocktails, themed, handsomely presented flights provide a crash course in, say, sparkling rosés. Meanwhile, the menu is both bigger and, especially if you stick to hors d'oeuvres, better than it has to be.

Sienna Wine Bar & Small Plates, 3422 E. 12th Ave., Denver, CO 80206; (303) 355-2202; www.siennawinebar.com. Romance fills the air at this Congress Park rendezvous. Parlor-cozy, low-lit, and alluringly appointed with Art Nouveau objets, it's run by serious oenophiles who pour what they like and wish to share, not what conventional market wisdom would recommend. Given nearly 30 wines by the glass, including an unusually high number of sparklers, to choose from, discovery is inevitable: a juicy, bubbly Brachetto d'Acqui here, a mineral-nosed Grüner Veltliner or an uncommon

Languedocienne Pinot Noir there. Among the hors d'oeuvres, a nicely done cheese plate suits us fine.

Sketch, 11 W. 1st Ave., Denver, CO 80223; (303) 484-9305; http://sketch-restaurant.com. Next door yet diametrically opposed to its rollicking Mexican sibling, **El Diablo** (p. 183), this European-style wine bar is at once ultra-stylish in glossy ivory and black tones and solidly neighborly, opening well before happy hour and finally shuttering at 2 a.m. In the interim, the polished crew pours some 50 wines by the glass that rarely fail to intrigue, be it a Pinot Noir from Brazil or a botanically infused Orange Muscat. Granted, since the arrival of veteran toque Brian Laird, the cellar's turning increasingly toward the Mediterranean in homage to his marvelous fresh pastas, while the backbar's no less well stocked with craft spirits for the cocktail set.

Vinue Food and Wine Bar, 2817 E. 3rd Ave., Ste. A, Denver, CO 80206; (720) 287-1156; www.denverwinebar.net; $$. Black, white, and red all over, this ultra-chic Cherry Creek lounge is indeed front-page newsworthy thanks to its central feature: card-operated banks of self-serve, pressurized wine dispensers—nearly 70 in all—that allow for the ultimate in customized flights (you can even control the size of each pour). A selection of comely small plates (hello, cheesecake dumplings) only furthers the interactive, mix-and-match experience—right down to the menu itself, featuring battery-powered LED screens that light up when you open it. Think of Vinue, in short, as a toy store for stylish oenophiles.

The Wine Loft, 1527 Wazee St., Denver, CO 80202; (303) 284-3493; http://wineloftdenverlodo.com. Laid out rather like a modern furniture showroom—all well-spaced clusters of leather sectionals and plush ottomans—this LoDo lounge is as refined yet accessible as its wine list, which occupies the middle ground between what you might call steak-house-style greatest hits and lesser-known labels to pique the grape geeks, both by the bottle and by the glass (pours number about 40). The accompanying hors d'oeuvres are reasonably interesting and adequately executed. Still, it's the serene yet sophisticated atmosphere we appreciate above all. Additional location: 7600 Landmark Way, #107, Greenwood Village, 80111; (720) 328-3810; http://wineloftdenverlandmark.com.

Recipes

Tapenade

Every time we visit Panzano, we swear we won't gorge ourselves silly on Elise Wiggins's signature bread dip—and every time we break our vow within seconds of its arrival. We bet it would make a splendid pasta sauce, too.

Makes just over a quart; serves about 12

1 cup sundried tomatoes	**1 cup Kalamata olives, pitted**
¼ cup capers	**¾ cup olive oil**
3 garlic cloves	**2 cups rice oil**
1 ounce anchovies	

With a meat grinder or food processor, mix tomatoes, capers, garlic, anchovies, and Kalamata olives. (If you don't have a grinder or a food processor, finely chop ingredients with a knife.) Then add oils and fold in. Allow 24 hours for flavors to meld.

Courtesy of Executive Chef Elise Wiggins of Panzano (p. 84)

Burrata

So nice a friend of ours once ordered it twice—first for an appetizer, and then again for dessert—Chef-Restaurateur Frank Bonanno's signature burrata, or ricotta-filled mozzarella, is an absolute must at Osteria Marco. But it's also worth a try for ambitious home cooks; even the less aspirational can pull it off with purchased curds, says Bonanno, whose notes are also to be found in parentheses.

Makes 4 8-ounce cheeses

For the ricotta:

1 cup plus ¼ cup heavy cream
2 quarts organic whole milk
5 lemons (1 cup lemon juice)

1 cup buttermilk
Pinch of salt

Tools needed: *cheesecloth*

In a saucepan, bring 1 cup cream and whole milk to a boil. Add lemon juice, buttermilk, and salt; reduce heat to low and simmer, stirring until thick.

Wrap the mixture in cheesecloth; knot the top and hang over the faucet of the kitchen sink. Drain for 24 hours.

With a bowl mixer, whip remaining cream into ricotta until it is the consistency of soft ice cream.

For the mozzarella curd:

2½ teaspoons powdered citric acid (available online or in specialty stores; otherwise, use double the amount of lemon or lime juice)

¾ teaspoon liquid rennet (vegetarian alternatives work as well as the animal-based original)

2 gallons nonhomogenized whole milk (www.realmilk .com, is a good resource)

Tools: *double boiler; cooking thermometer; 2 small glass bowls; cheesecloth*

Line a large colander with a generous amount of cheesecloth (enough to fold up and wrap the top of colander later). Set aside.

In a small glass bowl, dissolve citric acid in ½ cup cool water. In another bowl, mix the rennet with ½ cup water. Set bowls aside.

Warm the milk in a double boiler to 88°F. Remove from heat. Add citric-acid mixture; stir. Add rennet mixture; stir some more until curd forms.

Pour curd into lined colander; place in sink. Wrap cheesecloth all the way around the top of the curd. Set a plate on top of the cheesecloth; atop it, put something heavy (like a large can of tomatoes or a marble rolling pin) so that the weight will bear down on the curd and press all of the liquid into the sink and down the drain. Leave in sink overnight.

For the burrata:

14 ounces mozzarella curd, cut into half-inch cubes   **2 cups ricotta**

Tools: *four 8-ounce ramekins or plastic cupcake pan, greased with 4 teaspoons extra-virgin olive oil*

Put curd into large pot. In another pot, bring about 2 quarts heavily salted water to a boil. Pour the boiling water over the cubed curd and let steep for 10 minutes. While the curd is steeping, set out ramekins or pan.

Remove the curd from the pot, reserving the water, and place into a bowl. With a wooden spoon, knead the curd gently. As it starts to come together, set the spoon aside and use your hands to knead it into 3-ounce balls (about the size of regular meatballs).

Flatten out the balls to about ⅛ inch thick and 6 inches in diameter. Set over the rim of the ramekins.

Scoop 2 large tablespoons ricotta into the center of each piece of mozzarella, using the spoon as you go to gently press the mozzarella down and into the hollow. Fold the cheese that hangs over the edge over the top (if there is a lot of excess, trim with scissors so that it just covers the top; you do not want the burrata to be too thick).

Sprinkle the top of each filled mold with a little of the reserved water—just enough to form a wet seal. Remove and serve at room temperature. Burrata will keep, covered with plastic wrap, in refrigerator for 3 days.

Courtesy of Executive Chef and Owner Frank Bonanno of Osteria Marco (p. 83)

Samosas with Roasted Corn Sauce

You can—and we have—pair this sauce with just about anything on Chef Matt Selby's menu at Vesta Dipping Grill, but there's a reason it comes with the samosas by default.

Makes 16

For the corn sauce:

- 2 ears corn in the husk
- 1 carrot, peeled and chopped
- ½ red onion, peeled and chopped
- 1 rib celery, chopped
- ¼ cup chopped garlic
- 2 cups heavy cream
- 1 stick butter
- ¼ cup tomato juice
- Juice 1 lemon
- 1 teaspoon Worcestershire sauce
- 1 teaspoon Tabasco
- 1 pinch saffron
- ⅛ teaspoon turmeric
- Salt and pepper to taste

Heat oven to 500°F and roast corn for 20 minutes.

While corn is roasting, add carrots, onion, celery, and garlic to a saucepan over medium heat and cook until onions are translucent.

Remove corn from the oven; strip the husks. Cut the kernels from the cob and add them to the carrot mixture.

In a deep saucepan, add the remaining ingredients and bring to a simmer. Cook for 15 minutes.

Transfer the mixture to a food processor and puree. Adjust seasoning with salt and pepper and set aside.

For the samosas:

- 1 red bell pepper
- 1 tablespoon sesame oil
- ¼ cup peeled, diced carrots
- 1 teaspoon minced garlic
- 3 cups cold buttermilk mashed potatoes, your preferred method
- 2 tablespoons minced cilantro

- 1 tablespoon yellow curry paste
- Salt and pepper to taste
- 2 egg yolks
- ¼ cup milk
- 16 small, square egg-roll wrappers
- Cornstarch as necessary
- 3 quarts vegetable oil

Tools: *candy thermometer*

On a hot grill or over an open flame, roast the red pepper to char the flesh on all 4 sides. Place pepper in a bowl and cover with plastic wrap. When it is cool enough to handle—20 minutes or so—peel away the charred flesh; then seed, core, and finely dice.

Heat the sesame oil in a saucepan over high heat. Add the carrots and garlic and sauté until tender, about 3 minutes. Allow to cool slightly.

Place cold buttermilk mashed potatoes in a mixing bowl, and add pepper, carrots, and garlic as well as cilantro and curry paste. Combine and season to taste with salt and pepper. Cool mixture for at least 1 hour before making samosas.

Put egg yolks and milk in a small bowl and whisk to combine.

Lay out the egg-roll skins on a cornstarch–dusted surface, 2–3 at a time, so they resemble diamonds rather than squares before you. Brush a small amount of the egg mixture over each wrapper; then place about 1 tablespoon potato mixture in the center of each. Fold each corner in and over the filling, as though you were wrapping a Christmas (or Hannukah) present.

Place samosas on a cornstarch-dusted tray; lightly dust more cornstarch over the samosas. Chill for about an hour before frying.

Pour vegetable oil into a medium saucepan, and use a candy thermometer to bring temperature up to 350°F. Line a platter with paper towels.

Carefully add 3 to 4 samosas at a time to the hot oil. Use tongs to flip and move samosas to ensure even cooking. Fry for about 4 minutes and remove to platter. Pat dry any excess oil. Serve with roasted corn sauce.

Courtesy of Chef Matt Selby of Vesta Dipping Grill (p. 96)

Colorado Lamb Sliders

Elway's eponymous owner is a sports legend; no wonder, then, that the Cherry Creek flagship's exec chef, Tyler Wiard, has a knack for game-time grub.

Makes 16 sliders

2 pounds ground Colorado
lamb

3 Anaheim chiles

Sea salt and fresh black pepper

⅛ cup canola oil

1 clove fresh garlic

¼ cup cotija cheese (or grated
parmesan)

¼ cup toasted pumpkin seeds

½ cup olive oil

16 slider buns

¼ cup melted butter

16 slices pepper jack cheese
(cut to fit onto buns)

Divide ground lamb into 16 2-ounce portions and form into mini-hamburgers. Set aside. Coat chiles in canola oil and season with salt and pepper; roast on a hot grill or under broiler until charred. Place in a container with a lid and let stand 20–30 minutes so they can steam.

If your skin is sensitive, don gloves. Peel and destem the chiles and remove the seeds. Roughly chop chiles and garlic. Place both together with cotija cheese, pumpkin seeds, and olive oil in a blender. Season with salt and pepper and blend until mixture is smooth. Taste and adjust seasoning if necessary. Set pesto aside.

Butter both sides of the slider buns and toast on grill. Season lamb with salt and pepper, then cook on a grill to desired temperature. Place slices of pepper jack on the patties to melt; set atop bottom buns and add a spoonful of pesto to each one. Add top buns and serve.

Courtesy of Executive Chef Tyler Wiard of Elway's (p. 137)

Bella! Bella! Benny

In addition to the funky pancakes on which it's built an ever-expanding franchise, Snooze serves up a bevy of variations on eggs Benedict; heading up its culinary team, Scott Bermingham and Spencer Lomax put an Italian twist on this popular signature.

Serves 6

For the cream-cheese hollandaise:

4 ounces pasteurized egg yolks
1 tablespoon lemon juice
3 ounces softened cream cheese

1 teaspoon cayenne pepper
¾ pound melted butter, hot
2 teaspoons salt

In a stainless-steel mixing bowl, combine the egg yolks, lemon juice, cream cheese, and cayenne. Whisk ingredients together until combined; still whisking, add the butter in a slow, steady stream until the mixture is emulsified.

Season with salt to taste and keep warm; if the sauce becomes too thick, add a few drops of hot water to thin it out.

For the Benedict:

¼ cup white vinegar
12 eggs
12 slices ciabatta, halved
12 1-ounce slices prosciutto di
  Parma

12 ½-ounce slices taleggio
  cheese
6 ounces baby arugula
6 ounces balsamic vinegar,
  reduced by half

Bring 8 quarts water to a boil; reduce to a simmer and add vinegar. Place eggs in the water to poach, approximately 3–4 minutes for a soft, runny yolk.

While the eggs are poaching, toast ciabatta bread halves and transfer to a plate. Top each slice of bread with 1 slice of prosciutto di Parma; top the prosciutto slices with 1 slice taleggio; and place under a broiler, set on high, until the cheese begins to melt. Transfer onto plates.

Remove eggs from poaching water and place 1 egg on each piece of bread; top with 2 ounces cream-cheese hollandaise. Divide arugula among the plates and an even amount of balsamic reduction to garnish.

Courtesy of Snooze (p. 90)

Grilled Beef Ribeye with Beet Greens and Horseradish Aioli

Leave it to a Boulderite like Black Cat Bistro's Eric Skokan to lace a red-blooded American steak with fresh-picked produce from his own farm.

Serves 4

2 pounds beef ribeye
Salt and pepper to taste
1 tablespoon ground juniper
4 cloves garlic, roasted
Juice half a lemon
1 tablespoon ground fresh
    horseradish

1 egg yolk
1 tablespoon water
2 cups salad oil
1 clove fresh garlic, peeled and
    minced
2 tablespoons salad oil
½ pound beet greens, washed

Season beef with salt, pepper, and juniper. Grill over high heat, turning often, until meat is cooked to desired temperature. Reserve in a warm place.

Combine garlic, lemon juice, horseradish, yolk, water, and salt in the bowl of a food processor. Blend at high speed until homogenous. Slowly drizzle in oil until incorporated. Season to taste.

In a large sauté pan over medium-high heat, cook garlic in oil until it just begins to color, about 20 seconds. Add beet greens and cook until wilted, about 2 minutes. Season to taste with salt.

To serve, slice beef thinly and divide among plates. Garnish with wilted beet greens and horseradish sauce.

Courtesy of Owner and Chef Eric Skokan of Black Cat Bistro (p. 209)

Whole Grilled Trout with Autumn Vegetables in Brown Butter

For this showcase of the local bounty, Jax Executive Chef Sheila Lucero sources trout from Berthoud's E & J Fish Farm, mushrooms from Hazel Dell in Fort Collins, and heirloom pumpkins from Boulder's Munson Farms.

Serves 4

For the trout:

- 4 (1-pound) whole trout, head-on and gutted
- 1 lemon, thinly sliced (at least 8 slices)
- 4 sprigs rosemary
- 8 sprigs thyme
- 4 sprigs parsley
- Olive oil
- Salt and pepper

Rinse all four trout and pat dry; evenly distribute herbs and lemon inside their bellies. Liberally rub the fish on all sides with olive oil, salt, and pepper. Set aside in the refrigerator.

For the mushroom-pumpkin mixture:

- 1 small-to-medium heirloom pumpkin (2–3 pounds)
- Olive oil
- Salt and pepper
- 6 tablespoons butter
- 3 cups mixed mushrooms, coarsely but uniformly chopped
- 8 leaves sage, chiffonaded
- 1 tablespoon minced shallot
- 1 teaspoon minced garlic
- ¼ cup white wine
- 4 cups arugula

Heat oven to 350°F. Peel skin off pumpkin, using a knife; cut in half and remove seeds. Dice pumpkin into 1-inch pieces; toss with olive oil, salt, and pepper. Place on a sheet tray and roast until tender. Remove from oven and cool. Reserve 3 cups for recipe.

Over high heat, add butter to a small saucepan. When it begins to turn amber and give off a nutty aroma, pull the pan from the heat and skim any foam from the surface.

In a large sauté pan, heat brown butter; add mushrooms. Cook over medium heat until slightly softened. Add roasted pumpkin; sauté for another minute. Add sage, shallot, and garlic and cook until sage gets crisp (be careful not to burn the garlic). Deglaze with white wine and toss in arugula; season with salt and pepper. Remove from heat and set aside.

For the Yukon Gold potato puree:

2 pounds Yukon Gold potatoes, peeled and diced into 2-inch pieces

½ cup butter, softened
¾ cup heavy cream, heated
Salt and pepper to taste

Place potatoes in a pot of salted water and bring to a boil. Cook until fork-tender, about 12–15 minutes. Drain potatoes in a colander and return them to the dry pot. Add butter and cream and mash until very smooth (a hand mixer works great). Season with salt and pepper.

To assemble:

Place stuffed trout on a well-oiled grill and cook for 3 minutes. Turn trout 20 degrees to the right; cook for 3 more minutes. Flip trout and repeat the turning procedure.

Warm four large plates. Place a large spoonful of potatoes on the plate; lay grilled trout, belly-side down, on top. Arrange mushroom-pumpkin mixture around and over the fish.

Courtesy of Executive Chef Sheila Lucero of Jax Fish House & Oyster Bar (pp. 80, 217)

Nut Brown Ale Cake with Caramel Icing

Kim and Jake Rosenbarger use Ellie's Brown Ale from Boulder's own Avery Brewing Company, but any similar ale will do.

Makes 1 layer cake to serve 15

For the cake:

6 eggs
3 cups brown sugar
1½ cups oil
2 teaspoons salt
1½ teaspoons baking soda
½ teaspoon baking powder
1 teaspoon ground clove
1 teaspoon ground coriander
2 teaspoons vanilla

3 cups dark-brown ale (two 12-ounce bottles)
4½ cups flour
¾ cup toasted, coarsely chopped nuts (such as hazelnuts, pecans, almonds, and walnuts)
¾ cup processed dried fruit (such as chopped figs, blueberries, cherries, and cranberries)

Preheat oven to 300°F.

Combine first 9 ingredients in 6-quart mixing bowl. With the whisk attachment on speed 2, mix until a shiny batter forms.

Add half the beer to the batter, then all the flour, then the remaining bottle. When everything is incorporated, add nuts and fruit and mix on the same speed until blended.

Pour batter into two greased, wax-lined 9-inch pans and bake for 1 hour or until done (may take longer depending on your oven).

For the icing

2 pounds butter
8 cups brown sugar

2 cups milk
5 pounds powdered sugar

Melt butter and brown sugar in a 4-quart saucepan. When a low boil appears, add milk and bring to full boil. Pour the resulting caramel into a 6-quart mixer bowl and on speed 1, with the whisk attachment, slowly add powdered sugar. When all the sugar is added, bring speed up to 5 or 6 and mix until all the lumps are gone. Let cool.

For assembly:

When cake and icing are cool, turn cakes out of their pans and cut the tops off each layer so they are level. Put one layer on whatever serving plate you plan to use.

Gently apply a thin coat of caramel icing to the first layer. Add second layer to the top of the first. Cover the cake with the remaining icing.

(Note: Caramel will keep for 2–4 weeks in the refrigerator if stored in a plastic container with a tight lid. To use later, take out of fridge and let icing come to room temperature, or microwave the icing for no more than 30 seconds or so, checking every 10 seconds.)

Courtesy of Kim Rosenbarger, Co-Owner of Kim & Jake's Cakes (p. 253)

Funnel Cake—Fried Bananas with Peanut-Butter Caramel

Although the first and second times were too, the third time was a hell of a charm for Jennifer Jasinski and Beth Gruitch of Rioja and Bistro Vendôme. With the immeasurable help of chef de cuisine Jorel Pierce and pastry chef Eric Dale, they've made a smash success of LoDo gastropub Euclid Hall. This dessert is just one of many runaway hits.

Serves 4

For the batter:

7⅔ ounces all-purpose flour

1 teaspoon baking powder

1 tablespoon granulated sugar

¼ teaspoon kosher salt

2 whole eggs

8 ounces whole milk

½ teaspoon vanilla extract

Tools: *5-quart mixer*

In a large mixing bowl, sift together the flour, baking powder, sugar, and salt; set aside.

In the bowl of a 5-quart mixer, beat the eggs until aerated and frothy; gradually add in the milk and vanilla and beat to combine. Add the dry mixture to the wet in three stages, beating just to combine and scraping after each addition. Place batter in tightly covered container and refrigerate until needed. May be stored for 2 days.

For the peanut-butter caramel:

14 fluid ounces heavy cream
2 tablespoons peanut butter
1 cup water

2 cups sugar
¼ cup corn syrup

Combine the cream and peanut butter in a medium saucepan and bring to a simmer over medium heat. Whisk to emulsify; keep warm.

In a large saucepan combine the water, sugar, and syrup; with a wooden spoon, stir to combine. Over high heat, bring the mixture to a boil; continue heating until the mixture is golden-brown in color.

Bring cream mixture to a boil and add to the syrup (careful—it will splatter); whisk to combine.

For the bananas:

Peanut oil as necessary
4 bananas

4 wooden skewers
Powdered sugar as necessary

Add peanut oil to a medium stockpot until ⅓ full; heat to medium-high.

Slice bananas into 1-inch rings and thread them onto the skewers; dip into the batter until thoroughly coated. Fry until the batter is golden-brown.

Carefully transfer the skewered bananas to a serving plate that has been drizzled with ¼ cup peanut-butter caramel. Dust with powdered sugar and enjoy.

Courtesy of Jennifer Jasinski, Executive Chef and Partner of Euclid Hall (p. 76)

Sweet-and-Savory Bread Pudding on a Stick

How to account for the cult legend that is Andrew Novick? He was a member of the seminal, long-defunct-but-still-beloved local punk band the Warlock Pinchers. His mind-boggling found-art collection was displayed at a much-talked-about 2009 gallery exhibit titled "The Astounding Problem of Andrew Novick"; in 2011, he served as an expert witness on marshmallows at the infamous so-called Peeps Trial in Boulder (Google it to believe it). And now, the entertainment director of the Denver County Fair is also a chef-about-town who hosts pop-up dinners on themes ranging from cereal to surgery. Fresh off the success of his 2011 Thanksgiving on a Stick blowout, he offered us this related recipe.

Makes about 18 skewers

2 cups corn bread stuffing cubes

2 cups herbed stuffing cubes

2 tablespoons butter, melted

3 eggs

2 cups milk

½ cup dark brown sugar

½ cup organic sugar

2 teaspoons cinnamon

½ teaspoon nutmeg

½ teaspoon ginger

fleur de sel

2 jars prepared caramel sauce

Tools: *deep-fryer, wooden skewers*

Preheat oven to 350°F.

Grease a standard glass baking dish. Add all stuffing cubes to dish; drizzle melted butter over cubes and mix well.

In a mixing bowl, combine the remaining ingredients and beat well. Pour the mixture over the stuffing cubes and push down cubes to make sure they are all covered with egg mixture. Bake for 40–45 minutes or until the top is springy.

Use a mini–ice cream scoop to make balls of the bread pudding. Thread each ball onto a wooden stick and deep-fry at 375°F until the outside is crisp.

Sprinkle with a few grains of fleur de sel and serve with caramel sauce.

Courtesy of Andrew Novick

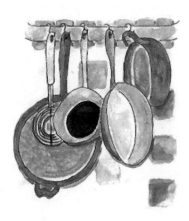

Aspen Highland

The owner and beverage director of Boulder's OAK at Fourteenth, Bryan Dayton, may be a nationally recognized barman, but his commitment to the community remains intact, as revealed by this Colorado-proud cocktail recipe.

Serves 1

2 ounces Stranhan's Colorado Whiskey

½ ounce Leopold Bros. Three Pins Alpine Herbal Liqueur

½ ounce honey (from Boulder's own Uncle Pete's Bees)

2 dashes Bittermens Xocolatl mole bitters

Orange peel for garnish

Place all ingredients into a mixing glass; add ice. Stir, then strain. Serve in an old-fashioned glass over 1 large piece of ice. Garnish with an orange peel.

Courtesy of Bryan Dayton, Owner and Beverage Director of OAK at Fourteenth (p. 225)

Pueblo Chili Flip

The bar at Root Down built its reputation on cocktails like this: at once earthy and airy, flirty and, yes, rootsy.

Makes 1

- ¾ ounce green chile-infused Espolón reposado tequila*
- ¾ ounce St. Germain elderflower liqueur
- ¾ ounce fresh squeezed organic lemon juice
- ½ ounce pasteurized egg white
- ½ ounce brown-sugar simple syrup**
- Dash Fee Brothers plum bitters
- ¼ ounce organic beet juice
- Sage leaf

Combine first 6 ingredients in a mixing glass. Dry shake without ice for 20 seconds.

Add ice and shake again.

Strain into chilled cocktail glass and drizzle beet juice over froth; garnish with sage leaf.

* Add fresh green chiles of your choice to the bottle and let sit for 2 days.

** Combine equal parts boiling water and brown sugar. Stir until the granules are dissolved and let cool.

Courtesy of Justin Cucci, Owner of Root Down (p. 43)

Appendices

Appendix A: Eateries by Cuisine

American

bang!, 22

Bastien's Restaurant, 161

Berkshire, The, 22

Buff Restaurant, The, 243

Chautauqua Dining Hall, 244

Coop de Ville at the Stingray
    Lounge, 26

DJ's Berkeley Cafe, 26

Dot's Diner, 245

Ellyngton's, 99

Hash, 33

Highland's Garden Cafe, 34

Interstate Kitchen & Bar, 186

Jelly, 141

Lou's Food Bar, 40

Market, The, 100

Mikes2 Kitchen, 15

Modmarket, 225

Pete's Kitchen, 165

Sam's No. 3, 103

Snooze, 90

Steuben's, 156

Syrup, 158

Tangerine, 237

Tocabe: An American Indian
    Eatery, 44

Walnut Cafe, 240

Argentinian

Buenos Aires Pizzeria, 65

Asian Fusion

Bones, 134

CholLon Modern Asian Bistro, 69

Izakaya Den, 187

Red Claw, The 120
TAG, 92
Zengo, 97

Bakery/Cafe
Breadworks, 211
Caffe, 212
Crave Dessert Bar & Lounge, 72
D Bar Desserts, 138
Devil's Food Bakery &
    Cookery, 182
Dolce Sicilia Italian Bakery, 268
Duffeyroll Cafe, The, 200
Gaia Bistro + Rustic Bakery, 184
Hi*Rise, 79
Les Delices de Paris, 202
Market, The, 100
Pajama Baking Company, 191
Paris on the Platte, 85
Rise & Shine Biscuit Kitchen &
    Cafe, 154
Spuntino, 44
Sugar Bakeshop, 204
Tasterie Truck, The, 17
Trompeau Bakery, 279
Udi's Bread Cafe, 46
Wooden Spoon Cafe & Bakery, 47

Bar & Grill
Billy's Inn, 48
Bonnie Brae Tavern, 195
Charlie Brown's Bar and Grill, 163
Cherry Cricket, The, 163
LoHi SteakBar, 38
My Brother's Bar, 101
Ship Tavern, 103
Sink, The, 247
Wazee Supper Club, 105
West End Tavern, 240

Barbecue
Big Hoss Bar-B-Q, 23
Boney's BBQ, 64
Jabo's Bar-Be-Q, 270
Russell's Smokehouse, 90
Shead's BBQ & Fish Hut, 275

Brazilian
Cafe Brazil, 24

Burgers
HBurgerCO, 78
Highland Tap & Burger, 35
Larkburger, 189
Park Burger, 192

Rueben's Burger Bistro, 233

Cajun/Creole
Lucile's Creole Cafe, 197, 246

Chinese/Taiwanese
Chef Liu's Authentic Chinese
    Cuisine, 265
China Jade, 266
East Asia Garden, 183
JJ Chinese Seafood Restaurant, 113
King's Land Chinese Seafood
    Restaurant, 114
Lao Wang Noodle House, 115
Star Kitchen, 122
Super Star Asian Cuisine, 122
Tao Tao Noodle Bar, 277
Zoe Ma Ma, 241

Contemporary
Aria, 132
Beatrice & Woodsley, 174
Bittersweet, 175
Black Cat Bistro, 209
Black Pearl, 178
cafe | bar, 179
Charcoal Restaurant, 68

Coohills, 71
Corner Office, The, 71
Deluxe, 181
Duo, 27
Empire Lounge & Restaurant,
    The, 268
1515 Restaurant, 77
Flagstaff House, 245
Fruition, 139
Fuel Cafe, 32
Kitchen, The, 81, 218
Mizuna, 145
OAK at Fourteenth, 225
Opus, 274
Palace Arms, 101
Potager, 152
Q's Restaurant, 246
Restaurant Kevin Taylor, 102
Root Down, 43
Row 14 Bistro & Wine Bar, 89
SALT the Bistro, 234
Satchel's on 6th, 154
Second Home Kitchen + Bar, 155
Strings, 166
Table 6, 159
Trillium, 94
twelve restaurant, 95

Vesta Dipping Grill, 96

Cuban
Cuba Cuba Cafe and Bar, 73
Cuba Cuba Sandwicheria, 214

Deli
Bender's Brat Haus, 264
East Side Kosher Deli, 201
Jimmy & Drew's 28th Street
    Deli, 201
Salvaggio's Deli, 235

Ethiopian
Abyssinia, 132
Arada Restaurant, 174
Queen of Sheba, 153
Ras Kassa's Ethiopian
    Restaurant, 232

French
Bistro Vendôme, 63
Brasserie Ten Ten, 210
Indulge French Bistro, 36
La Merise, 143
L'Atelier, 219
Le Central, 99

Le Grand Bistro & Oyster Bar, 81
Mateo, 221
Village Cork, The, 194
Z Cuisine & À Côté, 47

Gastropub
Colt & Gray, 70
Euclid Hall, 76
Ghost Plate & Tap, 77
Jonesy's EatBar, 141

German
Cafe Berlin, 66

Ghanian
African Grill & Bar, 261

Greek
Athenian Restaurant, 263
Axios Estiatorio, 21
Yanni's, 282

Hot Dogs/Sausages
Biker Jim's Gourmet Dogs, 62
Steve's Snappin' Dogs, 157
Über Sausage, The, 159

Hungarian
Budapest Bistro, 179

Indian/Himalayan
Azitra, 263
Jai Ho, 271
Masalaa, 273
Sherpa House Restaurant and
    Cultural Center, 276
Tiffin's, 239
Yak and Yeti, 281

Italian
Arugula Bar e Ristorante, 209
Barolo Grill, 133
Cafe Jordano, 264
Crimson Canary, 180
Frasca Food and Wine, 215
Gaetano's, 49
Gennaro's Cafe Italiano, 86
Il Posto, 140
Laudisio, 220
Luca d'Italia, 144
Lucky Pie Pizza and Tap House, 86
Osteria Marco, 83
Pagliacci's, 50
Panzano, 84

Parisi, 42
PastaVino, 226
Patsy's Inn, 51
Radda Trattoria, 232
Trattoria Stella, 45

Japanese/Sushi
Domo, 126
Izakaya Amu, 216
KiKi's Japanese Casual
    Dining, 189
Oshima Ramen, 190
Sushi Den, 197
Sushi Sasa, 91
Sushi Tora, 236
Sushi Zanmai, 237

Korean
Korea House, 272
Seoul BBQ, 275
Silla, 276

Mediterranean
Ambria, 61
Mediterranean Restaurant,
    The, 226
Olivéa, 146

Rioja, 88
Solera, 156

Mexican
Agave Mexico Bistro & Tequila
  House, 208
Brewery Bar II, 56
Casa Bonita, 282
Chili Verde, 25
Comida, 14
Efrain's II, 57
El Camino, 30
El Diablo, 183
El Olvido, 28
El Original Tacos Jalisco, 31
El Paraiso, 28
El Taco de Mexico, 195
Guadalajara Authentic Mexican
  Buffet, 269
Jack-n-Grill, 126
Lola Coastal Mexican, 39
Los Carboncitos, 40
Original Chubby's, The, 49
Patzcuaro's, 29
Paxia, 29
Pinche Tacos, 15
Santiago's, 57

Socorro's, 57
Tacos y Salsas #3, 123
Tamayo, 94
Tarasco's New Latin Cuisine, 124

Middle Eastern
Ali Baba Grill, 262
Amira Bakery & Deli, 173
Arabesque, 176
Boulder Dushanbe Teahouse, 243
Damascus Grill, 267
House of Kabob, 176
Jerusalem Restaurant, 196
Mecca Grill, 177
Phoenician Kabob, 151
Pickled Lemon, 228
Shondiz, 16
Ya Hala Grill, 177

Moroccan
Mataam Fez, 145
Palais Casablanca, 192
Tangier Moroccan Cuisine, 238

Nigerian
Hessini Roots International
  Cafe, 270

Organic
Mercury Cafe, 164
Stick It to Me, 16

Pan-Latin
Centro Latin Kitchen &
   Refreshment Palace, 213

Peruvian
Los Cabos II, 82

Pizza
Basic Kneads Pizza, 14
Brava! Pizzeria della Strada, 64
Ernie's Bar & Pizza, 31
Fat Sully's New York Pizza, 138
Hops & Pie, 36
Kaos Pizzeria, 188
Lala's Wine Bar + Pizzeria, 142
Marco's Coal-Fired Pizza, 83
Oven Pizza e Vino, The, 87
Pizzeria Basta, 228
Pizzeria da Lupo, 229
Pizzeria Locale, 230
Proto's Pizzeria Napoletana, 87
Virgilio's Pizzeria & Wine Bar, 280
Walnut Room, The, 87

Wazee Wood Fire Pizza, 97

Polish
Belvedere Restaurant, 62
Cracovia Restaurant and Bar, 266

Salvadoran
El Chalate, 222
Pupusas Sabor Hispano, 231

Sandwiches
Ba Le Sandwich, 118
Buchi Cafe Cubano, 24
Dish Gourmet, 214
Hutch & Spoon, 79
Las Tortas, 29
Las Tortugas, 115
Masterpiece Delicatessen, 41
Red Star Deli, 88
Salvaggio's Deli, 235
Vert Kitchen, 193

Seafood
GB Fish and Chips, 185
Highland Pacific, 33
Jax Fish House & Oyster Bar,
   80, 217

Small Plates/Tapas
Cafe Aion, 211
Chlóe Mezze Lounge, 68
Izakaya Den, 187
Linger, 37
Ondo's Spanish Tapas Bar, 144
Riffs Urban Fare, 233
TAG | Raw Bar, 93

Somali
Maandeeq East African Cafe, 273

Southeast Asian
Jaya Asian Grill, 187
Street Kitchen Asian Bistro, 277

Southern
CoraFaye's Cafe, 136
Denver Biscuit Co., 13, 138
Tom's Home Cookin', 104

Southwestern
Zolo Grill, 242

Steakhouse
Broker Restaurant, The, 98
Buckhorn Exchange, The, 125

District Meats, 74
EDGE Restaurant & Bar, 74
Elway's, 75, 137
Fort, The, 283
Pearl Street Steak Room, 227

Thai
Chada Thai, 162
Phat Thai, 151
Thai Avenue, 238
Thai Flavor, 278
Thai Food Cart, 17
US Thai Cafe, 280

Vegetarian
City, O' City, 135
Leaf Vegetarian Restaurant, 221
WaterCourse Foods, 160
Zudaka, 223

Venezuelan
Empanada Express Grill, 222
Quiero Arepas, 16

Vietnamese
Chez Thuy, 118
DaLat Vietnamese Cuisine, 113

Manna from Heaven, 15
New Saigon, 116
Parallel 17, 150
Pho Duy, 117
Pho-natic, 119

Pho 95 Noodle House, 119
Saigon Bowl (aka Dong
    Khanh), 121
T-Wa Inn, 119
Viet's, 119

Appendix B: Specialties & Specialty Food

In some ways, this is a Best of Denver/Boulder round-up; not every listing that could fall under a given category does. What's more, some listings appear under more than one category—they're just that worthy.

Baked Goods

Breadworks, 211
Caffe, 212
Crave Dessert Bar & Lounge, 72
D Bar Desserts, 137
Dah Won Rice Cake, 284
Denver Biscuit Co., 13
Denver Bread Company, The, 53
Devil's Food Bakery & Cookery, 82
Dolce Sicilia Italian Bakery, 268
Gaia Bistro + Rustic Bakery, 184
Happy Cakes Bakeshop, 54
Hi*Rise, 79
Kim & Jake's Cakes, 253
Les Delices de Paris, 202
Lovely Confections, 168
Omonoia Greek Bakery, 170
Pajama Baking Company, 191
Rheinlander Bakery, 288
Rise & Shine Biscuit Kitchen and Cafe, 154
Spruce Confections, 257

Sugar Bakeshop, 204
Taste of Denmark, 289
Tasterie Truck, The, 17
Tee & Cakes, 257
Trompeau Bakery, 279
Udi's Bread Cafe, 46
Vinh Xuong Bakery, 129
Walnut Cafe, 240
Wednesday's Pie, 111
Wooden Spoon Cafe & Bakery, 47

Beer

Ale House at Amato's, 311
Argonaut Wine & Liquor, 166
Avery Brewing Company, 293
Breckenridge Brewery & BBQ, 294
British Bulldog, The, 312
Bull & Bush Pub & Brewery, 294
Cheeky Monk Belgian Beer Café,
    The, 312
Copper Kettle Brewing Co., 295
Denver Beer Co., 296
Dry Dock Brewing Company, 297
Euclid Hall, 76
Falling Rock Tap House, 313
Freshcraft, 313
Great Divide Brewing Co., 297

Highland Tap & Burger, 35
Hops & Pie, 36
Kitchen, The, 81, 218
Liquor Mart, 254
Lucky Pie Pizza and Tap House, 86
Mountain Sun Pub & Brewery, 298
Rackhouse Pub, 314
Renegade Brewing Company, 300
Rueben's Burger Bistro, 233
Strange Brewing Company, 301
Twisted Pine Brewing Company, 301
Upslope Brewing Company, 301
West End Tavern, 8, 240
Wit's End Brewing Company, 302
Wynkoop Brewing Company, 302
Yak and Yeti, 281

Breakfast

Cafe Aion, 211
DJ's Berkeley Cafe, 26
Ellyngton's, 99
Hash, 33
Hutch & Spoon, 79
Jelly, 141
Lucile's Creole Cafe, 197, 246
Red Star Deli, 88
Snooze, 90

Syrup, 158
Tangerine, 237
WaterCourse Foods, 160

Cheese
Cured, 249
Osteria Marco, 83
St. Kilian's Cheese Shop, 59
Truffle Cheese Shop, The, 171

Chocolate
Chocolate Therapist, The, 184
Dietrich's Chocolate &
  Espresso, 199
Piece, Love and Chocolate, 255

Cinnamon Rolls
Duffeyroll Café, The, 200

Cocktail Bars and Noteworthy Cocktail Lists (see also Spirits)
Amaro Drinkery Italia, 303
Beatrice & Woodsley, 174
Bitter Bar, The, 304
CholLon Modern Asian Bistro, 69
Colt & Gray, 70

Cruise Room, The, 304
Green Russell, 305
Linger, 37
Mario's Double Daughters
  Salotto, 306
OAK at Fourteenth, 225
Peaks Lounge, 306
Root Down, 43
SALT the Bistro, 234
Steuben's, 156
TAG | Raw Bar, 93
Williams & Graham, 307

Coffee
Boxcar Coffee Roasters, 248
Buchi Cafe Cubano, 24
Common Grounds, 52
Crema Coffee House, 106
Huckleberry Roasters, 107
Kaladi Brothers Coffee, 201
Novo Coffee, 108
Pablo's Coffee, 170

Dim Sum & Dumplings
Celestial Bakery, Deli & BBQ, 127
East Asia Garden, 183
JJ Chinese Seafood Restaurant, 113

King's Land Chinese Seafood
Restaurant, 114
Lao Wang Noodle House, 115
Star Kitchen, 122
Street Kitchen Asian Bistro, 277
Zoe Ma Ma, 241

Empanadas & Pupusas
Buenos Aires Pizzeria, 65
El Chalate, 222
Empanada Express Grill, 222
Maria Empanada, 286
Pupusas Sabor Hispano, 231

Farm to Table
Bittersweet, 175
Black Cat Bistro, 209
Cafe Aion, 211
Fruition, 139
Kitchen, The, 81, 218
Potager, 152
SALT the Bistro, 234
twelve restaurant, 95
Vert Kitchen, 193

Fries
Jonesy's EatBar, 141

Manneken Frites, 285
Sputnik, 310

Game
Buckhorn Exchange, The, 125
Fort, The, 283

Happy Hour
Brasserie Ten Ten, 210
Broker Restaurant, The, 98
Charlie Brown's Bar and Grill, 163
Highland Pacific, 33
Jax Fish House & Oyster Bar,
80, 217
Lola Coastal Mexican, 39
Mediterranean Restaurant, The, 224
Ondo's Spanish Tapas Bar, 147
Panzano, 84
Row 14 Bistro & Wine Bar, 89
Strings, 166

Hot Dogs and Sausages (see
also Specialty Markets)
Bender's Brat Haus, 264
Biker Jim's Gourmet Dogs, 14, 62
Cafe Berlin, 66
Cracovia Restaurant and Bar, 266

Salumeria Cinque Soldi, 203
Steve's Snappin' Dogs, 157
Über Sausage, The, 13, 159

Ice Cream, Gelato & Frozen
Yogurt
Bonnie Brae Ice Cream, 198
Liks Ice Cream, 168
Little Man Ice Cream, 54
Pajama Baking Company, 191
Rush, 256
Spuntino, 44
Sweet Action, 204
Sweet Cow Ice Cream, 288
Two Spoons, 258

Late-Night Dining
Biker Jim's Gourmet Dogs (week-
    ends only), 62
City, O' City, 135
El Diablo, 183
Fat Sully's New York Pizza, 138
Original Chubby's, The (weekends
    only), 49
Pete's Kitchen, 165
Row 14 Bistro & Wine Bar, 89
Star Kitchen (weekends only), 122

Tacos y Salsas #3, 123
Williams & Graham, 307

Offal
Bittersweet, 175
Colt & Gray, 70
CoraFaye's Cafe, 136
Euclid Hall, 76
JJ Chinese Seafood Restaurant, 113

Oysters
Brasserie Ten Ten, 210
Jax Fish House & Oyster Bar,
    80, 217
Le Grand Bistro & Oyster Bar, 81

Prix-Fixe Menus
Barolo Grill, 133
Black Cat Bistro, 209
Frasca Food and Wine, 215
Opus, 274
Palace Arms, 101
Sushi Sasa, 91

Seafood (Retail)
Pacific Mercantile, 108
Pacific Ocean Marketplace, 129

Seafood Landing, 58

Specialty Markets

Arash International Market, 283
Caffe, 212
Carbone's Italian Sausage Market
  & Deli, 52
Continental Deli, 167
Cook's Fresh Market, 105
Cured, 249
East Side Kosher Deli, 201
EVOO Marketplace, 107
Little Saigon Supermarket, 128
Marczyk Fine Foods, 169
Oliver's Meat & Seafood
  Market, 169
Pacific Mercantile, 108
Pacific Ocean Marketplace, 129
Paris Baguette Bakery, 286
Parisi, 42
Pig & Block Charcuterie, The, 55
Rancho Liborio, 287
Salumeria Cinque Soldi, 203
Savory Spice Shop, 109
Tony's Market, 110
Vinnola's Italian Market, 289

Spirits

Agave Mexico Bistro & Tequila
  House, 208
Argonaut Wine & Liquor, 166
Billy's Inn, 48
Bull & Bush Pub &
  Brewery, 294
Cafe Brazil, 24
Divino Wine & Spirits, 199
El Diablo, 183
Liquor Mart, 254
Lola Coastal Mexican, 39
Mondo Vino, 54
Pints Pub, 299
Rackhouse Pub, 314
West End Tavern, 240

Tacos & Burritos

Comida, 14
El Original Tacos Jalisco, 31
El Taco de Mexico, 195
Jack-n-Grill, 126
Original Chubby's, The, 49
Pinche Tacos, 15
Santiago's, 57
Socorro's, 57
Tacos y Salsas #3, 123

Tocabe: An American Indian Eatery, 44

Tea
Boulder Dushanbe Teahouse, 243
English Teacup, The, 285
Ku Cha, 254
Tres Jolie, 289

Wine (Retail)
Argonaut Wine & Liquor, 166
Boulder Wine Merchant, 248
Divino Wine & Spirits, 199
Liquor Mart, 254
Mondo Vino, 54
r + d Wine, 202

Wine Bars & Noteworthy Wine Lists
Arugula Bar e Ristorante, 166
Barolo Grill, 133
Bittersweet, 175
Black Cat Bistro, 209
Caveau Wine Bar, 315
Cellar Wine Bar, 316

Corridor 44, 317
Elway's, 75, 137
1515, 77
Flagstaff House, 245
Fort, The, 283
Frasca Food and Wine, 215
Fuel Cafe, 32
Lala's Wine Bar + Pizzeria, 142
Laudisio, 200
Linger, 37
Luca d'Italia, 144
Palace Arms, 101
Pizzeria Locale, 230
Restaurant Kevin Taylor, 102
Row 14 Bistro & Wine Bar, 89
SALT the Bistro, 234
Sienna Wine Bar & Small Plates, 317
Sketch, 318
Table 6, 159
Village Cork, The 194
Vinue Food and Wine Bar, 318
Wine Loft, The, 319
Z Cuisine & À Côté, 47

Index

A

Abyssinia, 132
African Grill & Bar, 261
Agave Mexico Bistro & Tequila
   House, 208
Ale House at Amato's, 311
Ali Baba Grill, 262
Amaro Drinkery Italia, 303
Ambria, 61
Amira Bakery & Deli, 173
Arabesque, 176
Arada Restaurant, 174
Arash International
   Market, 283
Argonaut Wine & Liquor, 166
Aria, 132
Arugula Bar e Ristorante, 209
A Taste of Colorado, 10
Athenian Restaurant, 263
Avery Brewing Company, 293
Axios Estiatorio, 21
Azitra, 263

B

Ba Le Sandwich, 118
bang!, 22
Barolo Grill, 133
Basic Kneads Pizza, 14
Bastien's Restaurant, 161
Beatrice & Woodsley, 174
Belvedere Restaurant, 62
Bender's Brat Haus, 264
Berkshire, The, 22
Beware of Dog, 8
Bhakti Chai, 250
Big Hoss Bar-B-Q, 23
Biker Jim's Gourmet Dogs, 14, 62
Billy's Inn, 48
Bistro Vendôme, 63
Bitter Bar, The, 304
Bittersweet, 175
Black Cat Bistro, 209
Black Pearl, 178
Bones, 134
Boney's BBQ, 64

Bonnie Brae Ice Cream, 198
Bonnie Brae Tavern, 195
Boulder Brew Bus, 8
Boulder Distillery & Clear Spirit
    Company, 293
Boulder Dushanbe Teahouse, 243
Boulder Farmers' Market, 148
Boulder Locavore, 5
Boulder Wine Merchant, 248
Boxcar Coffee Roasters, 248
Brasserie Ten Ten, 210
Brava! Pizzeria della Strada, 64
Breadworks, 211
Breckenridge Brewery & BBQ, 294
British Bulldog, The, 312
Broker Restaurant, The, 98
Buchi Cafe Cubano, 24
Buckhorn Exchange, The, 125
Budapest Bistro, 179
Buenos Aires Pizzeria, 65
Buff Restaurant, The, 243
Bull & Bush Pub & Brewery, 294
buying local meat, 67

C
Cafe Aion, 211
cafe | bar, 179

Cafe Berlin, 66
Cafe Brazil, 24
Cafe Jordano, 264
Cafe Society, 5
Caffe, 212
Carbone's Italian Sausage Market
    & Deli, 52
Casa Bonita, 282
Caveau Wine Bar, 315
Celestial Bakery, Deli & BBQ, 127
Cellar Wine Bar, 316
Central & South American
    food, 222
Centro Latin Kitchen &
    Refreshment Palace, 213
Chada Thai, 162
Charcoal Restaurant, 68
Charlie Brown's Bar & Grill, 163
Chautauqua Dining Hall, 244
Cheeky Monk Belgian Beer Cafe,
    The, 312
Chef Driven, 14
Chef Liu's Authentic Chinese
    Cuisine, 265
Cherry Creek Fresh Market, 148
Cherry Cricket, The, 163
Chez Thuy, 118

Chili Verde, 25
China Jade, 266
Chlóe Mezze Lounge, 68
Chocolate Therapist, The, 284
CholLon Modern Asian Bistro, 69
City, O' City, 135
City Park Esplanade Fresh
    Market, 148
Civic Center EATS Outdoor Cafe, 9
Colorado Beer Week, 9
Colorado Dragon Boat Festival, 10
Colorado Winery Row, 295
Colorado Wino, 5
Colt & Gray, 70
Comida, 14
Common Grounds, 52
Continental Deli, 167
Coohills, 71
Cook's Fresh Market, 105
Coop de Ville at the Stingray
    Lounge, 26
Copper Kettle Brewing
    Company, 295
CoraFaye's Cafe, 136
Cork House Wine Restaurant, 316
Corner Office, The, 71
Corridor 44, 317

Cracovia Restaurant and Bar, 266
Crave Dessert Bar & Lounge, 72
Crema Coffee House, 106
Crimson Canary, 180
Cruise Room, The, 304
Cuba Cuba Cafe and Bar, 73
Cuba Cuba Sandwicheria, 214
Culinary Colorado, 5
Cured, 249

D

Dah Won Rice Cake, 284
DaLat Vietnamese Cuisine, 113
Damascus Grill, 267
D Bar Desserts, 137
Deluxe, 181
Denveater, 5
Denver Beer Co., 296
Denver Beer Fest, 11
Denver Biscuit Co., 13
Denver Bread Company, The, 53
Denver Dish, The, 5
Denver Food and Wine, 11
Denver International Wine Fest, 12
Denver Off the Wagon, 7
Denver On a Spit, 7
Denver Post, The, 7

Denver Pretzel Co., 250
Denver Restaurant Week, 8
Denver Street Food, 7
Denver Urban Homesteading
    Indoor Farmers Market, 149
Devil's Food Bakery & Cookery, 182
Dietrich's Chocolate &
    Espresso, 199
Dish Gourmet, 214
District Meats, 74
Divino Wine & Spirits, 199
DJ's Berkeley Cafe, 26
Dolce Sicilia Italian Bakery, 268
Domo, 126
Don's Club Tavern, 308
Dot's Diner, 245
Dry Dock Brewing Company, 297
Duffeyroll Cafe, The, 200
Duo, 27

E

East Asia Garden, 183
East Side Kosher Deli, 201
Eat Drink Denver, 7
EDGE Restaurant & Bar, 74
Efrain's II, 56
El Camino, 30

El Chalate, 222
El Diablo, 183
Ellyngton's, 99
El Olvido, 28
El Original Tacos Jalisco, 31
El Paraiso, 28
El Taco de Mexico, 195
Elway's, 75, 137
Empanada Express Grill, 222
Empire Lounge & Restaurant,
    The, 268
English Teacup, The, 285
Ernie's Bar & Pizza, 31
Euclid Hall, 76
EVOO Marketplace, 107

F

Falling Rock Tap House, 313
farmers' markets, 148
Fat Sully's New York Pizza, 13
Fat Sully's New York Pizza/Denver
    Biscuit Co., 138
Fermentedly Challenged, 7
1515 Restaurant, 77
First Bite Boulder, 13
Flagstaff House, 245
Fort, The, 283

Frasca Food and Wine, 215
Freshcraft, 313
Fruition, 139
Fuel Cafe, 32

G

Gaetano's, 49
Gaia Bistro + Rustic Bakery, 184
GB Fish and Chips, 185
Gennaro's Cafe Italiano, 86
Ghost Plate & Tap, 77
Glacier Homemade Ice Cream & Gelato, 252
Great American Beer Festival (GABF), 11
Great Divide Brewing Co., 297
Greek Festival, 10
green chile, 56
Green Russell, 305
Guadalajara Authentic Mexican Buffet, 269

H

Happy Cakes Bakeshop, 53
Harvest Week, 12
Hash, 33
HBurgerCO, 78

Helliemae's Salt Caramels, 250
Hessini Roots International Cafe, 270
Highland Pacific, 33
Highland's Garden Cafe, 34
Highland Tap & Burger, 35
Hi*Rise, 79
Hops & Pie, 36
House of Kabob, 176
Huckleberry Roasters, 107
Hush, 8
Hutch & Spoon, 79

I

Il Posto, 140
Indie Eats, 7
indie food producers, 250
Indulge French Bistro, 36
Infinite Monkey Theorem, The, 298
Interstate Kitchen & Bar, 186
Izakaya Amu, 216
Izakaya Den, 187

J

Jabo's Bar-Be-Q, 270
Jack-n-Grill, 126
Jai Ho, 271

Jax Fish House & Oyster Bar,
    80, 217
Jaya Asian Grill, 187
Jelly, 141
Jerusalem Restaurant, 196
Jimmy & Drew's 28th Street
    Deli, 218
JJ Chinese Seafood Restaurant, 113
Jonesy's EatBar, 141
Juneteenth, 10

K

Kaladi Brothers Coffee, 201
Kaos Pizzeria, 188
KiKi's Japanese Casual
    Dining, 189
Kim & Jake's Cakes, 253
Kinga's Lounge, 62
King's Land Chinese Seafood
    Restaurant, 114
Kitchen, The, 81, 218
Korea House, 272
Ku Cha, 254

L

Lala's Wine Bar + Pizzeria, 142
La Merise, 143

Lao Wang Noodle House, 115
La Popular, 56
Larkburger, 189
Las Tortas, 29
Las Tortugas, 115
L'Atelier, 219
Laudisio, 220
Leaf Vegetarian Restaurant, 221
Le Central, 99
Le Grand Bistro & Oyster Bar, 81
Les Delices de Paris, 202
Liks Ice Cream, 168
Linger, 37
Liquor Mart, 254
Little Man Ice Cream, 54
Little Saigon Supermarket, 128
LoHi SteakBar, 38
Lola Coastal Mexican, 39
Los Cabos II, 82
Los Carboncitos, 40
Lost Lake Lounge, 308
Lou's Food Bar, 40
Lovely Confections, 168
Luca d'Italia, 144
Lucile's Creole Cafe, 197, 246
Lucky Pie Pizza and Tap
    House, 86

M

Maandeeq East African Cafe, 273
Manna From Heaven, 15
Manneken Frites, 285
Marco's Coal-Fired Pizza, 83
Marczyk Fine Foods, 169
Maria Empanada, 286
Mario's Double Daughters
    Salotto, 306
Market, The, 100
Masalaa, 273
Masterpiece Delicatessen, 41
Mataam Fez, 145
Mateo, 221
meat, Colorado raised, 67
Mecca Grill, 177
Mediterranean Restaurant,
    The, 224
Mercury Cafe, 164
Mexican food, 28
Middle Eastern restaurants, 176
Mikes2 Kitchen, 15
Mizuna, 145
MM Local, 251
Modmarket, 225
Mondo Vino, 54
MouCo Cheese Company, 251

Mountain Sun Pub & Brewery, 298
My Brother's Bar, 101

N

New Saigon, 116
Noble Swine Supper Club, 8
Noosa, 251
Novo Coffee, 108

O

OAK at Fourteenth, 225
Olivéa, 146
Oliver's Meat & Seafood
    Market, 169
Omonoia Greek Bakery, 170
Ondo's Spanish Tapas Bar, 147
Opus, 274
Original Chubby's, The, 49
Oshima Ramen, 190
Osteria Marco, 83
Oven Pizza e Vino, The, 87

P

Pablo's Coffee, 170
Pacific Mercantile, 108
Pacific Ocean Marketplace, 129
Pagliacci's, 50

Pajama Baking Company, 191
Palace Arms, 101
Palais Casablanca, 192
Panzano, 84
Parallel 17, 150
Paris Baguette Bakery, 286
Parisi, 42
Paris on the Platte, 85
Park Burger, 192
PastaVino, 226
Patsy's Inn, 51
Patzcuaro's, 29
Paxia, 29
Peaks Lounge, 306
Pearl Street Steak Room, 227
Pete's Kitchen, 165
Pete's Satire Lounge, 309
Phat Thai, 151
Pho Duy, 117
Phoenician Kabob, 151
Pho-natic, 119
Pho 95 Noodle House, 119
Pickled Lemon, 228
Piece, Love and Chocolate, 255
Pig & Block Charcuterie, The, 55
Pinche Tacos, 15
Pints Pub, 299

pizza, 86
Pizzeria Basta, 228
Pizzeria da Lupo, 229
Pizzeria Locale, 230
Polidori Sausage, 251
Potager, 152
produce, Colorado grown, 6
Proto's Pizzeria Napoletana, 87
PS Lounge, 309
Pupusas Sabor Hispano, 231

Q
Q's Restaurant, 246
Queen of Sheba, 153
Quiero Arepas, 16

R
Rackhouse Pub, 314
Radda Trattoria, 232
Rancho Liborio, 287
Ras Kassa's Ethiopian
    Restaurant, 232
r + d Wine, 202
Red Claw, The, 120
Red Star Deli, 88
Renegade Brewing Company, 300
Restaurant Kevin Taylor, 102

Rheinlander Bakery, 288
Riffs Urban Fare, 233
Rioja, 88
Rise & Shine Biscuit Kitchen & Cafe, 154
Root Down, 43
Row 14 Bistro & Wine Bar, 89
Rueben's Burger Bistro, 233
Rush, 256
Russell's Smokehouse, 90

S

Saigon Bowl, 121
SALT the Bistro, 234
Salumeria Cinque Soldi, 203
Salvaggio's Deli, 235
Sam's No. 3, 103
Santiago's, 57
Satchel's on 6th, 154
Savory Spice Shop, 109
Seafood Landing, 58
Second Home Kitchen + Bar, JW Marriott, 155
Seoul BBQ, 275
Shead's BBQ & Fish Hut, 275
Sherpa House Restaurant and Cultural Center, 276

Ship Tavern, 103
Shondiz, 16
Sienna Wine Bar & Small Plates, 317
Silla, 276
Sink, The, 247
Sketch, 318
Snooze, 90
Socorro's, 57
Solera, 156
South Pearl Street Farmer's Market, 149
Spruce Confections, 257
Spuntino, 44
Sputnik, 310
Star Kitchen, 122
Steuben's, 13, 156
Steve's Snappin' Dogs, 157
Stick It to Me, 16
St. Kilian's Cheese Shop, 59
Stranahan's Colorado Whiskey, 300
Strange Brewing Company, 301
Street Kitchen Asian Bistro, 277
Strings, 166
Studio F, 8
Sugar Bakeshop, 204
Super Star Asian Cuisine, 122

Sushi Den, 197
Sushi Sasa, 91
Sushi Tora, 236
Sushi Zanmai, 237
Sweet Action, 204
Sweet Cow Ice Cream, 288
Syrup, 158

T

Table 6, 159
Table Talk, 8
Tacos y Salsas #3, 123
TAG, 92
TAG | Raw Bar, 93
Tamayo, 94
Tangerine, 237
Tangier Moroccan Cuisine, 238
Tao Tao Noodle Bar, 277
Tarasco's New Latin Cuisine, 124
Taste of Denmark, 289
Tasterie Truck, The, 17
Tee & Cakes, 257
Thai Avenue, 238
Thai Flavor, 278
Thai Food Cart, 17
Thin Man Tavern, The, 310
34°, 251

Tiffin's, 239
Tocabe: An American Indian
    Eatery, 44
Tom's Home Cookin', 104
Tony's Market, 110
Trattoria Stella, 45
Tres Jolie, 289
Trillium, 94
Trompeau Bakery, 279
Truffle Cheese Shop, The, 171
T-Wa Inn, 119
twelve restaurant, 95
Twisted Pine Brewing
    Company, 301
Two Spoons, 258

U

Über Sausage, The, 13, 159
Udi's Bread Cafe, 46
Upslope Brewing Company, 301
US Thai Cafe, 280

V

Vert Kitchen, 193
Vesta Dipping Grill, 96
Vietnamese restaurants, 118
Viet's, 119

Village Cork, The, 194
Vinh Xuong Bakery, 129
Vinnola's Italian Market, 289
Vinue Food and Wine Bar, 318
Virgilio's Pizzeria & Wine Bar, 280

W

Walnut Cafe, 240
Walnut Room, The, 7
WaterCourse Foods, 160
Wazee Supper Club, 105
Wazee Wood Fire Pizza, 97
Wednesday's Pie, 111
West End Tavern, 8, 240
Williams & Graham, 307
Wine Loft, The, 319

Wit's End Brewing Company, 302
Wooden Spoon Cafe & Bakery, 47
Wynkoop Brewing Company, 302

Y

Ya Hala Grill, 177
Yak and Yeti, 281
Yanni's, 282

Z

Z Cuisine & À Côté, 47
Zengo, 97
Zoe Ma Ma, 241
Zolo Grill, 242
Zudaka, 223